SHEIKH MUJIBUR RAHMAN

FROM REBEL TO FOUNDING FATHER

SHEIKH MUJIBUR RAHMAN

Syed Badrul Ahsan

NIYOGI BOOKS

Published by

NIYOGI BOOKS

D-78, Okhla Industrial Area, Phase-I
New Delhi-110 020, INDIA
Tel: 91-11-26816301, 49327000
Fax: 91-11-26810483, 26813830
email: niyogibooks@gmail.com
website: www.niyogibooksindia.com

Text © Syed Badrul Ahsan
Photographs © Father of the Nation Bangabandhu
               Sheikh Mujibur Rahman Memorial Trust

Editor: Jayalakshmi Sengupta
Cover Design: Shashi Bhushan Prasad
Layout: Sarojini Gosain

ISBN: 978-93-83098-10-1
Publication: 2014

Printed at: Niyogi Offset Pvt. Ltd., New Delhi, India

TO MY PARENTS

WHO GAVE ME UNRESTRAINED HORIZONS
TO EXPLORE AND TAUGHT ME TO DREAM BIG

Contents

Foreword

If there is one man to whom the emergence of the People's Republic of Bangladesh (1971) is indebted, whose contribution to history has made him a legend, it is Sheikh Mujibur Rahman. His patient endeavour and staunch belief in the rights of the Bengalis created a new milestone for them, giving them the opportunity to not only establish and uphold their cultural entity at last, but also the dignity to proclaim it on the world stage. The story of this great man's meteoric growth, and his equally tragic end, is part of Bengali folklore today, which continues to inspire millions of Bangladeshis across the globe.

Mujib was 'Bangabandhu', a friend of Bengal, an honorific a grateful nation bestowed on him in early 1969 after he was freed from incarceration in the Agartala Conspiracy case by the Pakistani military regime of Field Marshal Ayub Khan. He deserved the honour, for it was his dedication to the cause of Bengali autonomy within Pakistan and then independence from Pakistan that was to underline his political struggle, all the way to his assassination in August 1975.

A remarkable aspect of Bangabandhu's political character was the steady and sure evolution of his personality from one steeped in the communal politics of the Muslim League in the 1940s, to that of a political being, ready not only to embrace but inaugurate a secular order for his people by the mid-1960s. His Six-Point Programme of regional autonomy for Pakistan's federating units, as presented in early 1966, was the first clear sign of how he meant to steer politics towards a new frontier.

Mujib's significance in the politics of Pakistan and subsequently of Bangladesh came to be formally acknowledged when, for the first time in the history of a state carved out of British India in 1947, he emerged as the undisputed leader of the majority party at Pakistan's first general elections in December 1970. Of course, the results of those elections were to be subverted by the military regime of General Yahya Khan in league with the machinations of the leader of the minority Pakistan People's Party, Zulfikar Ali Bhutto. The conspiracy snowballed into a crisis that engulfed Pakistan in March 1971, followed by the genocide launched by the Pakistan army against its Bengalis later that month. It convinced Bangabandhu in no uncertain terms that his people needed to find their own way out of Pakistan. His declaration of Bangladesh's independence in the early hours of 26 March 1971, followed by his arrest at the hands of the army and his subsequent solitary confinement and secret trial in West Pakistan, were events which galvanised Bengalis into a necessary spirit of liberation.

Sheikh Mujibur Rahman remains that rare instance of a statesman in history in whose name, and in whose physical absence, a nation fought its way to freedom. The surrender of Pakistan in Bangladesh in December 1971 was indeed the culmination of Mujib's long struggle for the emancipation of his people. That was when the legend around the man took shape. In the following three and a half years in which he governed his new nation, Bangabandhu was buffeted by problems of an unprecedented nature inasmuch as he was fortunate in propelling his country into the councils of the world. He asked his nation to give him three years to turn the country around. His enemies made sure he did not survive. They killed him, with most of his family, on 15 August 1975.

Bangabandhu Sheikh Mujibur Rahman remains in death, as he was in lifetime, Bangladesh's foremost political symbol. For people outside Bangladesh, and indeed for the generations that came to life and adulthood after his passing, it is important that his story, the record of his times, be presented in a dispassionate manner. Syed Badrul Ahsan's work on the founder of Bangladesh, I am convinced, will do that job to the satisfaction of all.

A.F. SALAHUDDIN AHMED
National Professor
President, Managing Committee, Bangabandhu
Sheikh Mujibur Rahman Memorial Museum, Dhaka

Preface

My association with Sheikh Mujibur Rahman, Father of the Bengali Nation and 'Bangabandhu' to his grateful people, began in early 1968 when I heard my father speaking in whispers with his colleagues about the charge of conspiracy laid at Mujib's door by the Pakistan government. My father's conviction was absolute: Mujib, a believer in constitutional politics, was made of better stuff.

As the chief of the Awami League, he toured innumerable villages and towns in East Bengal, then known as East Pakistan, trying to impress on his people the belief that if democracy was the goal, and economic prosperity of the various regions of Pakistan was the overall national objective, the state of Pakistan would need to change. The change would necessarily have to be based on the Six Points he and his party offered to the country. The Six Points argued for a federal state where its constituent provinces would enjoy the highest degree of regional autonomy.

The Six Points were brushed aside despite the electoral triumph of the Awami League at Pakistan's first general election in December 1970. What followed the collapse of the tripartite talks, involving the Awami League, the Pakistan People's Party and the Pakistan Army in March 1971, was horror. Once again, Sheikh Mujibur Rahman was a prisoner of the state intent on demonstrating its ferocity in East Bengal. In the nine months that followed, three million Bengalis died at the hands of the army and two hundred thousand Bengali women were raped by Pakistani soldiers. Eventually, in December 1971, the *Mukti Bahini*, in alliance with the Indian Army, rammed through Pakistan's defence lines, to preside over the birth of a new, secular and democratic country.

The inspirational figure behind it all was Bangabandhu Sheikh Mujibur Rahman. There was heroism in him, along with the flaws which are often the hallmarks of great men, reminding one of a Greek tragic hero. If there is any truth to the notion that revolutions always consume their heroes, then the revolution that was Bangladesh claimed its founding father. And yet, in the broad perspective of history, Sheikh Mujibur Rahman remains a metaphor for Bangladesh and for its long sustained struggle for freedom. In life, he was the Bengalis' spokesman in the councils of the world. In death, he continues to be a powerful voice, forever ready and willing to speak for those who yearn for freedom and national self-dignity.

This is the story of a rebel who did not give up and because he did not, Bangladesh was born.

Acknowledgement

The writer gratefully acknowledges the cooperation of the Father of the Nation Bangabandhu Sheikh Mujibur Rahman Memorial Trust in making available copies of photographs for use in this book.

Prologue

It rained steadily that evening, the day of Sheikh Mujibur Rahman's burial by the soldiers in his village Tungipara of Faridpur district in Bangladesh. It was said by the village elders that there had been something about his death, the chilling nature of his murder, which was manifesting itself through the rains. The skies, they said, were knowingly weeping tears. And yet the fact remains that on that day, as on the day preceding it, few Bengalis were seen weeping in public, at the passing of the man who had come to symbolise Bangladesh.

The shock and the terrible sense of fear that had come over Bangladesh on 15 August 1975, when news poured in at dawn that the founder of the country, the leader revered as *Bangabandhu* or friend of Bengal by his people, had been assassinated, precluded an immediate outpouring of grief. The sense of disbelief was too overpowering to allow for any display of emotion. While it was shocking to accept that someone who had galvanised a whole nation into being fearless should be dying thus, it was dreadful to realise that the military had once again taken over the lives of the Bengalis. It was not supposed to be this way!

Having spent nearly his entire political life struggling to end military rule in Pakistan, of which Bangladesh had been the eastern province called East Pakistan, Sheikh Mujibur Rahman, or Mujib or Sheikh Shaheb as many knew him, had set into motion a train of events that would not only see Bangladesh emerge as a free and secular country but also ensured that never again would constitutional rule be overturned by military intervention in politics.

Clearly, neither Mujib, nor the nation whose fortunes he presided over after its liberation from Pakistan, had foreseen a situation where a Bengali army would replicate the Pakistan military and take over the state. In the pre-dawn hours of 15 August 1975, when a small yet well-organised band of army officers launched their assault on Mujib's residence in Dhaka, the Pakistani experience had clearly been improved upon—the soldiers had swiftly put everyone on the premises to death. Only his two daughters, travelling in Europe at the time, survived the massacre. If the 1958 and 1969 coups d'état that marred politics in Pakistan had avoided being bloody affairs, the Bangladesh coup was plainly a horrific instance of murder and mayhem. It did not go with the notion of Bengalis being a society of polite people who spent long hours debating politics and reciting poetry.

Mujib's body and those of other members of his family lay where they had fallen, till late in the evening. The men who had done the deed had by then installed their man in office as the president. The man was none other than Mujib's long-time political associate and commerce minister, the right-winger Khondokar Moshtaq Ahmed. The chiefs of the army, navy, air force, police and the para-military *Jatiyo Rakkhi Bahini* (JRB), had already declared their allegiance to the new regime, after being escorted to the radio station by the coup leaders to do so. As night fell in Dhaka, with soldiers moving in and out of Mujib's house, it was clear that politics in Bangladesh had taken a violent and unpredictable turn. Moshtaq had earlier set the tone of the political change in a broadcast to the country. He described the young officers who had murdered Mujib and his family as 'children of the sun' who had saved the nation. He ended his speech by invoking the slogan 'Bangladesh Zindabad', a clear throwback to the times when politicians in East and West Pakistan were wont to employ 'Pakistan Zindabad', a non-Bengali expression, in their speeches.

On the day Mujib died, his murderers made certain that '*Joi Bangla*', the old slogan he had coined and effectively used as a way of buttressing Bengali nationalist aspirations in their struggle against Pakistan, was put to an end. It did not matter that 'zindabad' was an Urdu term, an anachronism in Bengali-speaking Bangladesh. '*Joi Bangla*', victory to Bengal, had a ring of rebellion and defiance about it.

As it rained on the evening of 16 August, resistance to the coup was conspicuous by its absence. Those political leaders, who could have put up resistance to the commandeering of power by the soldiers, were on the run. And those who did not resist were already in the cabinet headed by their colleague, Moshtaq. Only four men remained outside the cabinet and did not run. They were Syed Nazrul Islam, Tajuddin Ahmed, Mansoor Ali and A.H.M. Quamruzzaman. Close to Mujib, these men had cobbled the provisional government of Bangladesh into shape while in exile in 1971, and planned and executed the guerrilla struggle against the Pakistani military.

On the morning of the coup they found themselves under house arrest. A few days later all four were to be carted off to Dhaka Central Jail, where less than three months later they would be murdered in their cells by the very men who had killed Mujib. A fifth man in the Mujib circle, Foreign Minister Kamal Hossain, was on the day of the coup on an official visit to Yugoslavia. He would not return to Bangladesh for some years after the assassination of Mujib.

Hours after the news of the coup reached him in Islamabad, Pakistan's prime minister, Zulfikar Ali Bhutto, cheerfully recognised the 'Islamic Republic' of Bangladesh (though the country had turned into no such thing), and declared his intention of dispatching rice as a goodwill gesture to the country that had broken away from Pakistan three and a half years earlier.

In New Delhi, Prime Minister Indira Gandhi, newly into the job of administering a state of emergency, fell silent when informed of the Bangladesh leader's assassination. She was at that point overseeing Independence Day celebrations in New Delhi.

A few days later, the sovereign nature of Bangladesh as a state was duly recognised by Saudi Arabia and China. In the brief period in which Mujib had wielded power in Bangladesh, these two countries had made it a point to publicly stay away from recognising his government and his country. With Mujib's policies reversed, they nearly cheered the violent overthrow of the administration in Bangladesh.

—◦◉◦—

PART

1

Initiation into Politics

The rise and fall of Mujib is a tale which continues to intrigue not just Bangladeshis but also others in the rest of South Asia. It has been argued that his emergence into the limelight was phenomenal and almost a result of fortuitous circumstances; through the twists and turns of the times, he had been catapulted to the top. Apart from his admirers, there have been a plethora of critics, many of them Bengalis, who have lost no opportunity in dismissing Mujib as a demagogue who rose to political prominence through sheer display of oratory, without much of political insight into the problems that defined his era. While it is quite legitimate to argue that Mujib was no intellectual in the sense that India's Jawaharlal Nehru was, it would be quite incorrect to believe that he did not have a comprehension of what politics was all about. The steady manner in which he was to rise to the top, over nearly three decades, gives the lie to the argument that it was circumstances alone that made the man. In more instances than one, it was Mujib who shaped circumstances for his country.

Politics for Mujib began in school. In the late 1930s, when the struggle for Indian independence mounted and the British colonial power found itself dealing increasingly with a rising crescendo of Indian nationalism, Mujib was in high school. A keen student of history, as the head of a students' delegation, he confronted A.K. Fazlul Huq and Huseyn Shaheed Suhrawardy, two prominent politicians of undivided Bengal, with the demand that development work be undertaken in his native Faridpur district. The two men, at first surprised and then charmed by the seriousness in the young man, quickly recognised the political spark in him. Mujib was not yet twenty. Born on 17 March 1920 in Tungipara to an affluent middle-class Muslim family, he struggled with bad eyesight, the result of beriberi he had suffered at a very young age. Not a particularly gifted student, Mujib nevertheless managed to finish high school at the age of twenty in 1942, which was about the time he found himself greatly charged by the idea of Pakistan. The two-nation theory put forward by Mohammad Ali Jinnah and his All India Muslim League envisaging the creation of an independent state for India's Muslims was an idea that seized the imagination of young Muslims like Mujib.

As the countdown to Partition approached, before the country was divided along communal lines under the supervision of Lord Mountbatten, Mujib found himself an active worker of the Muslim League in 1946. There was a roughness in him, the kind Indian politicians often gainfully employed to intimidate their opponents. In Mujib, politicians like Suhrawardy, a man who was to provoke and preside over the Great Calcutta Killings of August 1946, saw a human weapon they could use every time politics needed to be backed up by the insolence of youth. It was not clear, at that point, if Mujib would make his way to exalted heights in future. He was the diligent, faithful political worker the likes of whom who were to come in handy as the riotous struggle for Pakistan gathered steam. What was certainly evident was the tremendous enthusiasm in him about promoting the idea of Pakistan among those he consorted with. He was in Calcutta (now Kolkata), which at the time, as always, was the hub of Indian politics. For the young Mujib, life in Calcutta nominally centred on a half-hearted pursuit of education at the Islamia College, an institution many Muslim parents from eastern Bengal preferred to dispatch their male children to. What increasingly gained a place in Mujib's life at that point was the relation he established with Suhrawardy. It was an association that would define the course Mujib would take in the years ahead.

Suhrawardy, prime minister of Bengal and a prominent figure in the All India Muslim League, was an active participant in the movement for Pakistan. In August 1946, when the leader of the Pakistan movement, Mohammad Ali Jinnah, decided to give his political concept a fresh push by announcing what he called a 'Direct Action Day' for Muslims all over India, Suhrawardy acted with alacrity. He declared a state-wide holiday in Bengal so that the Muslims of the province could participate in the events of the day. It was a decision that was to have terrible consequences for the province and, by extension, the rest of India. On 16 August 1946, within minutes of the Muslim League rally in central Calcutta having come to an end, Muslims and Hindus, driven by communalism and armed with lethal weapons, took up position against one another. Over the next four days, mobs of rioters moved all over the city, killing people subscribing to faiths other than their own, and damaging property indiscriminately. A stunned Suhrawardy was unable to rein in the forces he had unleashed. His party, the Muslim League, was not prepared to help him. They seemed to be satisfied with the outcome which came as definitive evidence that a Muslim Pakistan was only a matter of time. In its terrible totality, the Calcutta riots had clinched the argument for Pakistan.

The Cabinet Mission Proposals, a set of suggestions made by Britain's Sir Stafford Cripps and the political mission he led to India to help the country's politicians arrive at a consensus on a federal arrangement that would keep Hindus and Muslims as part of a united India following the departure of the British colonial power, had already lost meaning in July 1946. The collapse of the mission came through some of the larger ironies of the Indian nationalist movement. The Cabinet Mission having successfully brought around Jinnah and the Muslim League to agreeing to a federal India through a guarantee of wide-ranging autonomy for the Muslim majority regions of the country presumed that it had solved the India puzzle. The rudest of shocks came from the Congress' Jawaharlal Nehru. He stunned all Indians, and delighted all Pakistan enthusiasts, by making the dramatic announcement that his party reserved the right to modify the proposals made by Sir Stafford Cripps and his colleagues. The statement irrevocably ruined any chances that India might have had of remaining a single country. Nehru was clearly driven by the feeling that a free India of the kind envisaged by the Cabinet Mission Proposals would leave the centre weak and ineffectual, and would at the same time leave it at the mercy of those areas that Jinnah would have under his control. He was ready to cut the Muslim League with its own Muslim majority areas adrift, unwilling to witness the spectre of secession gather steam in a post-colonial India. Nehru's announcement was just what Jinnah needed to salvage his own reputation. He had been accused by sections of his party of having frittered away Pakistan by agreeing to a federation deal. He quickly declared that given the Congress leader's announcement, the Muslim League was no more bound to abide by the agreement it had subscribed to earlier. The murder and mayhem in Calcutta came a month later.

In the build-up to the vivisection of India, Mujib spent much of his time in Calcutta. For him and others of his age and political beliefs, the times were glorious. The birth of a Muslim Pakistan for the followers of the Islamic faith in India could only be regarded as a fantastic moment in history—an event for which Muslims had Jinnah to thank for. In those early days, Mujib was a fervent admirer of Jinnah. A rather apocryphal story has been given out of his cycling all the way to distant Delhi to have a glimpse of the man about to create Pakistan. It is pretty telling that in his future struggle for Bengali political self-assertion and eventual freedom from Pakistan, Mujib never commented on the personality of Jinnah. His youthful admiration for Pakistan's founder, while it may have dimmed with age, never lost the respect it came wrapped in. But then, in those dramatic times, Mujib admired all Muslim politicians who appeared to be articulating the historical injustices, as he saw them, their community had been suffering from.

Huq, the Bengali politician who had moved the resolution for Pakistan at the Lahore conference of the All India Muslim League in March 1940, was another figure who aroused his respect as the countdown to Pakistan progressed. Then there was Syed Badrudduja, a spellbinding orator and former mayor of Calcutta, held in deep respect by Muslims in Bengal and elsewhere in India. Badrudduja, who opted to remain in India and not go to Pakistan in 1947, was in his heydays in the late 1940s. His home, on European Asylum Lane in Calcutta's Park Circus region, was often a focal point for young Muslims eager to hear him speak on the issues affecting the country. Mujib was a frequent visitor and always came away quite mesmerised by Badrudduja's eloquence. When he died in 1974, Mujib arranged for one of his sons, who had settled in Bangladesh, to fly to Calcutta to take part in his last rites.

Awami Muslim League

The creation of Pakistan on 14 August 1947 brought about a seismic shift in the politics of the South Asian region. The consequences of Partition were huge and tragic. It was particularly in Bengal and the Punjab that the terror of political division was felt acutely. It was to leave lasting scars on the image of a subcontinent, too sordid to put behind. The unabashed hurry with which Lord Louis Mountbatten went into the job of dividing India, thus bringing British rule over the country to an end, was an exercise that was clearly flawed.

The trauma of Partition was not merely in the spectacle of millions of Muslims, Hindus and Sikhs leaving their homes they had inhabited for generations. It was also in the rather insensitive way in which men like Cyril Radcliffe, with little idea of Indian history and its social structure, were employed in the task of carving up Bengal and the Punjab into their religious communities. There are supposed to be instances, where to their great horror, households woke up one morning to discover their bedrooms apportioned to India while the kitchens were with Pakistan. These results were to be felt more in what became the new state of Pakistan than in the India which Nehru and Patel now prepared to govern. Almost the entire leadership of Pakistan comprised a Muslim refugee class, men who found themselves saying farewell to their homes in India as they moved to take charge of Pakistan. Jinnah, a man from Gujarat, just as Gandhi was, left behind a home he loved in Bombay and shifted to Karachi, the port city that would now be the capital of Pakistan. Liaquat Ali Khan, the country's first prime minister and Choudhury Khaliquzzaman, a leading Muslim League figure in united India, in company with scores of others trekked off to Pakistan.

In the east, such migrations of political leadership were relatively less pronounced since individuals such as Fazlul Huq and Moulana Abdul Hamid Khan Bhashani, a firebrand preacher-cum-politician, hailed from areas that in any case had been part of eastern Bengal, now Pakistan's eastern wing. Only Suhrawardy, from Calcutta, who needed to relocate to Dhaka, seemed to be in no hurry. A prime reason for this were his ties with Gandhi for stemming the communal violence which raged in West Bengal where the Muslims were in a particularly vulnerable position after the establishment of Pakistan. By the time Suhrawardy was ready to move over to Pakistan—which was after Gandhi's assassination at the hands of Hindu extremists on 30 January 1948—he discovered to his dismay that Pakistan's ruling classes, especially Jinnah, were not favourably disposed towards welcoming him there. When Suhrawardy did make it to the new state in 1949, the rot in Pakistan's politics had already set in. Jinnah succumbed to cancer in September 1948. His successor Khwaja Nazimuddin, a weak politician, was finding it hard to cope with the forcefulness of Prime Minister Liaquat Ali Khan. It did not take much time or reflection on Suhrawardy's part to convince himself that the new state was drifting away from the ideals the Muslim League set in the early 1940s.

The increasingly arbitrary nature of government by the Liaquat Ali ministry manifested itself early. Anyone demonstrating a readiness to criticise the actions of the government was quickly dubbed a traitor and an agent of foreign powers, that of Hindu India, across the frontier. For Mujib, now a student of law at Dhaka University, those early days of the Pakistan state must have been a pointer to the years ahead. By and large such a feeling was beginning to take root among the entire East Pakistan population, which was a disturbing thought. The Bengalis of East Pakistan happened to form the majority, fifty-six per cent to forty-four, of the population of Pakistan. That political and demographic reality was given short shrift when Jinnah, in the only visit he made to East Pakistan, loudly proclaimed the intention of the government to have Urdu as the language of the state. The statement was fraught with risks and how incendiary Jinnah's remarks were was soon made clear. Even as he spoke before the teachers and students of Dhaka University in March 1948, Pakistan's creator found himself squarely up against a spontaneous expression of protest from a section of students assembled in the hall. Cries of 'No! No!' were heard.

A stunned Jinnah heard the protest and saw the young men behind it. For the first time in his life and only months into the creation of Pakistan, Jinnah could not comprehend the audacity of the slogan-raisers. If there was any feeling in anyone that the protest would lead to a softening in his attitude to the language issue, it turned out to be misplaced. A couple of days later, Jinnah reiterated his view that Urdu indeed would be the state language. For good measure, he also made it clear that the people of East Pakistan needed to be cautious of agent provocateurs in their midst and had to be on guard to defend the integrity of Pakistan if it came under assault. It was, for Bengalis, a haughty Jinnah who refused to take note of the political realities in East Pakistan. When a delegation of university students met him to present the case for Bengali as the language of the state, he brushed them aside. Abdur Rahman Chowdhury, one of the students who would in time serve as a judge of the Bangladesh Supreme Court, was unwilling to take Jinnah's brusqueness lying down. Telling Jinnah that his attitude was all wrong, Chowdhury and his friends stormed out of the great man's presence.

For Mujib, however, the first step in his growing disillusionment with politics in Pakistan was not the language issue. In the same month that Jinnah visited East Pakistan, Mujib found himself at the head of a protest over working conditions by menial workers at Dhaka University. He was promptly sent off to jail. It was to be an initiation into a political process that would involve Mujib for as long as Bengalis remained part of Pakistan. The fiery nature of his radicalism would soon lead to his rustication by Dhaka University, an act that effectively deprived him of a chance to finish his law studies. But the expulsion did not appear to have greatly affected Mujib. He showed scant interest in going back to university and demonstrated the least desire to offer any apologies for his political activities on the campus. Politics, in effect, was what was increasingly beginning to define his behaviour. While the Calcutta days, in pre-Partition India, had been only about activism on the streets as a staunch follower of the Muslim League, in independent Pakistan, however, the young man sought a larger role for himself. But at that early stage, there was hardly any well-known politician he could look up to or serve as a loyal follower of.

Suhrawardy, who would in time become his idol and under whose tutelage he would refine the rough edges of his radicalism, was still in Calcutta dealing with the aftermath of the 1947 riots. There was Huq, a political giant, now looking for a niche in a political structure which was being largely commandeered by politicians based in West Pakistan. Mujib, though deeply respectful of Huq, was not drawn to him politically in the way he was to Suhrawardy. Even at that early stage, he had the good sense to note the differences between Suhrawardy and Huq. While the former appeared to him to be a politician focused on the issues (even if his judgement was not always correct), the latter had already committed too many flip-flops to be taken seriously. Mujib's fortunes took, as it were, a sudden surge in 1949. With Suhrawardy finally making his way to Pakistan, it was clear that a political polarisation was at work.

The secretiveness of the Muslim League government and its sensitivity to dissent had convinced Pakistan's still small intellectual society of the bankruptcy the rulers were pushing themselves into. Political and economic differences between East Pakistan and West Pakistan, separated by a thousand miles of Indian territory, were also coming up surreptitiously. The intake of Bengalis in the newly constituted civil service of Pakistan was hideously low. In the armed forces, there appeared to be not much of enthusiasm in the recruitment of Bengalis, whereas there was a constant pressure to have recruitment of men from the provinces that comprised West Pakistan. The controversy generated over the state language was still unresolved at the time Suhrawardy entered Pakistan. Above all, the new state had made no headway in the drafting of a constitution for itself, with the British-ordained Government of India Act serving as the basis of political administration.

Jinnah had played a powerful role, combining the offices of governor general, president of the constituent assembly and chief of the Muslim League all in himself. His death led to a division of authority between the new governor general, Khwaja Nazimuddin, and the prime minister, Liaquat Ali Khan. Having never been a mass-based political organisation, the Muslim League was now clearly in a state of creeping atrophy. In West Pakistan, the party was dominated by the feudal classes and refugee politicians from pre-1947 India; in East Pakistan, a middle-class leadership with Nurul Amin, as the chief minister, ruled the roost. Little talk of political change went around. It was time for men like Suhrawardy to do something.

On 23 June 1949, Suhrawardy and Bhashani, with a clutch of younger politicians, formally announced the establishment of the Awami Muslim League as a political party. The word *Awami* was an Urdu term that meant 'popular' or 'people's'. The name of the party suggested, in extremely strong terms, the desire on the part of its founding figures as well as their followers to convince the country that it was indeed a new Muslim League—a consequence of the perceived decay of the party which had achieved Pakistan. Mujib was one among the hordes of youth who flocked to the new organisation. In the first few months after the party came into being, Mujib demonstrated admirable organisational skills that impressed Suhrawardy and other senior leaders of the party. For Mujib, a political career now did not seem like a hard bargain. He quickly made his way to the hamlets and villages of East Pakistan popularising the programmes of the Awami Muslim League. It was a style that would remain for the rest of his life. The contacts he made in the course of his political apprenticeship, if they could be called that, and the ease with which he related to the poor as well as the middle class in a typical Bengali rural structure, were to serve him in good stead in subsequent years. There are stories aplenty of how he remembered faces and recalled names decades down the road. It was during these early journeys to the countryside that Mujib showed a prodigious capacity for work. He was indefatigable and worked the crowds in the manner of a politician seeking office.

There were other young men in the new party, but not many of them could match Mujib's stamina for work and ability in disseminating party propaganda. Tall for a Bengali, with his six-foot plus frame he towered above most other politicians around him. Mujib also made good use of his deep voice to present his views in the dialect of the people. He deliberately eschewed the urbane Bengali that other politicians of East Pakistan employed in their speeches. The deep chord that his words were to strike among Bengalis, between the late 1940s and early 1970s, had for their underpinning the common, earthy language he used in his dealings with them. Even in his more mature years his speeches often displayed a language mangled at unexpected points. But his message was never lost on anyone. An early political trait that emerged in Mujib was his indifference to the western part of Pakistan. He was clearly not much enthused by the idea of exploring a political career on an all-Pakistan basis, even in those early days when the chasm that was to lead Bengalis and West Pakistanis down their separate ways was yet to cast its long shadow on national politics.

For Mujib, the politics of the Awami Muslim League fundamentally signalled the emergence of the Bengali voice in Pakistan. It was at once an expression of his disillusion with Pakistan, only a couple of years after he had excitedly cheered its birth, and also a growing belief that Pakistan's Bengali population could not expect to enjoy its political rights unless it asserted its distinctive presence on the national stage. Besides, with the leaders of the new party drawn from East Pakistan, it did not need much convincing for Pakistanis to believe that for all the changes and transformations to come in future, the Awami Muslim League would essentially be rooted in Pakistan's Bengali-speaking province. Mujib was among the earliest of individuals to recognise this truth.

Pakistan after Jinnah

The state of Pakistan was beginning to fall in disarray by the end of 1951. In October of that year, Prime Minister Liaquat Ali Khan was assassinated at a public rally in Rawalpindi. Immediately after the death of Jinnah, in September 1948, it was Liaquat who took full charge of the country. Indeed, the more cynical among observers of Pakistan in its early stages have consistently believed that the prime minister's takeover of effective authority occurred even before Jinnah had actually passed from the scene. Days before Jinnah's death, Liaquat made it a point to pay him a visit, more out of courtesy than a political need. The dying, frail old man made it clear that he did not appreciate the manner in which his prime minister had been usurping his authority. Liaquat said nothing, but only smiled. Some thought it was more of a smirk than smile. At that point, there was hardly anyone strong enough to resist Liaquat's ascendancy.

Only days later, with Jinnah finally dead, Liaquat knew his path to the future was wide open. He took swift steps to have Khwaja Nazimuddin, the Urdu-speaking feudal landlord from Dhaka long involved with Muslim League politics, installed as Pakistan's new governor general. But there was little doubt that where Jinnah had exercised overall control over the country as governor general, Nazimuddin could only hope to play to Liaquat's tune. In pre-Partition Bengal, Khwaja Nazimuddin's role in politics, while being contemporaneous with that of stalwarts of the stature of Suhrawardy and

Fazlul Huq, had been relatively less illustrious in terms of popularity as well as intellectual appeal. By the time he became Pakistan's governor general, however, Nazimuddin had gone quite a few notches ahead of Suhrawardy and Huq, ostensibly because the latter had by then found themselves in opposition to the governing Muslim League.

The circumstances of Liaquat's assassination have remained shrouded in mystery. The man who fired the shots at him was immediately pounced upon by the crowd and lynched. In all the years that have passed since that tragic moment, no inquiry has been conducted into the murder and there have in fact been suspicions voiced about the involvement of powerful circles within Pakistan's political class in the assassination. In the meanwhile, a rather curious turn of events occurred when Nazimuddin, having been governor general for three years, stepped down to take charge as the country's new prime minister. Into the governor general's office stepped in Ghulam Muhammad. It was the beginning of a process that would inexorably lead Pakistan to a long series of political adventurism, followed by predictable bouts of instability.

The Nazimuddin ministry was sent packing by Ghulam Muhammad in 1953—a year which is generally regarded as a trendsetter in the gathering spate of political mishaps. The governor general's action, stunning as it was for the country, was followed by behaviour that was plainly quixotic. He recalled Mohammad Ali, a Bengali then serving as Pakistan's ambassador in Washington, to Karachi and installed him as the new prime minister. Events took place so quickly that the country's political classes were left guessing as to where the governor general wished to take the country.

Mohammad Ali (he later came to be known as Mohammad Ali Bogra), was not destined to serve long as prime minister as he developed clear disagreements with Ghulam Muhammad. But as long as he served as Pakistan's prime minister, Ali enjoyed it. There was a certain flamboyance in his style of leadership. Men like General Ayub Khan—who was both the commander-in-chief of the Pakistan Army and minister of defence—were in his cabinet. This was the first subtle indication of increasing military influence over national politics. Of greater significance was the inclusion of Suhrawardy, the former chief minister of Bengal, as minister for law, in the Bogra cabinet. Suhrawardy had by then become a focal point of political opposition through the formation of the Awami Muslim League. Suhrawardy's entry into the cabinet was the first time that the Awami Muslim League had come into government.

Strategically, Suhrawardy's appointment was important. Having been forced to stay out of Pakistan by Liaquat in the first two years following the establishment of the country, Suhrawardy now saw a real chance to regain the kind of foothold he once had in pre-1947 Bengal politics. His party was enthusiastic about his new role. The young Mujib, by now busy travelling the length and breadth of East Pakistan to publicise the political message of the Awami Muslim League, thought he could foresee a time when the new party would dominate the arena. In a way, Mujib saw in Suhrawardy's cabinet position an opportunity for Bengali grievances to be aired in the corridors of central authority in Karachi. He was to be disappointed, for Suhrawardy was unwilling to cast himself in a provincial role. Having lived through the bitterness of his years as a provincial Muslim League politician in Bengal, as the momentum for Pakistan built up, he was now determined to seize the opportunity that the Bogra ministry provided him with. For the remainder of his life he would consciously fashion a political role for himself more suited to politics at the national level.

The Awami League (the term 'Muslim' would be done away with in 1955 as a way of refurbishing the party in a secular mould) had, by the time Suhrawardy entered the cabinet, been giving out the signs of being a Bengali or rather an East Pakistan oriented party. All its important figures—Moulana Bhashani, Fazlul Haq and Mujibur Rahman—were Bengalis and as a result much inclined to dealing with Bengali issues rather than those that affected the entirety of Pakistan. But none of this detracted from Suhrawardy's growing belief that his place was in the central scheme of things in Pakistan. The reality of the growing nature of Pakistan's problems was beginning to make a deep, worrying impression on him. Foremost among the issues confronting Pakistan in the sixth year of its statehood was the failure of the politicians to frame a constitution for the country. While Pakistan stumbled in its search for a constitution, neighbouring India had clearly moved ahead. Prime Minister Jawaharlal Nehru's Congress government had steered a constitution through parliament in 1950, which had subsequently been followed by the first general elections in the country in 1951. While India was clearly on its way to an institutionalisation of Westminster-style parliamentary democracy, Pakistan found itself lurching from one crisis to another. The death of Jinnah and Liaquat had removed in pretty quick succession the two powerful men who mattered in the country. In the rise of Khwaja Nazimuddin, Ghulam Muhammad and Mohammad Ali Bogra, Pakistan faced a formidable political test. None of these three men were equipped to deal with governance owing to their glaring shortcomings where a comprehension of realities and an exercise of political judgement were concerned.

In Suhrawardy, however, Pakistanis saw a different proposition altogether. He possessed the kind of charisma that Pakistan missed with Jinnah's death. Moreover, he was suave, well read and self-assured to the point of arrogance. In a society that treated powerful men with deference, Suhrawardy was an individual who truly emitted sparks of brilliance. In his own mind, he knew the road he wished to take, and even if uncomfortable serving under the neophyte Mohammad Ali Bogra and Ayub Khan, he realised that any thought on his part of playing a leading role on the stage depended on patience and endurance. The portfolio of law was, as he saw it, an important as well as a challenging one. On the one hand, it was about drafting Pakistan's constitution which was essentially in his hands. On the other, it promised an opportunity for him to exercise all his intellectual energy and physical powers of persuasion in actually overseeing the framing and adoption of the constitution. For all the daunting nature of the job, however, Suhrawardy enjoyed being part of the power circle. He had always been in his element in office in the days before the division of India. He was now in a similar state in the cabinet of

Prime Minister Mohammad Ali Bogra. Framing the constitution would, however, take three more difficult years.

The failure of Pakistan's politicians to enact a constitution and the extent to which such a failure was responsible for the slide that would eventually result in its collapse in East Pakistan in 1971, has been debated by many. One of the major difficulties with framing the constitution was the increasing controversy generated around the nature of the Pakistan state. The 1940 resolution of the All India Muslim League, which demanded an independent entity for India's Muslims, did not say or even suggest that the Islamic religion would have a role to play in politics or governance. The Pakistan question in the early 1940s was riddled with many ironies. It was paradoxical that Jinnah, who was essentially a westernised man, should be spearheading the movement for a Muslim Pakistan and be destined to be acknowledged as the father of Pakistan. A devoted Anglophile, Jinnah drank wine, ate pork, spoke no Urdu and observed none of the Islamic rituals that his followers thought would serve as the guiding principles of the state they looked forward to being part of. It was not surprising therefore, that his concept of a Muslim Pakistan was essentially one of a secular state where there would be no room whatsoever for theocratic rule. Jinnah's vision of Pakistan was made abundantly clear on 11 August 1947. Speaking before the constituent assembly created for the new country that was to take formal shape three days later, he made it clear that the pursuit of religion would strictly be a matter of personal faith and would have nothing to do at all with the business of the state. He set out a clear signal that the Pakistan he envisioned would be a democracy fashioned on the secular Western model and not the Islamic state that many around him wished for. Here too the irony could not be missed. In all his years spent struggling for the creation of Pakistan, Jinnah had hammered away at the theme of Hindu–Muslim incompatibility in a united India. But once Pakistan became a real possibility, Jinnah readopted a position he had espoused in the 1920s and 1930s when he was hailed for his efforts to forge Indian national unity across communal lines.

The struggle for Pakistan's soul commenced soon after Jinnah's death in 1948. It seemed that the passing of the founder of the state had released some pent-up emotions among many of his own followers, who could not bring themselves to conceive of a Pakistan without the attendant Islamic characteristics they thought came with the earlier struggle for it. In this matter, fundamentalist parties like *Jamaat-e-Islami* of Moulana Abul A'la Moududi enormously added to the rising frenzy for an Islamic state. Despite the incontrovertible fact of the Jamaat's having opposed the creation of Pakistan, the party now appeared to take a position which clearly advocated Pakistan as a theocratic state, to a point where by 1953 things would come to a head with the agitation against the relatively small Ahmadiyya community in the country. The Ahmadiyyas, a peaceful congregation, also known as Qadianis, followed the founder of their faith, Mirza Ghulam Ahmed of Qadian and believed him to be the last prophet of God—a position that set the community on a confrontational course with other Muslims. Moududi and his men were bellicose in their stand and demanded that the Ahmadiyyas should be declared a non-Muslim sect, and treated as other religious minorities in the Muslim state of Pakistan were. Its frenzied propaganda eventually pushed Lahore, considered Pakistan's cultural capital, into chaos with the entire Ahmadiyya community fearing for its security. It was not until martial law was declared in Lahore by General Azam Khan that the riots came to an end. Moududi was arrested, tried and sentenced to death. He was not to walk to the gallows, however. In one of those twists and turns Pakistan's politics has been known for, he soon emerged free and went back to his mission of demanding that Pakistan be modelled along purely Islamic lines. His party would later join hands with the Pakistan Army in attempting to brutally put down the Bengali struggle for independence in 1971.

The struggle for the constitution, while on the surface a battle for dominance by the secularists and communalists, had another dimension to it. That was the matter of how the Bengalis of East Pakistan and their fellow citizens in West Pakistan would define their relationship in a federal scheme of things. West Pakistan, despite comprising the provinces of Sind, Baluchistan, the North West Frontier Province and the Punjab, altogether was home to forty-four per cent of Pakistanis. In contrast, the Bengali-speaking East Pakistan was palpably conscious of its status as the country's majority province. The homogeneity of the province was another important factor in its belief that in any constitutional scheme of things it ought to have the upper hand. The Bengalis, acutely aware of the disdain with which West Pakistanis often held them because of what was generally perceived as their non-martial appearance and behaviour, nevertheless prided themselves on the clear cultural advantages they enjoyed.

While the Partition had also left the province of Bengal divided into distinct Hindu and Muslim parts, the fact remained that Bengalis on both sides of a divided Bengal continued to see themselves as the heirs of a single, powerful cultural tradition. All Bengalis revered the poetry of Rabindranath Tagore, who had won the Nobel Prize for Literature in 1913. The poetry of Kazi Nazrul Islam, a Muslim whose militant lyrics had been extremely inspiring in the years of struggle against British colonial rule was also equally popular among Hindu Bengalis and Muslim Bengalis. By the early 1950s, therefore, the Bengalis of Pakistan, while aware of their contributions to the creation of Pakistan as members of the Muslim community, were slowly but surely reigniting the old notions of their linguistic-cultural traditions in a subcontinent now severed in two. Conversely, the Islamic links that Bengalis shared with West Pakistanis were beginning to go through strains as questions of politics slowly overshadowed everything else.

―◦◌◦―

Language Movement

By the early 1950s, there were unmistakable signs of a chasm developing between Bengalis and other Pakistanis in the western part of the country over the language issue. If Bengalis had thought that Jinnah's death would neutralise the controversy and that his successors would adopt a more conciliatory approach to Bengali demands about the position of their native language in the national scheme of things, they were mistaken. Both Khwaja Nazimuddin and Liaquat were brusque in their rejection of Bengali sentiments on the state language issue. They were part of a politically small yet powerful minority which continued to advocate the introduction of Urdu as the national language on the ground that the country needed a lingua franca to conduct business.

Conveniently ignored was the important position enjoyed by the English language, a legacy of British colonial rule, in the new country as well as in India. India opted for Hindi as the national language while at the same time making provisions for English to function as the official language of government for as long as Hindi did not permeate all sectors of life. In Pakistan the ground realities were quite different. Other than Bengali, spoken in East Pakistan, there were the provinces in the western wing of the country with their own distinctive linguistic patterns. Punjabi, Sindhi, Pushto and Baluchi were the languages, with their many dialects, spoken in West Pakistan. As for Urdu, it was essentially the language of people—Muslim politicians as well as general citizens—who had in the aftermath of the 1947 Partition, chosen to migrate to what could be called the promised land of Pakistan. A rich literary and cultural tradition had developed around Urdu since the times of the Mughal dynasty in places like Lucknow, Delhi, Hyderabad, Patna and Aligarh, places which had come to be part of the new Republic of India. In Pakistan, those who spoke Urdu were minuscule in number and were largely based in the capital city Karachi. At the same time, there was a healthy smattering of Urdu speaking people who belonged to the Indian state of Bihar but, post-1947, had been permitted to make their homes in Bengali-speaking East Pakistan. It was largely in the northern towns of Dinajpur, Saidpur and Rangpur that these Urdu speaking people, all Muslims drawn to the promise of Pakistan, settled. In time, Pakistan's Urdu speaking population would come to be referred to rather disparagingly as muhajirs or refugees, in its western wing, and as Biharis in East Pakistan.

But between 1947 and 1952, an overriding goal of Pakistan's government remained the imposition, as many saw it, of Urdu as the leading medium of national expression. It was especially in East Pakistan that the emphasis on Urdu appeared to be intense. This was owing to the misperceived feeling among the Karachi-based ruling classes that a process of Islamisation among the Bengalis could be aided by having Urdu play a larger role in Bengali life. The results of the effort were to be dire. It was not only men like Mujib who comprehended the nature of the approaching crisis, it was also others. Chief Minister Nurul Amin clearly felt that pushing things too far would only exacerbate conditions and could in time push Bengalis into alienation from the rest of the country. Amin was a staunch Muslim Leaguer, proud of Pakistan, believing fully in the idea that the new country was a place where the Muslim community could release all its latent energies towards promoting its intellectual and social development. But even he remained wary about the impact of the growing crisis over Urdu on the country as a whole.

The earliest statement on record about Bengali occupying an important perch in the structure of the state came from Dhirendranath

Dutta in the Pakistan Constituent Assembly in March 1948. It was around the same time that Jinnah was landing himself in hot water in Dhaka over his determination to have Urdu as the national language. Dutta, a Hindu and a refined Bengali who had seen little reason, like so many thousands of others in his community, to leave his native East Bengal for Calcutta after the province became part of Muslim Pakistan, argued the case for Bengali in logical terms. He suggested that Bengali being the language of the majority of Pakistan's population be placed alongside English as the official language in the constituent assembly. His suggestion was not entertained. In the event, the authorities in Karachi, aided by their friends holding political authority in Dhaka, undertook what was obviously a bizarre programme of reshaping the Bengali language through introducing Urdu terminologies in it. The motive behind such a move was, of course, to stress the distinctive nature of Muslim nationalism among Bengalis. It was also a message that the Bengalis of Pakistan had effectively severed links with the Bengalis of the Indian state of West Bengal. Bengali news bulletins broadcast by the state-controlled Radio Pakistan in Dhaka went to ludicrous extremes in their enthusiasm to infuse Urdu phraseology in its content. The sparks for a future confrontation between Pakistan's Bengali speaking people and the rest of the country were beginning to ignite and looked like an approaching twilight of gloom.

The showdown came in early 1952. By then, Mujib had already acquired something of a reputation as a political agitator and was increasingly beginning to be a thorn in the side of the government. His frequent forays in jail and the alacrity with which the administration shifted him from one prison to another in East Pakistan were the earliest indications of a political life destined to be spent more in incarceration than in freedom. It was significant that while the senior leaders of the Awami League, namely, Suhrawardy, Bhashani, Ataur Rahman Khan, and others, by and large, conformed to the traditions and rules of parliamentary politics, Mujib remained a rebel. He had convinced himself rather early that politics in Pakistan was gradually mutating into an activity that favoured the more affluent classes in West

Pakistan. If he entertained any notion that Suhrawardy, the man he idolised, was not exactly willing to notice the growing chasm between the eastern and western parts of the country, he kept it to himself. But there was no mistaking the predilection on Mujib's part to stay focused on politics in East Pakistan even as his mentor did otherwise.

A growing measure of shrewdness and political acumen was characteristic of young Mujib at that stage in his career. He had hitched his wagon to Suhrawardy's star, even if he did not share his leader's views on quite a few national issues. He just might have gone over to Fazlul Huq or Moulana Bhashani, for his brand of politics appeared to be more in tune with theirs than what Suhrawardy espoused at the centre. However, Mujib knew that politics of flip-flops could go only in circles. Huq's politics was of the kind he could not be comfortable with. He admired the calm reserve of Suhrawardy, even if his own lack of the same qualities quite clearly set him apart from his guru. As for Bhashani, politics was largely a temperamental thing. Bhashani's approach to the issues confronting Pakistan was an odd mixture of religion, socialism and general unpredictability. The consequence being, while Mujib would shoot ahead in his career, Bhashani and everyone else who Mujib looked up to would either fall by the wayside or dwindle into insignificance. Suhrawardy was the standard Mujib held fast to and it was an association that would pay him rich dividends in the times to come.

Overzealous fans of Mujib, since the liberation of Bangladesh, have made tall claims of Mujib's deep involvement in the gathering momentum around the Bengali language issue in 1952. It has also been suggested that when Jinnah spoke in defence of Urdu at Dhaka University's Curzon Hall in 1948, Mujib was one of the students who had raised his voice in an immediate demonstration of protest. There has so far been no documentary evidence, however, to show that he was part of the audience that defied Jinnah in March 1948. As far as the events of 1952 go, the entire movement around the language issue was shaped by the students of Dhaka University and was little influenced by politicians. In fact, agitated students had defied the

Awami Muslim League's advice to adopt a peaceful approach to the language issue. To his credit, however, Mujib made certain that he did not become identified with the moderate elements in his party. The fears of the moderate elements in the Awami Muslim League were understandable. They were not willing to be seen to encourage or engage in violent confrontation with the government over the language controversy. It was the infancy of the Awami Muslim League that was a crucial factor in the stance adopted by the party. The party was still wet behind the ears.

Mujib, in the midst of the gathering, was free to adopt his own position on the language issue. The opportunity was provided by a period of incarceration in which he had been placed by the Pakistani authorities on 1 January 1950. On that day, the Awami Muslim League planned an anti-famine rally to draw attention to the reports of growing hunger in parts of the province. Strategically, the party organised the rally to coincide with a visit to East Pakistan by Prime Minister Liaquat Ali Khan. Predictably led by Mujib, the rally was quickly pounced upon by the police and Mujib found himself in prison, yet once again. The authorities, clearly rattled by what they saw as a rabble-rouser in the young Bengali politician, put him behind bars for a period of two years. By the time the Language Movement gathered pace, Mujib had already spent slightly over two years in jail. But there was little cause to believe that these spells in prison were in any way softening the streak of rebellion in him. If anything, the agitational nature of his political character was being reinforced by imprisonment, to a point where both the provincial and central authorities in Pakistan began to smell danger in the activities of the young Awami Muslim League politician. In prison, Mujib maintained the reputation of a man with deep political instincts. He was still only thirty and was rapidly coming round to the idea that if Pakistan was to survive, its leaders would need to satisfy the demands of the Bengali population first. Those demands were once more brushed aside by Prime Minister Khwaja Nazimuddin.

On 26 January 1952, barely three months after the assassination of Liaquat, Nazimuddin restated the government position of decreeing

Urdu as the national language of Pakistan. It was an incendiary comment that quickly led to a fresh hardening of position among the Bengalis. Mujib's response from prison was to go on a hunger strike on 14 February as a protest against Nazimuddin's attitude. Mujib's refusal to eat in Dhaka Central Jail was proving to be an embarrassment for the government. It was shrewd enough to understand that the young man could cause more problems if his health was seriously affected. A clearly unnerved administration quickly shifted Mujib to a new prison, in the distant northern town of Rajshahi. Mujib's hunger strike lasted thirteen days and was to include the moment when the police actually fired on the students of Dhaka University in the expectation that a demonstration of firepower would quell the rising rebellion of the Bengalis over the language issue.

21 February 1952—the day on which the Language Action Council, a body of university students, planned to stage a protest demonstration against the imposition of Urdu—dawned bright but was soon steeped into dark foreboding. The previous evening, a section of politicians largely belonging to the Awami Muslim League had tried dissuading the students from precipitating action as the authorities had already banned any gathering of people under Section 144 of the Criminal Procedure Code. Ironically, the law was a holdover from British colonial rule and was now handy for the government. Early in the morning, the organisers of the protest as well as general students began to gather warily before the arts faculty building of Dhaka University which houses the government medical college today. The mood was one of barely concealed anger owing to the restrictions in place. It gradually became uglier as consensus developed among the students that Section 144 needed to be violated and the demonstration needed to be carried on. Talk of consensus soon led to decisive action. The students marched in clear defiance of all restrictions and felt there could be no turning back. The police took immediate action. Without warning they randomly fired into the crowd. Four young men died. The stunned marchers taken by surprise, scattered. For the first time since the creation of Pakistan, a real sense of gloom suddenly descended

on the country. For Bengalis, the four dead young men became the earliest of heroes in a long procession of martyrs that would intensify the national cause in subsequent years.

The shootings of 21 February were to be a watershed in the history of the Bengalis of East Pakistan. The spirit of nationalism it engendered in the province was to be the first sign of a progressively strong Bengali movement for autonomy that would lead to a full-fledged war of independence against Pakistan nineteen years down the road. In the immediate aftermath of the shootings, Bengalis across the board were made aware for the first time that politics in Pakistan, especially the future of the country's eastern province, headed downhill. A young journalist, Abdul Gaffar Chowdhury, captured the spirit of the moment and penned a brief elegy on the four martyrs. The poem, '*Amar bhaiyer rokte rangano ekushey* February /*Aami ki bhulite pari*' (Can I forget 21 February, soaked in the blood of my brothers?), quickly became a rallying song all over the province. Initially set to a defiant martial tune by the singer Abdul Latif, the song soon became a dirge at the hands of musician Altaf Mahmood. Every 21 February since 1952, Bengalis have sung the song as Altaf Mahmood set it to musical score.

In March 1971, as the Pakistan Army cracked down on the Bengalis, one of the first targets of the military rulers of the time was to hunt down Mahmood. He was killed in the earliest moments of what would in time turn into genocide. Abdul Gaffar Chowdhury would, in 1974, move out of Bangladesh and settle in London, from where he would write for newspapers back home. But all of this was to be in the future. In February 1952, the demand by Bengalis to have their language given the status of a national language in Pakistan and the subsequent murder of their young students severely jolted the political structure in the country. Also, it was the first time that the government of the free state of Pakistan had taken recourse to extreme measures to ensure a continuation of its authority in Dhaka. Things would never be the same again. Mujib was freed from prison five days after the killings of 21 February. The two years he had spent in jail could not but have reinforced his growing antipathy to Pakistan. The shootings of February 1952 could only have helped recharge his batteries. He now had all the reasons in the world to persuade himself that Pakistan had really little place for its Bengali citizens in its politics.

Emerging Star

Politics in East Pakistan as a whole took a new turn in 1953. The Awami Muslim League, sensing an opportunity to take on the ruling Muslim League at the elections scheduled for early 1954 in the province, went into a concerted drive to take its policies to the Bengali masses scattered all across the villages of the province. Interesting, perhaps intriguing as well, elections were being organised in only one of the five provinces of the country, a sign of the volatility that had crept into the political system in Dhaka. Chief Minister Nurul Amin and his administration had since the early days of Pakistan demonstrated a measure of incompetence that was unique even at that wobbly stage of Pakistan's national entity. Food shortages had resulted in near famine conditions in the province, the consequence of which had been an angry outcry in the small towns of East Pakistan.

The Awami Muslim League, and more specifically Mujib, took clear advantage of the conditions to embarrass the provincial administration at every opportunity that made itself available. At a particular stage in the early 1950s, a steep hike in the price of salt, an essential item of everyday necessity, led to ugly demonstrations against Amin and his government. Worst was an outbreak of fresh communal riots, the first after the division of India, in East Pakistan. Thousands of Hindu families, almost all of whom were aligned to such professions as medical science and teaching, along with a sizeable number of businessmen, simply closed shop in the province and made their way to Calcutta. The repercussions were felt in West Bengal, where the appearance of all these new refugees from East Pakistan convinced local Hindus that a systematic move was on to push the Hindu religious minority out of Pakistan as a scheme to turn the country into a land only for the followers of the Islamic faith. The riots in East Pakistan quickly led to violence against Muslims in a number of districts in West Bengal, the result of which was a new influx of Muslim refugees into East Pakistan.

All of these factors had together combined to create a situation where the base of popular support for the government, poor at the best of times, underwent further erosion. The Opposition, led by men like Moulana Bhashani, the president of the Awami Muslim League, demanded provincial elections as a way of reversing the situation. The administration had already passed into atrophy owing to its rather long and unimpressive record in office. The Nurul Amin ministry, in effect, was a microcosm of the larger malaise that was developing all across Pakistan, especially at the centre. The Muslim League, never having been a mass-based political party, despite the significant role it played in the Partition, was proving incapable of holding the centre together. The tragic happenings of 21 February 1952 also told badly on the reputation of the administration. After the shootings of the students, Nurul Amin was seen as a Bengali stooge of the West Pakistan based central government, unable or unwilling to uphold the interests of his people. It was the helplessness of the provincial authorities which, more than any other factor, led to a rapid decline of the government. Things were beginning to fall apart and a clear impression grew of the party having reduced itself into a coterie which was out of touch with the country. Such an impression was most acute in the east, where it was obvious to all except the ruling class that a simple push was what was needed for the Muslim League administration to fall on its face. For Amin, as also for his friends in West Pakistan, the developing situation was a mere conspiracy resorted to by an Opposition desperate in its drive for political power. Worse, Muslim League politicians began, as if in tandem, to peddle the notion that the Opposition was bent on striking at the integrity of Pakistan by the dissemination of its political agenda. It was an attitude that would for years be adopted by the ruling classes of Pakistan. This was also probably a reason why the necessary elements of mutual trust and political accommodation never came to be part of the process in Pakistan, either before its eastern province broke away from it to form the independent state of Bangladesh or after it began its fresh journey on an ostensible democratic path in the years of Zulfikar Ali Bhutto.

The Awami Muslim League was much energised by the turn of events in the province. The beleaguered state of the provincial administration was precisely what a young politician like Mujib needed to galvanise support for what was yet a fledgling Opposition. His fiery speeches at public rallies throughout the country were already being remarked upon. The down to earth, often rustic language he employed in explaining the ground realities to his essentially rural audience was revealing of the transformation he was going through as his political career assumed newer dimensions. The abrasiveness which had earlier been a characteristic of the student in him was by 1953 largely a thing of the past as he made conscious attempts to carve a niche for himself in Bengali politics. But if the raw edges were beginning to peel away, Mujib made certain that his radical streak stayed with him. Deep down, for all his adherence to the constitutional politics his mentor Suhrawardy epitomised, Mujib was an admirer of such past Bengali heroes as Subhas Chandra Bose, the pre-Partition Congress political leader who had mysteriously disappeared in the Far East where he had gone to solicit Japanese imperial support for the cause of Indian independence.

For Mujib, like a large number of other Bengalis, Subhas Chandra Bose was an apt metaphor for courage. Mujib had on at least one occasion felt the power and energy flowing from Bose. On 3 July 1940, as Bose prepared to speak before a crowd in Calcutta to demand the removal of the Holwell monument, built by the British in the centre of the city to commemorate what was considered the controversial massacre of Englishmen in the Black Hole episode of 1756, he was placed under arrest. The meeting at the city town hall went ahead despite Bose's arrest, with Hindus and Muslims spontaneously converging on the place to demand that the British remove the monument by 16 July or face a *Satyagraha* organised by an action council already in place to whip up an agitation over the issue. The youth front of the Muslim League, with Mujib in a leading role, was eager to demonstrate its solidarity with Bose. Mujib came away from the rally marvelling at the ability of a Bengali politician to cut across communal lines and rally Bengalis to what was patently a national cause. It was an admiration that was to last as long as Mujib lived. There was one other politician who evoked similar admiration from Mujib, but he died in 1925 when Mujib was five years old. Chittaranjan Das, an urbane Bengali politician clearly destined for great heights in Indian national politics, died of a cardiac arrest at the relatively young age of fifty-five.

By the time Mujib was creating ripples in the politics of Pakistan, he was conscious of how Bengali aspirations, and consequently the Indian dream of unity and freedom, had been laid low by the unfortunate loss of such stalwarts as Chittaranjan Das and Subhas Chandra Bose.

PART

2

1954, Politics in Crisis

In the year 1953, politics in Pakistan offered little hope for the country to step out of the myriad problems it was entangled in. Politicians at the centre wrangled over issues that looked more like a clash of egos than principled arguments over policy. There was, as yet, little sign of any constitution being framed any time soon, and in the absence of the constitution, governance was turning into a difficult proposition.

Prime Minister Mohammad Ali Bogra, elevated to his position by Governor General Ghulam Muhammad, was beginning to feel distinctly uncomfortable with the latter's high-handed manner of running the show. To add to Pakistan's problems, two other men who would soon be exercising a considerable measure of influence on the Pakistani political scene, General Mohammad Ayub Khan and Major General Iskandar Mirza, were beginning to show all signs that would in time place Pakistan's tottering democracy in jeopardy. Ayub Khan, the army commander-in-chief, who also happened to be cabinet minister for defence, saw in the weakness of the civilian politicians the first hints of a situation that could most likely call for change of a drastic kind. That change would come five years later, but already in 1953 Ayub Khan was inclined to dominate cabinet meetings, often to a point where his rudeness became palpable to his political colleagues around the table.

Where Ayub Khan foresaw a future that would be defined by political change, Iskandar Mirza gradually had developed the notion that the politicians were up to no good. A former officer of the British Indian Army, he traced his ancestry back to Mir Jafar, the man placed on the throne of Bengal by Lord Clive after the murder of Nawab Siraj-ud-Daulah at the hands of local British agents. Mirza had subsequently moved to the civil service and now called many of the shots in the Pakistani civilian structure. Mirza did not conceal his contempt for the damage, in his view, the civilians were doing to his country. A pompous man whose aping of British manners and mannerisms was to be a defining feature of his personality, he nevertheless lacked the shrewdness of Ayub Khan. It was no coincidence, therefore, that only a few years down the road, he was bumped off by Ayub Khan. But in 1953 Ayub Khan gave Mirza all the reasons in the world to think he was beholden to him, a bait for which he would pay later.

It was in the province of East Pakistan, however, that politics was moving at a faster pace in 1953. Armed with the knowledge that elections to the provincial assembly had been scheduled for early 1954, the Awami Muslim League briskly went about putting its house in order. A principal reason behind such activity was of course the fact that the party was, for the first time, poised against the ruling Muslim League and actually believed that it had a good chance of bringing down Nurul Amin and his administration from power. The East Pakistan Awami Muslim League met in council in July. The clear objective was a thorough election-oriented reorganisation of its structure which included the political programme the party would present before the electorate in the run-up to the elections. For Mujib, the council meeting turned out to be richly rewarding. He was elected general secretary of the provincial Awami Muslim League (which by then was already being referred to simply as 'Awami League'), a position that clearly testified to the increasing confidence party elders like Suhrawardy and Bhashani demonstrated in his ability to organise the party at the grass-roots level. His elevation was both a recognition of his abilities and an opening for him to take higher responsibility. The recognition of his role came, not merely because of the ease with which he propagated party programmes throughout the province but also in the clear populism he had, increasingly and carefully, begun to adopt in his approach to the electorate. Mujib understood, more than anyone else in his generation, that if the Awami League was to beat the Muslim League at the elections, it would need to hold itself back from embracing the elitism which now worked as an albatross around the neck of the Muslim League, instrumental in the birth of Pakistan.

In the years after August 1947, Muslim League politicians and workers all over the country had grown complacent, with a large number of them having already developed a reputation of being corrupt or inept or both. As Mujib saw it, it was this growing isolation of the Muslim League from the masses that needed to be focused on in the Awami League's drive for votes. Despite the wariness with which the party had approached the language crisis of February 1952, it was now time for the Awami League to connect with the electorate on the specific issue of Bengali culture. To observers of the Language Movement, the shootings of 21 February had ignited, even if tentatively, the sparks of a nationalistic sentiment that would in time take the Bengalis of Pakistan towards shaping their political aspirations. Young Mujib was certainly one of the first of his generation to comprehend the momentous opportunities the language crisis had opened up for any politician willing to espouse a nationalist Bengali cause. It was a brand of politics which had never actually been toyed with earlier, either in British-controlled India or in the truncated parts of Bengal in the aftermath of the Partition of 1947. Even as he considered the idea of developing a decidedly Bengali approach to politics in mid-1953, Mujib remained aware of the pitfalls of such an approach at that stage.

Suhrawardy, on the other hand, having contributed immensely, sometimes controversially, to the creation of Pakistan, was the last person who could be led into believing that one of its provinces should begin thinking in terms of carving a separate niche for itself in the future. Suhrawardy's faith in Pakistan remained steadfast till the end. If the nature of politics in the country disappointed him—and it disappointed him nearly all the time—he hardly ever allowed that feeling to translate into second thoughts about the state of Pakistan as a whole, which in his case meant playing a central role within that larger picture. Having never been permitted to influence politics in pre-Partition India beyond Bengal, Suhrawardy was determined to ensure that in Pakistan he emerged as the voice of a whole country and not just of one of its provinces. Even though Mujib spontaneously chose to respect this sentiment, he found a timorous rise of feelings that Pakistan may not, after all, be the best option for Bengalis at a later stage. In the hot and humid Bengali summer of 1953, Mujib understood the reality of how far he could go in playing the cultural card before the provincial constituency of the Awami League without in any way upsetting the cart for Suhrawardy.

The latter half of 1953 was used by the Awami League in looking for ways to forge a consensus among secular Bengali politicians on how best to approach the provincial elections. One of the clearer streams of thought tended to favour the formation of a united front. It was a surefire way of defeating the ruling Muslim League, giving East Bengal an administration which would be seriously involved in improving the conditions of the province, especially those that still affected the lives of its peasantry. The Awami League was fortunate in having Bhashani as its president. Like many of his contemporaries, Bhashani had been educated in madrasas. His entire life had been spent living, studying and working in the villages of Bengal, which was how his closeness to the people at the grassroots level became reinforced over time. In 1953, there was hardly anyone better placed than Bhashani to popularise the agrarian-oriented policies of the Awami League. Even so, Suhrawardy, Bhashani and Mujib clearly realised there was little point in the Awami League's going it alone at the elections. It was thus that these men turned to another pivotal figure in Bengali politics, Fazlul Huq.

By 1953, Huq's glorious years were largely behind him. He had, in the years before the division of India, served in a number of positions, including that of prime minister of Bengal. In 1940, as one of the pre-eminent figures in the Bengal Muslim League, Huq presided over the March session of the All India Muslim League in Lahore which officially adopted a resolution for the creation of Muslim states in those areas of India where the followers of the Islamic faith happened to be in a majority. It was as a result of his role at the session that Huq was accorded the honorific *Sher-e-Bangal*, Urdu for 'tiger of Bengal'. The irony is that the individual who addressed Huq as Sher-e-Bangal was Mohammad Ali Jinnah at the very 1940 session of the Muslim League. As Jinnah addressed the Muslim League councillors, Huq made a rather dramatic entry, drawing everyone's attention and forcing Jinnah to pause. It was at that point Jinnah mischievously said, 'Now that the tiger of Bengal is here, I shall retire'. Jinnah might well have been recalling the day, decades earlier, when Gandhi, enthused by his oratory, had described Jinnah as *Quaid-e-Azam*, or the great leader. The title had stuck, as would the one Jinnah gave Huq. To this day, people in Pakistan find it offensive to refer to their founding father as anything other than Quaid-e-Azam. In both Pakistan and Bangladesh, Fazlul Huq is still known as Sher-e-Bangal and Sher-e-Bangla.

In independent Pakistan, Huq achieved instant popularity by playing an instrumental role in the abolition of the antiquated *zamindari* or landlord system. The system had fundamentally been a method by which the old British colonial power had distributed its largesse to Hindus and Muslims loyal to its regime. The largesse, formalised by the Permanent Settlement policy of Lord Cornwallis, comprised handing over prime land in Bengal to British loyalists in perpetuity. In time, the system had led to gross abuse and corruption with the landlords, or *zamindars,* exercising increasingly high levels of exploitation upon the peasants who worked on their land. Indeed, in the early 1940s, conditions turned so bad that leftist as well as Muslim religious figures shaped a radical response to the rapacious behaviour of the landlords. Known as the *Tebhaga* Movement, the plan was to force landlords to hand over a third of the produce from their agricultural lands to the peasants who worked on them. Predictably, the landlords put up resistance and sought the aid of the colonial authorities to quell the rebellion. The British administration duly obliged. By the late 1940s, after the establishment of Pakistan, demands grew in East Bengal for the zamindari system to be abolished altogether. In 1950 with Huq at the forefront, the antiquated, exploitative system of wealth distribution introduced by the British colonial power was finally abolished.

Given such a background, it made sense for Suhrawardy, Bhashani and Mujib to rope in Huq into the job of cobbling a United Front into shape, to challenge the ruling Muslim League at the elections. On 14 November 1953, the Awami League met in a special council session to adopt a resolution authorising the formation of the United Front. The way was now clear for the political Opposition in East Pakistan and it was to plunge into the election campaign. From day one of the United Front, known as *Jukto* Front in Bengali, there was never any question about the immense popularity the leaders of the front enjoyed. To observers, the electoral triumph of the United Front was a foregone conclusion, though there was hardly anyone ready to predict the scale of victory. Curiously enough, the ruling Muslim League gave every impression of complacency, with its leaders and workers not quite prepared to read the writing on the wall. In the end, it was the sheer weight of the combined political appeal of Suhrawardy, Huq and Bhashani that carried the day for the United Front. For Mujib, the 1954 elections were a baptism in the sense that the untiring campaigning he undertook all over the province, to make the United Front a household phrase in the rural interior, burnished an already growing reputation for his organisational skills.

The elections took place all across the province on 10 March 1954. The results, when they came in, demonstrated the deep inroads the United Front had made in the popular perception. The Muslim League had been thoroughly routed and even Chief Minister Nurul Amin lost his seat to a young politician not particularly known in the area. With voting conducted for a total of 237 seats in the provincial legislature, the United Front garnered altogether 223 seats. More surprising was the decisive stamp the Awami League now cast on the future of Bengali politics by winning 143 of the total seats. In the immediate aftermath of the election results, two significant and obvious conclusions were drawn. First, the triumph of the United Front had effectively exposed the political bankruptcy of the Muslim League in East Pakistan and also served as a broad hint on the decline of the party in the perspective of the whole of Pakistan. Second, the elections demonstrated in a decisive manner the links the Awami League had established with Pakistan's Bengali population, a reality that could only have added to the nightmares of the politicians based in the national capital Karachi.

At a personal level, Mujib defeated the powerful Muslim League politician Wahiduzzaman in his native Faridpur region, by a margin of 13,000 votes. It was only to be the beginning of a long political journey for the young general secretary of the provincial Awami League. He would never lose any election as long as he lived. The elections were to bring another boon for Mujib. On 15 May, more than two months after the United Front had beaten the Muslim League and formed a new government for the province, he was given a berth in the cabinet now led by the new chief minister, Fazlul Huq. As minister for agriculture and forests, Mujib was for the first time in his political career in an administrative position, a job he may not have quite enjoyed given that he had always been more comfortable with work that challenged his organisational abilities. Yet it was important that he did not stay away from the administration that needed the skills of all the members of the United Front to prove it a credible and competent government. With the exception of the chief minister, who had administered the undivided province of Bengal in the 1930s, everyone else in the cabinet was a tyro. It was only too obvious that the new arrangements would soon run into trouble. The United Front government would shortly find itself up against all the problems that political coalitions often throw up. The decision to set up the front in the prelude to the March elections had been dictated by a paramount need to send the Muslim League government packing. Now that the objective had been fulfilled, the inevitable strains that often characterise a regime of men with many differing points of view began to surface into the open. It did not quite help that Suhrawardy and Huq, for decades engaged in political rivalry in the years leading to the establishment of Pakistan, were once again faced with real prospect of coming to a head over policy making for the province. Suhrawardy, unwilling to give up his place in central Pakistani politics in Karachi, nevertheless maintained a huge interest in the new provincial government in which his party, the Awami League, wielded rather inordinate authority through its sheer numbers in the legislative assembly.

The teething problems of the United Front ministry could not but have cheered the central government in Karachi, still in the hands of the Muslim League. The defeat of Nurul Amin and the provincial Muslim League in East Pakistan had delivered a staggering blow from which the governor general and the prime minister found it hard to recover. Consequently, when within weeks of the United Front taking over in Dhaka trouble broke out in the country's largest jute mills, Adamjee, in Narayanganj, a river port and industrial town on the outskirts of the provincial capital, the central authorities detected the earliest sign of trouble that could lead to the collapse of the new administration. Over the years since 1954, arguments have raged around the extent of the role the central government and its loyalists may have played in the creation of the crisis at Adamjee as a means of undermining Huq's administration. Seventeen years later, as Mujib led what was beginning to shape up as a struggle for an independent Bangladesh in 1971, he would refer to the removal of the United Front government as one of the grossest instances of the West Pakistani political classes trying to deprive the Bengalis of their constitutional right to govern themselves in their own province. The chief minister compounded the crisis for himself and his government when, on a visit to Calcutta only days after taking over, he emotionally recounted the old days when Bengal was a single entity in British-controlled India. Ever the sentimental man, Huq told his West Bengal audience what they probably wanted to hear—that despite the division of 1947, Bengalis across their severed land remained united around their cultural and political heritage.

Such sentiments were heresy to the ruling classes of Pakistan, who had since Partition strenuously gone into the task of shaping what they saw as a Pakistani ideology for the country, especially for East Bengal, where a streak of Bengali rebelliousness had always been pronounced. Huq, once his Calcutta comments made their way back into Pakistan, was quickly reviled as a traitor to the cause. Open accusations began to be made about a deep conspiracy between the Bengalis and a hostile Indian government to dismember the country. On his return to Dhaka, Huq lost his nerve and attempted damage control by trying to explain away that his remarks as quite innocuous. Where the chief minister should have given short shrift to the accusations, knowing as he did the motives involved, he opted to make rather tame rebuttals of the charges laid at his door. For his part, Mujib saw little reason to be defensive about Huq's statements in Calcutta. But as a young new minister in the provincial cabinet, he was discreet enough to keep his feelings to himself. In private conversations, though, he clearly foresaw what the central government was aiming at. Mujib had developed a sense of certainty about the United Front government eventually being thrown out by the administration in Karachi.

On 29 May, less than three months after winning the provincial elections and forming its government, the United Front ministry was summarily dismissed by the central government of Prime Minister Mohammad Ali Bogra under the terms of Section 92-A, a law that authorised the central administration to take action in a situation it thought threatened the peace and security of any or all parts of the country. The irony in the action of the central government was that it had long waited, somewhat impatiently, to see the last of the United Front government but was now putting up the pretence of having been led to such a drastic action by the ineptitude of the provincial government. Mujib, in the national capital at the time of the dismissal of the government, decided to fly back to Dhaka within hours of the collapse of the United Front ministry. He was placed under arrest as soon as he stepped off the plane at Dhaka airport. The assumption on the part of the authorities was obvious. They felt that with Mujib remaining free, there was a possibility of his galvanising the population in opposition to the imposition of

Section 92-A and thereby putting up the kind of roadblocks before the central authorities that Karachi was not willing to face.

A strong sign of the ham-fisted measures the Pakistan government now planned to undertake in East Pakistan came through the appointment of Major General Iskandar Mirza as the new governor. He was a man who had always suspected Bengalis of harbouring secessionist tendencies and felt they needed firm handling hereon. A measure of how he believed he should be going about his new job came when Mirza publicly declared his wish to shoot the respected Moulana Bhashani, president of the Awami League, a force behind the United Front, like a dog. Mirza was also one of the earliest bureaucrat-politicians in Pakistan to see the dangers in men like Mujib. Such men, he reasoned like many others who followed him, were best kept locked up. Mujib, transported directly from the airport to prison, was not to re-emerge into freedom until 23 December of the year.

The permutations and combinations of politics in Pakistan, over the next year, were to lead to changes of considerable political import. On 21 September 1954, Pakistan's central government in Karachi fell into disarray. Increasingly irked by what it saw as irrational behaviour on the part of Governor General Ghulam Muhammad, the administration of Prime Minister Bogra proceeded to sound out other politicians in the constituent assembly on possible moves towards stripping the governor general of the broad authority he enjoyed. In all fairness to Ghulam Muhammad, it must be said that the powers he enjoyed as governor general were the same that Mohammad Ali Jinnah had exercised in the thirteen months he had been governor general after Pakistan's birth. No one, from Liaquat Ali to Khwaja Nazimuddin, had ever seriously considered the possibility of such unadulterated authority vested in the governor general precipitating a crisis in governance someday.

The governor general, as head of state, was really the head of the administration owing to the powers he wielded in respect of the appointment and dismissal of the prime minister, and the convening and dissolution of parliament. By mid-1954, Bogra had become a trifle exasperated with Ghulam Muhammad who, it was widely rumoured, was already displaying schizophrenic behaviour. It was a brave Bogra who convinced the constituent assembly that the wings of the governor general needed clipping. This meant a clear introduction of the provision in the interim constitution relating to the governor general acting only on the advice of the prime minister. The assembly acted swiftly, taking advantage of the absence of Ghulam Muhammad, who was away on a tour of the northern regions of West Pakistan. Shortly afterwards, the prime minister jetted off to Washington on an official trip, obviously happy that his coup had succeeded. At that point, neither he nor anyone else around him had any way of knowing just how circumstances would transform even as the prime minister toured the United States.

Returning to Karachi as soon as he could, Ghulam Muhammad immediately declared a state of emergency as in his view the constitutional machinery had collapsed, thus rendering the government unable to function. The constituent assembly, which only days earlier had voted to strip him of his powers, was now a fugitive across the political landscape. The governor general made it clear that a new constituent assembly would need to be forged and the government would require to be reconstituted. With a single stroke, therefore, Ghulam Muhammad had shown who had the final say in political governance. He had taken the legislature's action against the powers of the governor general personally and he was now determined to humiliate the prime minister, possibly by sacking him. By a rather curious coincidence, Prime Minister Bogra, Army Chief Ayub Khan and Iskandar Mirza, the new governor of East Pakistan, were all abroad at the time Ghulam Muhammad made his sweeping moves. Bogra and Ayub were both in the United States, on separate missions, while Mirza was in London for medical treatment. The prime minister, as he rushed back to Pakistan, stopped over in London, where Mirza met him. Ayub Khan also turned up there and together the trio travelled back to Pakistan. It is not difficult to see the different strands of thoughts that would have been going through the minds of the three men as they made that long journey from London to Karachi. For Bogra, it was a matter of saving his position as prime minister, now that the governor general had struck back so viciously. For Ayub Khan, who had never concealed his contempt for politicians, there was finally the possibility that the army he commanded could begin to call the shots. If he meant to remain part of the political scene, Ayub Khan would have to make sure that some dramatic development ensured his continuation as army commander-in-chief, a position from which he was scheduled to retire in 1955.

In the late 1960s, Ayub would make it clear in his memoirs as Pakistan's president that had he wished he could have taken over the country in 1954. It is therefore reasonable to suppose that in October 1954, as Ayub Khan made his way back to Pakistan with his two compatriots, he might already have been toying with the possibility of introducing military rule in the country. As for Mirza, who had always relished the chance to be at the centre of things, there was the rather pretty prospect of his playing the role of a kingmaker in the whole new drama about to unfold in Karachi. His inflated ideas about his own indispensability would always blur the realities before him and would one day lead to his unceremonious exit from power as well as from Pakistan. For now, however, he indulged in the happy thought that whatever the nature of the changes on the way, he could not but have a focal place in them. Bogra managed to retain his position as prime minister, but his authority had greatly shrunk. He did not demur when the governor general moved to have a new constituent assembly to replace the one he had already pushed out into the cold. Iskandar Mirza, after only a few months as governor of the country's eastern province, was taken into the cabinet as minister for interior. Bogra plodded on as prime minister until 7 August 1955, when ill health compelled Ghulam Muhammad to quit, temporarily as it was put about, in favour of Mirza. On that day, Bogra resigned from the office of prime minister. He was soon reappointed to his old job as Pakistan's ambassador to the United States. Life would treat him in rather mysterious ways. As ambassador in Washington for a second time, it would be his job to welcome, in 1957, Prime Minister Huseyn Shaheed Suhrawardy (who had been law minister in his cabinet) to Washington. More surprisingly, in the early 1960s, Bogra would be offered the position of foreign minister in the military regime of President Ayub Khan, which he would accept. When he died in early 1963 he would be replaced by the young Zulfikar Ali Bhutto.

Pakistan, on the whole, would be pulled inexorably and dramatically in quite a few directions. But all of that was in the future. By mid-1955, politics was once more hotting up in East Pakistan and Mujib was clearly on his way to playing a role, as a Bengali, on the national stage in Karachi.

At the Epicentre

Pakistan's Bengalis were given new ammunition in the autumn of 1955 to wage battle against, what for them, was increasingly becoming a pattern of political perfidy on the part of the West Pakistani-dominated central government. A new constituent assembly was already in place, replacing the one that had tried stripping the governor general of his enormous powers in the structure of the state. One of the new members of the refashioned constituent assembly, established without exercising universal adult franchise, was Mujib.

After his release from imprisonment at the end of 1954, he was thus placed firmly on the national stage, clearly through the patronage of his leader Suhrawardy. At that particular stage, Suhrawardy needed all the support he could get and naturally was inclined to think that having Mujib in Karachi as a lawmaker would strengthen the case for the Awami League at the centre. Suhrawardy had by then made no secret of his ambition to take charge of Pakistan as prime minister. His difficulty was that his party was in a minority in the legislature and could only form a government if it managed to manoeuvre a coalition with other parties. The bet was that Mujib the organiser could be a dependable hand for Suhrawardy, though he also remained convinced there was yet a streak of radicalism about Mujib which needed to be curbed. For his part, Mujib did not give any impression that he enjoyed being part of the constituent assembly, although he took due advantage of its sessions to draw attention to issues that affected his province. It is significant that a few days after taking his seat in the Pakistan Constituent Assembly, Mujib was instrumental in organising a public rally for the Awami League in Dhaka. The objective was the placement of demands relating to the question of autonomy for the province within the parameters of Pakistan. The 21-point programme of the party, announced at the rally on 17 June 1955, was the first instance of a formalisation of the demands and needs that Bengalis felt ought to be met by the ruling circles. In light of the fact that Mujib's later demands for autonomy would go far beyond, the Awami League's demands in June 1955 were rather tame. But the autonomy demands of the East Pakistan politicians were looked upon as a cool, premeditated way of undercutting the Pakistan ideology. It did not help that one of the powerful voices behind such demands was Suhrawardy's. The suspicions lingered.

Then came a move which aroused even more suspicion among Bengalis about the motives of the rulers in Karachi. On 30 September 1955, the constituent assembly voted to lump the provinces of the Punjab, Sind, Baluchistan and the North West Frontier together into a single unit to be known as West Pakistan henceforth. At a single, swift stroke, the preponderance that East Bengal/East Pakistan had enjoyed in terms of population was struck down. What replaced the old system was euphemistically given about as parity, which was essentially a move to strike a balance in the relationship between the two parts of the country. Mujib's discomfiture was close to the point of despair. He was one of the few Bengali politicians to comprehend the repercussions of the One Unit scheme, as it came to be known, primarily because he saw in the plan a watertight system that would for good prevent his province from asserting its political rights by drawing attention to its distinctive political and economic problems. The fact that the constituent assembly would from now on have an equal number of members from East and West Pakistan only added to Bengali concerns about how much of a hold, if at all, the province would continue to have in the state.

The signs of disquiet were already in the air. The country's civil service was being stacked with officers from the west, with a mere smattering of individuals from the east. In recruitment to the armed forces, conditions were worse. With the army chief himself being of the view that the Bengalis, descendants of India's ancient Dravidians, were not a martial race in the way the 'Aryan' West Pakistanis were, it was fairly easy to see the groundwork in progress to keep the people of East Pakistan marginalised in the military. It would be quite revealing, when East Pakistan finally chose to break away from the rest of the country in 1971, that Bengalis had few officers in the armed forces, none of whom held a high position in the military hierarchy.

More than a month before the constituent assembly voted in favour of One Unit in the western part of Pakistan, Mujib made his concerns known at the 25 August session of the legislature in Karachi: 'Sir, you will see that they want to place the words "East Pakistan" instead of "East Bengal". We have demanded so many times that you should use (East) Bengal instead of (East) Pakistan. The word "Bengal" has a history, has a tradition of its own. You can change it only after the people have been consulted. If you want to change it, then we have to go back to Bengal and ask them whether they accept it.' Mujib's words fell on deaf ears. There was little he could do given that his own party seemed rather reticent about taking any action that resembled radicalism where the position of Bengalis was concerned. As already seen, the assembly adopted the One Unit resolution along with the proposal of formally renaming the country's eastern province as East Pakistan. Such moves were only to add to the discontent already brewing among Bengalis.

While in East Pakistan a growing sense of political deprivation was gradually taking root, within the centre itself things were moving fast, almost disturbingly so. Bogra was out and his place as prime minister had been taken over by Chaudhri Mohammad Ali. The acting governor general, Iskandar Mirza, proved to be more astute than Ghulam Muhammad in that he was successfully playing off one politician against another. Mirza remained steadfast in his belief that the Bengalis of Pakistan were yet to become fully attuned to the ideology of the Muslim state. He made little attempt to conceal his contempt for their leaders and made dark hints about their lack of loyalty to Pakistan, going so far as to suggest that they had one foot in Pakistan with the other planted firmly in India. Mirza clearly had Mujib, among others, in mind. Mujib did not need much persuasion to know that men like Mirza represented a potent threat not only to Pakistan's Bengalis but also to the concept of democratic governance in Pakistan as a whole. Even Suhrawardy, a man whose political beliefs had been shaped in the explosive circumstances of British India, comprehended the risks that Mirza and his ilk posed to Pakistan and especially to Bengalis. But he was shrewd enough to know that antagonising Mirza would only keep him out of the power circle in which he had already begun moving with ease. Suhrawardy reassured himself that the future was his and that Chaudhri Mohammad Ali, who was in office with the support of the Awami League, was doomed to fall. In the topsy-turvy world of Pakistan's politics, there was no one other than Suhrawardy, at that point, to take charge.

Before the Awami League could bring Chaudhri Mohammad Ali down, there was an immediate need for the party to get its own house in order. In the years after its establishment in 1949, it had clearly evolved into a political organisation that shared few principles with the ruling Muslim League. Translated into simpler terms, the Awami League kept faith with the concept of Pakistan, despite the growing misgivings of Moulana Bhashani and Mujib about the future of the country in relation to its Bengalis. Apart from such adherence to the idea of Pakistan, the party had begun veering off into a direction that portrayed it as everything the Muslim League was not. Fundamental among the ideas that the party's politicians seriously toyed with was the need to give the Awami League a secular turn. This was of course seen as a political necessity, even an imperative, if the electorate were to distinguish between it and the Muslim League at national elections, whenever they took place. In essence, the Awami League had in the years since the Language Movement of 1952 and particularly after its participation in the United Front progressively taken on the appearance of a secular organisation. It was of small consequence that it officially continued to be known as the Awami Muslim League. The truth was that it was beginning to think in terms of reaching out to all religious and sectarian communities in Pakistan as a demonstration of its increasingly secular dimensions. By 1955, the country's constituent assembly adopted One Unit and renamed it East Pakistan in what was largely seen as a move towards strengthening the Islamic roots of the state. The party that Suhrawardy and Bhashani had founded in 1949 seemed ready and willing to formalise itself as a secular entity. On 21 October 1955, the party officially saw its communal skin peel away when it discarded the term 'Muslim' from its name and renamed itself the Awami League. Mujib was re-elected general secretary of the East Pakistan provincial Awami League.

In terms of Pakistan's history, 1956 was a mixed blessing. The constituent assembly, nearly nine years after the creation of the country, was finally able to adopt a constitution for the state. Promulgated on 23 March, the document represented somewhat of a break from the system that had until then been the foundation of governance in the country. The Government of India Act 1935, with suitable modifications, had served as the basis for constitutional politics in Pakistan. But in 1956, the constitution that came to be adopted and accepted by both wings of the country envisaged a republic, which signified a replacement of the office of the governor general with that of a president. But such a change was not as far-reaching as the two other changes—the definition of the state, for the first time, as the Islamic Republic of Pakistan, and the introduction of a Westminster-style of parliamentary government for the country. The adoption of the constitution also happened to be a windfall for Iskandar Mirza, who soon found himself elected by the legislature as the first president of Pakistan. The clear sentiment all over the country was that Pakistan would finally move towards the next phase in its independent existence through elections at the national level. It was assumed that elections to a future national assembly would be held by late 1958 or early 1959. But before the country could indulge in such luxury, there was the small matter of ensuring that the central government functioned in Karachi.

Prime Minister Chaudhri Mohammad Ali certainly took pride in the fact that it was during his tenure in office that the country had come by a constitution for itself, but the larger and ominous fact was that his administration was adrift. Having been a bureaucrat for much of his life, the prime minister was something of a fish out of water in the palace intrigues which continued to define politics in Pakistan. It was not just Suhrawardy's manoeuvrings that were undermining him. The prime minister was under attack from his own Muslim League, who made little secret of their contempt. As for the party itself, it was now largely controlled by its new president, Sardar Abdur Rab Nishtar, a man given to believing that the country was in absolute need to be governed along the principles laid down in Islam. Nishtar was only one of the men who sought to take advantage of the situation, now that Pakistan had officially been defined as an Islamic republic. Faced with such challenges from Nishtar, and also from the more fanatical Jamaat-e-Islami of Moulana Abul A'la Moududi, Chaudhri Mohammad Ali could not but observe his circumstances get increasingly complicated.

By early September, the prime minister was at the end of his tether. Meanwhile, in East Pakistan, the Awami League had clearly been on the offensive in the days and weeks leading to the adoption of the constitution. In early February, party leaders, including Mujib, made the demand that the constitution incorporate provisions of meaningful regional autonomy for the provinces, which at that point referred only to East and West Pakistan, the latter having already been transformed into a single unit. For Bengali politicians, the draft of the constitution offered little in terms of autonomy. Most subjects or portfolios remained in the hands of the central government in Karachi while the provincial administrations looked as if they were to be dependent on the largesse offered by the central authorities in their efforts to run themselves. The Awami League was worried about the role of the military in the nation's politics and adopted a resolution four months after the constitution had been adopted, advocating a slicing away of military influence in the government.

It did not need much wisdom to know where the party was pointing its fingers. President Mirza, having been part of the army, and General Ayub Khan, the army chief, were two individuals who cast their long shadows on politics despite the impression that Pakistan was now well and truly on the way to being a parliamentary democracy. It was Mujib more than any other leading figure in the party who adopted a tough line towards any signs of the army hovering around what he considered was a business for civilian politicians alone. Apart from dealing with constitutional issues, Mujib remained with his ears firmly to the ground. As reports of a possible food shortage in East Pakistan began to make their way to Dhaka, Mujib switched back to agitation and organised demonstrations demanding swift government action to handle the crisis. He relished, or so it appeared, confrontation with authority. The fact that he was now a member of the Pakistan Constituent Assembly and the fact that he had been a minister in the short-lived United Front provincial government were realities he did not allow to come in the way of what he loved doing best, which was to strike a populist position on issues concerning Bengalis at the grass-roots.

On 4 September 1956, even as his leader Suhrawardy struck what would be decisive blows against Prime Minister Chaudhri Mohammad Ali, Mujib defied government imposed restrictions on processions and demonstrations in Dhaka to lead an anti-famine march in the city. When the police opened fire on the procession in Dhaka's Chawkbazar area, three persons lay dead. Predictably, the killings pushed up the tension by several notches and left the provincial administration red in the face. Mujib's politics, by 1956, had begun to be exasperating for his more experienced colleagues in the Awami League. Moulana Bhashani, the president of the party, was continually irked by what he saw as brashness in the young politician. Moreover, Mujib, for all his respect for Bhashani, remained distrustful of his politics and could not quite rid himself of the feeling that the old man was a maverick who was doing little good to the party. Bhashani, for his part, was disturbed by Mujib's fanatical sense of loyalty to Suhrawardy, especially when their politics complemented each other. It was not just Bhashani whom Mujib left simmering in indignation. The mild-mannered Ataur Rahman Khan, an influential Awami League politician, later to be chief minister of East Pakistan, was almost regularly offended by what he considered as Mujib's brashness and lack of respect for senior party leaders. Khan and Mujib clashed often on policy. It was Khan's belief that Mujib's brand of fiery populism would in the end undercut the party and leave it surrounded with more enemies than it could handle. There was in Khan a strong belief that the Awami League needed to broaden its base to cover both the wings of Pakistan. For Mujib, the priorities related to the party's digging deeper roots among Bengalis. In his political beliefs, Khan was closer to Suhrawardy. But it was Mujib who had the great man's ear.

Huseyn Shaheed Suhrawardy took over as Pakistan's prime minister on 10 September 1956 when conditions became untenable for Chaudhri Mohammad Ali to continue as head of government. It was with considerable reluctance that President Mirza asked the leader of the Awami League to form a new government in coalition with the Republican Party. A pronounced reason for Mirza's ire was his long-standing suspicion that Bengalis were not the model citizens the state of Pakistan wished them to be. In his brief period as governor of East Pakistan, Mirza had made it seem that his authority in Dhaka was more that of a viceroy come from abroad than of a politician with roots in the same country. In 1954, Mirza's exercise of influence in the dismissal of the elected United Front government had been patent. Subsequently, his outburst against Bhashani made it clear to Bengalis that Mirza validated their argument that their province was being treated in the manner of a colony. For Mirza, it was plainly outrageous that the eastern province was systematically making it clear that its politics was at complete variance with that of West Pakistan.

A measure of the difference was reflected in the demand of the Awami League that the electorate not be divided along communal lines. The presence of a large number of Hindus in East Pakistan, over ten per cent of the provincial population to be exact, had convinced successive Pakistani administrations that a communal approach to electoral politics would ensure that the country's religious minorities did not have any perceptible influence on the overall course of national politics. The goal for Pakistan's rulers remained a promotion of a rather vaguely put Pakistan ideology and this ideology could not be tampered with by permitting Hindus and other minorities in Muslim Pakistan to have a say in the affairs of the state. The best they could look forward to was some form of representation for themselves in the national as well as provincial legislatures, restricted only to minority issues. Unfortunately for Pakistan, the Bengalis in the east tended to disagree, over a fairly good number of issues. One of these was the slow but steady re-emergence of the notion that despite the division of 1947 along religious lines, Bengalis on both sides of the frontier remained a distinct cultural body with common roots in literature, history and social mores. It was a problem that would assail even Suhrawardy, despite the fact that his political authority sprang from his base in East Pakistan. As prime minister, Suhrawardy was unwilling to make any move that could be construed as parochial. His struggle for power had been long and hard and when he assumed charge of the government, it was fundamentally the fulfilment of a dream that had been interrupted in 1947 when Partition led to his natural removal from office as chief minister of united Bengal. Suhrawardy served as Pakistan's prime minister for a mere year before his coalition collapsed in October 1957. But within that year, his government made some pretty sweeping changes in the country, especially where its foreign relations were concerned. The prime minister made a highly publicised visit to the United States, where the Eisenhower administration left no stone unturned to demonstrate its faith in Pakistan as a natural ally. It was his government that underscored Pakistan's role in such US sponsored anti-communist regional blocs as the South East Asia Treaty Organisation (SEATO) and the Baghdad Pact, which later was renamed the Central Treaty Organisation (CENTO). In his overriding zeal to take Pakistan closer to the West, Suhrawardy managed to upset sensibilities elsewhere.

His failure to come to the support of Egypt's Gamal Abdel Nasser in the 1956 Suez crisis certainly did not go down well with a majority of Pakistanis. However, in what seemed like a moment of high drama, Prime Minister Zhou En-lai visited Dhaka on a trip that clearly marked the beginning of a new trend in the country's approach to the world outside its frontiers, a feat never before attempted by earlier Pakistani administrations. It was Mujib who delivered the address of welcome to the Chinese prime minister at a civic reception in the East Pakistani capital of Dhaka. There was symbolism in that act too. No one was left in any doubt as to where Mujib stood in relation to Suhrawardy. The prime minister, by 1957, clearly looked upon Mujib as a future standard bearer of the Awami League.

The assumption of power in Karachi by Suhrawardy had brought with it a change in the fortunes of Mujib. The firebrand Bengali politician was inducted into the East Pakistan provincial cabinet as minister for commerce, labour, anti-corruption and village aid. But it was a job that Mujib would keep for only a few months, until May 1957. With his noted penchant for organisational work within the party, he had little difficulty in knowing where his responsibilities primarily lay. The Awami League only helped him make up his mind. On 30 May, the party formally asked him to take charge of the organisational programme, which he did with alacrity. Resigning from the cabinet, Mujib plunged into a programme of refurbishment of the party. In fact, the party's falling back on him was the result of fissures that had begun to develop within, with Bhashani and Suhrawardy publicly disagreeing on the course Pakistan was taking in foreign policy under the prime minister. Though Bhashani, a clear leftist in his views, had welcomed Zhou En-lai's visit to Dhaka, he nevertheless felt that under Suhrawardy, Pakistan was mortgaging its diplomacy to the Americans. Suhrawardy, of course, thought differently. But he could hardly ignore the fact that an angry Bhashani was also a dangerous Bhashani. The sheer populist appeal of the preacher-politician could jeopardise the future of the Awami League as a political organisation. With the Awami League undermined in such a way, Suhrawardy reasoned, prospects for democracy in Pakistan and his own future would be dealt a severe blow. Despite the fact that other political parties, such as the Republicans and the Jamaat-e-Islami, had in the previous few years emerged to challenge the dominance of the ruling Muslim League, it was the Awami League, with its tactical strategy and growing mass appeal, largely in East Pakistan, which represented a potent and perhaps necessary threat to the entrenched ruling classes. If Suhrawardy and Bhashani were unable to reach a compromise or bridge their differences, there was a dire possibility of the party coming apart soon. It was in such a context that Mujib's organisational skills were once more drawn upon. But if there was any hope that the younger politician could prevent the coming calamity, it was quite offset by the clear feeling in Bhashani and his followers that Mujib was Suhrawardy's man and would therefore not be willing to do anything that might undercut the prime minister. And yet the curious fact remained that Bhashani and Mujib pursued similar populist, closer-to-the-masses themes in their politics. The big difference between the elderly politician and young Mujib was the former's penchant for volatile unpredictability.

In 1957, Bhashani's politics would take him along a whole new course in Pakistan's politics. The break between Bhashani and the Suhrawardy-Mujib camp came at a conference organised by the fiery moulana in early February 1957 in rural Kagmari, where Bhashani demonstrated two new important features of his evolving political transformation. The first concerned what he and a whole swathe of Bengalis perceived as the growing chasm between West Pakistan and East Pakistan in the social, economic and political spheres. Bhashani, never so forthright as he was to be in this year of dramatic developments, warned West Pakistan that if it failed to undertake serious engagement with its eastern province, a time might soon arrive when Bengalis would have to say 'Assalam-o-Alaikum' or goodbye to Pakistan. It was the first time that a politician in the east was openly suggesting that relations between the two provinces had reached such a low point that talk of separation was no more an untenable proposition. Beyond the element of drama, however, Bhashani's outburst was more an angry denunciation of the way politics was shaping up, or collapsing, in the country. Personally, he was getting, or so his followers thought, marginalised in the political process. The Awami League, with Suhrawardy at the centre, was clearly embracing all those policies that were anathema to him. The party had clearly embarked on a capitalistic, middle-class oriented, pro-western course that to the moulana epitomised a rejection of the principles of egalitarianism upon which it was founded in 1949. Such observations of the scene around him led Bhashani into demonstrating the second feature of his politics at that point, which was to leave the Awami League in July of the year and form a new, certainly left-wing political party. He called it the National Awami Party (NAP). And he made it plain that the new party would cater more to the interests of the peasantry and industrial workers than what he perceived as bourgeois interests.

Moulana Bhashani's departure from the Awami League was for Mujib a matter of relief since it signalled an end to the long simmering conflict between the moderate and extreme left wings of the party. Suhrawardy, though hardly in a position not to recognise the damage the split in the party and the departure of Bhashani had caused him, would surely have felt the same way as Mujib did. Finally, the organisation was under his control. A majority of Awami League politicians and workers had chosen to remain with Suhrawardy. One reason for that was the national stature, in addition to his earlier importance in India, that Suhrawardy had by then come to acquire in Pakistan. Another factor was the presence of men like Mujib around him, which was a signal to the country that while Bhashani may have personified populism—and populist politics mattered in impoverished East Pakistan—it was a theme he could not expect to monopolise since young politicians like Mujib had already begun to make inroads into the rural Bengali psyche.

Prime Minister Suhrawardy resigned in October 1957 when the president did not permit him to seek a vote of confidence in parliament.

Mirza lost little time in placing I.I. Chundrigar, an unknown, in the job at the head of a new coalition. One of the first moves made by the new government related to the announcement of a schedule for Pakistan's first general elections in November 1958. But even before the Chundrigar administration could settle down, the coalition began to come apart. Suhrawardy, outraged at the fall of his government, went about trying to recreate conditions that would place him back in office. The year was turning out badly for him. With Bhashani gone and with the Awami League holding power in East Pakistan amidst a state of infighting between Ataur Rahman Khan, the chief minister, and Mujib, and finally with his central government dismissed, the veteran politician was for the first time in a decade faced with the prospect of being sidelined. Suhrawardy was well aware of how much Mirza distrusted him. To make matters worse, the governor of East Pakistan, Fazlul Huq, was getting exasperated with the muddle the Awami League provincial government was. He sent out signals of wanting to eventually send the chief minister and his cabinet out to pasture. It was this predicament that forced Suhrawardy into the politics of intrigue, an exercise he had last indulged in immediately prior to the partition of India. The Chundrigar ministry soon fell, but that did not make matters any easier for Suhrawardy. The man who took over from Chundrigar was Malik Firoz Khan Noon, who gave the impression of taking up from where his predecessor had left off. He went rather seriously into the business of preparing for the elections that would come in about a year's time.

Martial Law and Tagore

Pakistan's experiment with parliamentary democracy came to a resounding end on the evening of 7 October 1958 when President Iskandar Mirza, with the active support of the army commander-in-chief, General Ayub Khan, placed the country under martial law. It was a lightning action that saw the constitution, prepared so painstakingly over a period of nine years before being adopted in 1956, abrogated. The central government and the two provincial governments were sacked and their powers handed over to senior military officers, who now formed the core of the new regime. Ayub Khan not only took charge as chief martial law administrator but also in effect became the head of government. Mirza, in his naiveté, did not realise that the extreme step he had taken in league with the army chief would soon create the perfect conditions for his own ouster by the latter, a mere twenty days later. In the first few days of military rule, politicians were swiftly rounded up and transported to jails across the country. Mujib, naturally, was one of the earliest victims of the new circumstances. More elderly political figures, such as Suhrawardy, Bhashani and Huq, were spared prison, though a lid was placed on their political activities. Within a few weeks, however, Bhashani would be packed off to jail and Huq pushed into a situation where he would increasingly become redundant. As for Suhrawardy, Ayub Khan and Mirza were yet reluctant to take any precipitate action against him for fear that it might lead to wider ramifications.

The ramifications of martial law came, of course, but on a different plane. The army takeover, with the obvious support of the air force and navy, resulted in a state of fear enveloping the whole country. Given that Pakistanis had not expected or experienced anything like it before, the imposition of martial law created a grave sense of insecurity among the population. On a more specific level, the business classes and the civil bureaucracy and, of course, the politicians were forced into a situation where they clearly feared for their future. The kind of equanimity with which future spells of military rule in Pakistan would be met was absent in 1958 because it was the first time that Pakistan's citizens had been confronted with a situation they did not quite know how to respond to. All that was clear was that politics as usual had ground to a halt and the word of the army was law. On Mirza's part, there was a degree of satisfaction that he had acted in what he believed was the larger interest of the country. In the couple of months before the army took over, Mirza and Ayub had deliberated on the need for action against the politicians. Mirza, ironically, was the one who had suggested to Ayub that the constitution of 1956 had become unworkable and needed to be replaced by a new one. He was thus advocating the demise of a document on the basis of which he had taken over as Pakistan's president in March 1956. For Ayub Khan, Mirza's dark mutterings about the constitution and the politicians could not have come at a better time. He had, since 1954, been busy reflecting on a takeover and now Mirza was the man who seemed to be making matters easier for him. Apart from Mirza's conspiratorial nature and Ayub Khan's ambitions, the chaos into which Pakistan had descended owing to the doings of its politicians was an undeniable factor behind the entry of the army into politics. The rapidity with which governments fell in Karachi, with prime ministers passing through what were revolving doors, and the intrigue that had become a feature of coalition building and destruction in the centre as well as the provinces, played into the hands of the army. When Ayub Khan ordered the soldiers out into the streets on 7 October, he was quite certain about what he needed to do. Part of his plan related to jettisoning of President Mirza from the new set-up he had already lined up. On 27 October 1958, a group of senior military officers that included General Mohammad Musa, General K.M. Shaikh, General Azam Khan, General W.A. Burki and General Yahya Khan turned up at the presidential residence in Karachi to demand that Iskandar Mirza resign and hand over full authority to Ayub Khan. When Mirza demurred, one of the generals drew a gun to convince him the group meant business. Mirza got the message. Once he had affixed his signature to the resignation letter that had already been drafted by the officers for him, he was put on a plane along with his wife and flown to the south-western city of Quetta, capital of Baluchistan. A few days later, the deposed president and his wife were flown to Karachi, put on a plane bound for London and sent off into a long exile. Mirza would never be allowed to return to Pakistan for the remainder of his life. When he died in November 1969, the new military regime of General Yahya Khan refused him burial in Pakistan. His family, with help from the Shah of Iran, laid him to rest in Tehran.

Within Pakistan, immediately after the imposition of martial law, the army swiftly divided the country into martial law zones and placed senior generals in charge. Into the central cabinet came military officers, along with a smattering of civilians. Before he was forced out of power, Mirza had engineered the entry of a bright young lawyer from Sind, Zulfikar Ali Bhutto, into the cabinet as minister for commerce. It was a position the thirty year-old political novice would hold on to even after Mirza was sent off into exile. In the early days of the military government, the soldiers went after what they considered troublesome politicians with a degree of ferocity that left people surprised and in a state of trepidation. Mujib was arrested on 11 October and soon became a particular target of the army's wrath. The fiery nature of his politics and his focus on Bengali grievances in the previous years had not gone unnoticed by the army. It now boiled down to a situation where it became necessary to lock him up even if his mentor Suhrawardy stayed out of jail. The military regime instituted a number of cases against him and kept him in prison for a stretch of fourteen months. When a judicial order finally led to his release, he found himself taken into custody again as soon as he stepped out through the gates of prison. It was a pattern that would become part of Mujib's political career over the next decade and beyond.

In early 1959, General Ayub Khan, who was now president of Pakistan in addition to being chief martial law administrator, promulgated the Elective Bodies' Disqualification Ordinance (EBDO), under the provisions of which nearly every leading player on the country's political stage was barred from contesting any elections in the foreseeable future, unless of course the military regime decided otherwise. Suhrawardy, Chaudhri Mohammad Ali, I.I. Chundrigar, Bhashani, Mian Mumtaz Daultana, Mujib, Ataur Rahman Khan, Abdul Ghaffar Khan, Khan Abdul Wali Khan, Hamidul Haq Chowdhury, A.K. Fazlul Huq, Sardar Bahadur Khan, Ayub Khuhro, Nawab Akbar Bugti, Abdus Samad Achakzai and a host of other political figures were barred from taking part in politics. More pointedly, they would not be permitted to take part in any elections the regime might plan on organising. It was made clear, as the army consolidated its hold on political power, that there was little prospect of the country returning to democracy any time in the foreseeable future. Ayub Khan, an ambitious man, was also a tough soldier who was convinced that the travails Pakistan faced were largely the doing of the politicians. It was from such a premise that his regime went into forging a new alliance, not with politicians, but with the country's civil bureaucracy. In the next ten years, which would be entirely dominated by Ayub Khan, the army and the civil service would gradually and happily come together in a new enterprise to administer the country. That would in time lead to pretty bizarre and unfortunate results. With the army already holding power by sheer force of arms, the bureaucracy was now led to believe that the nation's political classes were not to be trusted. A conscious effort was put into the programme to discredit politicians, to which the bureaucracy happily contributed and just as happily reaped benefits.

A particularly disappointing feature of the Pakistan civil service in the Ayub years was the sense of elitism it developed about itself.

Such a development happened in parallel with the other elitism that was quickly coming to define the military. The declaration of martial law had placed military officers in political charge of the country. But the army ensured that the implementation of administrative plans was left to bureaucrats, who were only too willing to oblige the soldiers. In a ten-year period, therefore, Pakistan went through a transformation of sorts in the sense that new recruitment into the armed forces and the civil service was marked by an increasing number of individuals opting to join either of the two sectors. For the civil service particularly, the Ayub era was one of clear power-grabbing. The president and his regime made it clear through their words and actions that they were not willing to undermine the civil service. In truth, the administrative authority given to civil service officers, even at the provincial levels, allowed bureaucrats to exercise the powers that in a normal democracy would be the prerogative of elected members of parliament and local government bodies combined. A natural result of the nexus between Pakistan's army and civil service was in time, at first subtle and then an overt entry of corruption into the whole system. It would leave Pakistan and, later, Bangladesh trapped in a system that would become entrenched.

The Ayub Khan regime in time began to demonstrate all the classic symptoms of a government progressively sucked into a quagmire of its own making. Apart from a new set of laws introduced under the Family Laws Ordinance (in 1961), pertaining to divorces and inheritance laws for women and orphans, in clear opposition to traditional Islamic rules followed till that point in time, the regime really had little to show for dynamism or modernity. In a period of ten years, even as industrialisation picked up pace and President Ayub Khan could rightly be proud of having injected dynamism into the economy, the population became poorer. The burgeoning economy quickly threw up a number of families, all based in West Pakistan, who came to dominate the national economy. Described pejoratively as the twenty-two families these nouveau riche quickly became the butt of popular ridicule as also one of the strongest bases of support for the regime. In the final stages of Ayub's rule, these families would acquire a degree of power that would provoke nearly all political classes into promising action against them should they make it to power someday. The level of disapproval was sharp and regional exploitation was acute.

The ten years of Ayub Khan were, in contrast to what happened before and after it, a time when the Bengalis of East Pakistan moved further away from the centre. Bengali recruitment in the civil service remained pitifully low. In the military, it was paltry. The number of senior Bengali bureaucrats in the central government, given the nature of recruitment, was negligible. Such deprivation might have been checked or at least deliberated upon had a constitutional state structure been available. Politicians and civil society members in East Pakistan began to grumble about the way the province was made to feel like an alms seeker despite the fact that its cash crop, jute, happened to be the major foreign exchange earner for the whole country. The feeling that West Pakistan was being developed economically with the earnings of East Pakistan, a sentiment that sprouted in the years before martial law, took deeper roots in the Ayub era. In time, Mujib would seize on the idea as his political theme and go forth into developing his own notions of how Bengalis could on their own try to reverse conditions for themselves.

By 1961, dissatisfaction with military rule was gathering strength all over East Pakistan, though the same could not be said about West Pakistan. Bengali politicians across the spectrum chafed under the EBDO regulations, unable to mount an open public offensive against the regime. The rigorous martial law regulations precluded any overt demonstration of political fervour, and politicians by and large were reduced to silence in the confines of their homes. Even as 1961 began and progressed, Mujib, however, kept going into detention, obtaining freedom through judicial action and going back to jail. The regime seemed particularly sensitive to the idea of Mujib being out on the streets—and he clearly seemed to have developed a capacity for defiance of the military—in its view instigating public discontent. It was also a time when for the first time in his developing political career Mujib began to entertain serious notions of Bengali political freedom. Such ideas were in embryonic form and could not be advanced because of serious obstacles in his way. One of these was the continued presence of Suhrawardy, a strong believer in the territorial integrity of Pakistan. Another was Mujib's as yet minor role as a politician on the provincial as well as national canvas. He was yet to reach a position whereby he could influence Bengali opinion on a large scale. Besides, for all their disillusionment with Pakistan, the Bengalis remained attached to the state and certainly did not harbour thoughts of independence at that point. Mujib's failure to make any headway was also due to the harsh control the armed forces and the bureaucracy exercised over the whole country.

Mujib was well aware of the risks of any action that even remotely looked like secessionism and could be construed as an act of treason. And yet there were the secret links he was beginning to establish with a core group of young people, largely students of Dhaka University, about putting the idea of an eventual Bengali independence to the test. The *Shwadhin Bangla Biplobi Parishad* or Free Bengal Revolutionary Council, established in utmost secrecy, often met to debate the academic aspects of a probable struggle for freedom in future. There was little doubt that Mujib provided incentive to these young thinkers, though he scrupulously maintained a public distance from the organisation. The Ayub Khan regime was not being able to put its finger on what precisely he was up to. Mujib knew the army did not look kindly upon him and he was more than willing to repay the compliment. In all the years that remained of united Pakistan, relations between the army and Mujib would grow extremely fraught and would in the end reach a point of severe collision.

Mujib's suspicions that the military government was determined to prevent Bengalis from enjoying political authority had first been stirred with the dismissal of the United Front ministry in 1954. They were reinforced over the subsequent years. When Iskandar Mirza and Ayub Khan placed Pakistan under military rule in October 1958, Mujib drew the pertinent conclusion that the action had been aimed at destroying the possibility of the general elections that were being planned for between late 1958 and early 1959. The elections, had they been held, would in all probability have thrown up the Awami League as the majority party, or at the least as the party with the highest number of seats, in the national assembly and Suhrawardy would have taken over as the first elected prime minister of Pakistan. With the Awami League in East Pakistan having increasingly come under the influence of Mujib, it was quite likely that he would have opted to play a provincial role, possibly as chief minister, and moved on with his demands for regional autonomy for the province. The 1958 coup came in the way of all the plans the Awami League and Mujib may have had about the future. Right till the end, Mujib was unable to forgive the Pakistan army. It had already achieved the dubious distinction of being described by Justice M.R. Kayani, a respected jurist of the country, as being one of the few armies in the world that had occupied their own countries, for what he saw as its perfidy in subverting democratic politics.

In 1961, two clear parallel streams of thought had begun to course through East Pakistan. The first was the regime's transparent feeling that more of a sense of Pakistani nationhood needed to be injected into the Bengali consciousness; and the second was the slow but sure Bengali realisation that its secular heritage called for a defence of traditional Bengali values of politics and culture. The Bengalis, though enthusiastic about Pakistan in the 1940s, had increasingly demonstrated their clear reluctance over the years to have their essential secularism subsumed to the kind of Islamic puritanism Pakistan's ruling classes wished to impose on the province. More than ten per cent of East Pakistan's seventy million people comprised Hindus, and a large segment of the population consisted of Christians, Buddhists and the various indigenous tribes peopling such areas as the Chittagong Hill Tracts and Mymensingh. Bengali Muslims, especially in the tens of thousands of villages that constituted the province, were devout practitioners of their faith and yet remained non-communal and non-sectarian in their social behaviour. There were none of the violent sentiments that caused commotion of the kind first noticed in the anti-Ahmadiyya riots in the Punjabi city of Lahore in 1953. Neither were the Bengalis much taken in by the sectarian Shia-Sunni divide that often punctuated religious discourse in West Pakistan. On the political level, the simmering and vocal West Pakistani obsession with Kashmir vis-à-vis India did not impress the Bengalis, for whom a struggle for their own political and social rights was of greater importance than a dispute that was looking like a ploy by the ruling classes to grab and hold on to power.

The centenary of the birth of poet Rabindranath Tagore, a universally accepted Bengali icon, was observed in West Bengal and East Pakistan in 1961. For the people of the latter region, the celebrations held special significance in view of the Ayub Khan regime's carefully initiated measures to undercut the Bengali cultural basis as it gradually consolidated its hold on the country. Tagore had been the first Indian and first Bengali to be awarded the Nobel Prize for Literature in 1913. His poetry had, during his long literary career as well as after his death in 1941, resonated with Bengalis on both sides of the frontier. For the Pakistani ruling classes, however, a continued attachment of East Pakistan's Bengalis to the poet were an indication of how weak the Bengali commitment to the Muslim state could soon become unless it was checked. The designs of the rulers were not lost on educated, urbane Bengalis. They swiftly went about organising a committee for the observance of Tagore's centenary. The action would perhaps have merited little attention had it not been for the fact that none but Justice Syed Mahbub Murshed, chief justice of the East Pakistan High Court, agreed to chair the committee. Murshed was, even in that stifling period of military rule, a man of independence and integrity not at all unwilling to put the regime in its place when it came to deliberating on constitutional and political questions before the judiciary. The degree of respect he enjoyed among Bengalis was extremely high. His role in the Tagore celebrations thus clearly sent out a strong message from East Pakistan about the reassertion of cultural values that the Bengalis had clearly set their hearts upon. In the absence of politics, the Tagore centenary celebrations provided an unmistakable outlet for an expression of Bengali sentiment where the plans of Ayub Khan's government were concerned. Predictably, the celebrations and Justice Murshed's participation in them did not amuse the regime or its small-time camp followers in the country. Over the coming years, the army would be forced to deal with increasing doses of rebellion in East Pakistan, a task that would leave it enervated over time.

But the regime and the civil-military bureaucracy would not forget 1961. Rabindranath Tagore had obviously become an obstacle to the mission of promoting national integration and so needed to be dealt with severely. Six years later, Khwaja Shehabuddin, Ayub Khan's minister for information and younger brother of Pakistan's second governor general and also second prime minister, Khwaja Nazimuddin, would decree a ban on Tagore's music all over Pakistan as a measure towards protecting Pakistan's 'Muslim' Bengalis from what it considered the contaminating influence of Hindu culture as represented by the poet. The banning of Tagore would only serve to inflame Bengali passions further and add momentum to the popular struggle to push Ayub Khan from power. The move against Tagore would be fresh proof for the Bengalis that their suspicions about the establishment's designs against their cultural and political heritage had turned out to be true.

Taking Charge after Suhrawardy

President Ayub Khan decided to lift martial law in Pakistan in mid 1962. In the preceding two years, he and his regime had carefully gone into the job of drafting a new constitution for the country. He was little inclined to restore the 1956 constitution he and Iskandar Mirza had abrogated when they unleashed the army against the politicians in 1958. There was in him the undoubted feeling that Pakistan was in need of a firm system of government, which in his conception meant a powerful presidency with him in charge. But it would be a presidency that need not be upheld by the accepted standards of universal adult franchise. With advisors like Manzur Quader, who for a time served as his foreign minister, and former prime minister Mohammad Ali Bogra, Ayub Khan settled upon a concept of restricted democracy he called Basic Democracy. Under the scheme, 80,000 Basic Democrats, with 40,000 for each of the two provinces of the country, would be elected through direct voting. In their turn, these 80,000 elected Basic Democrats would constitute the electoral college, responsible for electing the president of the country. Members of the national and provincial assemblies would also be elected by the Basic Democrats. The president, once elected, was free to appoint ministers to a cabinet responsible to him. Likewise, the governors of East and West Pakistan would have their provincial councils of ministers serving at their pleasure. To all intents and purposes, the constitution which the regime drafted and then imposed on the country was a clear contravention of the fundamental principles of democracy, an act that was quickly denounced by politicians across the spectrum.

Politics remained in a state of ferment in the months before martial law was finally lifted. On 6 February 1962, Mujib was taken in for one more spell of detention under the Public Safety Act and was not freed until 18 June. In fact, it was a time when the government went about in a concerted manner after nearly every Awami League leader and did not spare even Suhrawardy, who was hauled off to prison, where he would spend the next few months. A few days after his release, Mujib joined other political leaders, who now finally had an opportunity of re-emerging in public as a result of a liberalising of politics, to issue a joint response to the government's proposed constitutional measures. On 5 July, days after the new constitution had taken effect, Mujib was at Dhaka's Paltan Maidan delivering a bitter tirade against the regime. He was, like nearly every other politician of repute in the country, dismissive about the president's brand of democracy and insisted that democracy would have to be restored to the form it had operated in before the army seized power in 1958. On 24 September, he accompanied Suhrawardy to Lahore, where politicians straddling the right and right of centre quickly engaged themselves in the business of forging a common front against the government. Taking advantage of the withdrawal of martial law, these opposition political figures were evidently of the view that the constitutional measures President Ayub had introduced were tailored to keep him and the army in power for an indefinite period of time, which effectively precluded any possibility of the political classes driving the regime from power in the near future. Largely through the efforts of Suhrawardy, Khwaja Nazimuddin and Chaudhri Mohammad Ali (Fazlul Huq had died in April of that year), the National Democratic Front (NDF), was launched as a platform on which the opposition would take its case for a restoration of parliamentary democracy to the country.

On his release from detention in the middle of 1962, Suhrawardy played an instrumental role in the formation of the NDF. Towards the latter part of the year, he travelled to London before making his way to

Beirut. It was in the Lebanese capital that Suhrawardy died in a hotel room on 5 December 1963, apparently from a heart attack. For years afterwards, his loyalists, including Mujib, voiced the suspicion that the Awami League leader had died under mysterious circumstances. Suhrawardy had likely been murdered by agents of the military regime in Beirut. In the years since his death, however, nothing by way of evidence has as yet emerged to suggest that Suhrawardy's passing away was a result of foul play on the part of the Pakistani government. What was made amply clear by his death was the poverty into which opposition politics suddenly found itself. Suhrawardy, by any measure, was the single most significant figure in the NDF and therefore was regarded as the one man who could put up resistance to the military regime. His demise threw the opposition into disarray, a situation that could only have pleased Ayub Khan and his loyalists.

Indeed, the year 1963 had for the president been rather pivotal, seeing that he had formally made his entry into politics by doffing his army uniform. He and his government inaugurated the process by calling a session of the old Muslim League, in a clear bid to divide the party and encourage its members into not only deserting the party but also bringing a big chunk of it with them for Ayub to take over. A section of the Muslim League called a convention and in a prearranged manner voiced their dissatisfaction with such leaders of the party as Chaudhri Mohammad Ali and Mian Mumtaz Daultana. The next course of action was predictable—the participants at the convention formally declared that their faction of the Muslim League was the only true Muslim League. Ayub Khan, again on cue, was invited to join the party, which he duly accepted. The man who had subverted constitutional politics thus presented himself in a new attire as the president of a political faction which to Pakistanis now began to be known as the Convention Muslim League. Into it streamed all those who were in time to develop a reputation for the sycophants, hangers-on and flunkeys they were.

A second important part of the rise of the Convention Muslim League in the shadow of Ayub Khan was the increasing influence of the young Zulfikar Ali Bhutto. Having joined the cabinet through the personal efforts of Iskandar Mirza soon after the coup of 7 October 1958, Bhutto had been shrewd enough to switch his loyalties to Ayub Khan twenty days after Mirza was overthrown. In the years since then, he had come to acquire a reputation as one of the foremost loyalists of Ayub Khan. In 1960, Bhutto had been moved from the commerce portfolio to industries and natural resources and in that capacity had concluded an energy deal with the Soviet Union during a trip to Moscow. An intensely ambitious man, Bhutto had made no secret of his ambition to head the country's Foreign Office. When Foreign Minister Mohammad Ali Bogra (the prime minister under whom Ayub Khan had served in the early 1950s and who then, in a twist of fate, joined the Ayub regime as foreign minister in 1962) died in early 1963, Bhutto was swiftly given the job. Sometime later, he was also made general secretary of the Convention Muslim League, in which capacity he publicly made the suggestion that Ayub Khan be elected president of Pakistan for life.

The death of Suhrawardy, for the vacuum it created in the politics of Pakistan's opposition, turned out to be a blessing in disguise for Mujib. In all the years he had spent in the Awami League, it was loyalty to Suhrawardy that had kept Mujib under restraint. While he had grown to share Suhrawardy's passionate belief in parliamentary democracy and a need to wage a struggle for its restoration, Mujib was also pulled in a direction that saw him gradually and imperceptibly loosening his links to all-Pakistan politics and instead focusing more on the advantages that the Bengalis could derive from a return to democracy. The introduction of Basic Democracy, which brought in its wake a tighter stranglehold of the military on democratic politics, only added to his suspicion that the economic exploitation of East Pakistan could only lengthen itself with Ayub Khan in power. An additional complaint in Mujib was the reluctance of his fellow politicians in the Opposition to avoid being seen to be undertaking programmes that would lead them into a frontal assault on the government. Most components of the NDF felt that the entrenched nature of the regime precluded any meaningful, popularly backed movement against it on the part of the Opposition. More tellingly, they were not persuaded by Mujib and others like him into accepting the idea that the focus of politics needed to shift to questions of autonomy for the provinces. The overriding thought among Opposition politicians, by and large, was a restoration of parliamentary representative government for Pakistan. For Mujib, politics was increasingly growing to be a matter of making life better for his fellow Bengalis. By the end of 1963, he had already begun referring to his province as *Shonar Bangla*, Golden Bengal, in his speeches. It was a palpable demonstration of his growing belief that if Bengalis were to regain the prosperity that they had once enjoyed as a society, as evident in folklore, they simply had to put up a struggle for their rights in Pakistan.

It was yet too early to think aloud on eventual freedom for the province. But what was becoming a priority for Mujib was establishing wide-ranging autonomy for East Pakistan. He was in need of a programme that would pave the way, in good time, for East Pakistan to move out of Pakistan or, if that proved difficult to achieve, for a loose confederation that would allow Bengalis to control their economic well-being. The thoughts that had made their way into his political conscience back in 1961, around the surreptitious activities of an embryonic Free Bengal Revolutionary Council, remained. But 1963 was too early for anyone and for Mujib in particular to think too far ahead. Mujib had to move one step at a time. He had already come under the government's suspicion and quite a few individuals in the corridors of power were already seeing in him the first tentative signs of a politician inclined to separatism.

The first step Mujib took towards creating his own niche in politics came only a month after Suhrawardy's death. In late January 1964, a large number of Awami Leaguers, many of whom had not taken kindly to the submergence of the party in the NDF in 1962 and had instead wanted the Awami League to maintain its distinct identity, met at Mujib's residence in Dhaka to revive the organisation. Once the deed was done, the NDF lost steam. By taking the Awami League out of it, Mujib was making it clear as to who was in charge of the party after Suhrawardy's death. He was also sending out the message that the Awami League was about to jettison its moderate approach to politics in favour of a radical new programme. The meeting elected the respected Moulana Abdur Rashid Tarkabagish, a senior Awami Leaguer and a cleric acclaimed for his interpretations of Islamic religious laws, as the new president of the Awami League. Mujib remained general secretary of the party.

There was little question about the dominance Mujib was henceforth to exercise in the party. His position was further buttressed by a younger crop of Bengali nationalist politicians, all of whom would, in subsequent years, assist him in reshaping politics in Pakistan and eventually prepare the grounds for Bengali political sovereignty. Among these men were Syed Nazrul Islam, a soft-spoken, able lawyer from the district of Kishoreganj; Tajuddin Ahmed, a former student of economics with a brilliant academic record behind him; M. Mansoor Ali, a former officer in the national guard, and A.H.M. Quamruzzaman, an affable, respected politician from the northern district of Rajshahi. Kamal Hossain, a young lawyer trained in Britain with clear inclinations towards a political role alongside Mujib, would be another entrant. One senior Awami League politician who resented Mujib's ascendancy but who nevertheless chose to stay on was Moshtaq. Older than Mujib by a few years, Moshtaq was uncomfortable in the former's shadow and would eventually be a contender. But in early 1964, Moshtaq pushed his personal feelings aside and joined the new bandwagon, as did a young politician named Mizanur Rahman Chowdhury. From the ranks of former student leaders came the likes of K.M. Obaidur Rahman and Shah Moazzam Hossain.

That first meeting of the revived Awami League began and ended with something of a bang. The party adopted a resolution demanding a return to parliamentary democracy on the basis of elections that in turn would be held on the basis of universal adult suffrage. Over the next couple of months, the party went into a mass contact programme undoubtedly aimed at projecting itself as a truly viable vehicle in the struggle to drive Ayub Khan from power. When communal riots against East Pakistan's Hindu minority broke out in the first half of 1964, Mujib and his party seized the opportunity to present themselves as an organisation which could be trusted to ensure the security of life and property of all sections of the population. Local units of the Awami League in the towns and cities went about reassuring Hindus about their safety in East Pakistan, many of whom had by then fled to India (the third such movement of the community towards West Bengal since the earlier communal riots of 1947 and 1950). The zeal with which Mujib and his followers attacked communalism in 1964 was to result in political dividends for them in future. The Hindu community could now look to a party that did not discriminate between religious communities but instead appeared keen on promoting a secular framework for East Pakistan, if not for the rest of the country. For the party, a certain satisfaction lay in the new perception of it as a political organisation that spoke for all Bengalis. Mujib knew which path he wanted to take in his new role, even if others did not.

Between 1964 and 1965, Mujib remained a regular target of the government's wrath. The authorities continued their unending exercise of arresting him under the provisions of one law or another. If it was once the Criminal Procedure Code under which he was hauled off to prison, it was the Defence of Pakistan Rules under which he was put behind bars again, once he had been bailed out of the earlier arrest. He used every spell of freedom to make increasingly inflammatory speeches against the government of Ayub Khan. Followed everywhere by intelligence agents of the government, he was prepared to be arrested anywhere and at any time of the day. The death of Suhrawardy seemed to have released him from all obligations relating to his need to keep his radicalism bottled up. He thus managed to alienate senior figures in the rest of the opposition camp, especially men like Mian Mumtaz Daultana, Sardar Bahadur Khan, Khwaja Nazimuddin and, to a certain extent, Bhashani. But he had his supporters too, in such men as G.M. Syed, the long-suffering veteran of Sindhi politics who had opposed the creation of Pakistan and remained true to his convictions.

Mujib was also coming by a certain measure of respect from the father-and-son team of Khan Abdul Ghaffar Khan and Khan Abdul Wali Khan, Pathan politicians whose espousal of the secessionist Pashtunistan cause in Pakistan's North West Frontier Province had long been an irritant for successive Pakistani administrations. In the mid-1960s, as the stridency of Mujib's Bengali nationalism went up by quite a few notches, all these men saw in the Bengali leader a reflection of what they might have been and who they could still be if Mujib could attain his goals.

Mujib, however, had other priorities in 1964. As the year progressed, the Opposition coalesced around the idea of confronting President Ayub Khan at the presidential elections slated for early January 1965. The president, so the Opposition felt, had to be challenged politically. Despite being outraged by the system of Basic Democracy, the Opposition came round to the conclusion that the regime needed to be attacked through an application of its own device. What better opportunity than fielding a candidate to run against Ayub Khan in 1965? In the autumn of 1964, therefore, Pakistan's disparate opposition political parties and factions came together to form a front described as the Combined Opposition Parties (COP), its principal objective being to put up a candidate to take on the president at the presidential elections. Interestingly, Khwaja Nazimuddin, the former governor general and prime minister who had earned the wrath of the Bengalis with his strident defence of Urdu as the national language in the late 1940s and early 1950s, was the leading figure around whom the opposition built up formal resistance to the Ayub Khan regime. The death of Huq in 1962 and Suhrawardy in 1963 had removed two of the more prominent men who could have injected a pronounced level of energy into the anti-regime campaign. By 1964, except for Nazimuddin, all other politicians clearly turned out to have been individuals whose appeal on the national stage was conspicuous by its absence. For his part, Nazimuddin, a member of the Bengal aristocracy that had played an instrumental role in the establishment of the All India Muslim League in 1906 in Dhaka, had in the years since his dismissal from the office of prime minister in 1953 managed to regain some of his appeal through a conscious alignment with Opposition politics, particularly in the matter of resisting the military regime.

The COP, as it came to be known, then moved to execute a masterstroke by nominating Fatima Jinnah, sister of the country's founder Mohammad Ali Jinnah, as its candidate for the office of president. Ms Jinnah, in her sixties, was a spinster who had trained to be a dentist but had eventually opted to be at her brother's side as he took his movement for Pakistan forward in the 1940s. Held in reverence by Pakistanis across the board, she had lived the life of a recluse since Jinnah's death in September 1948. When General Ayub Khan seized power in 1958, she had initially welcomed the take-over owing to her dismay at the chaos the country's politicians had led the country to through their internecine struggle for political dominance. Over the next few years, however, Ms Jinnah had grown increasingly disillusioned with Ayub Khan but managed to keep her opinions from making their way into the public domain. It was not for her, as Jinnah's sister, to be seen indulging in partisan politics. But by 1964, she was ready to take on Ayub Khan at the elections despite the apprehensions that the Basic Democracy system did not promise her a victory over the military ruler. For those who had nominated her, there was a clear calculation at work, which was simply that the appeal of the Quaid-e-Azam's sister would work profoundly into making the electoral college turn to her and, hopefully, dislodge Ayub Khan. There was a fair degree of logic in the argument, especially in East Pakistan, where the iniquities the Bengalis had gradually become prey to in the seventeen years since Pakistan's creation were beginning to convince them that change was called for. In such light, it was expected that a majority of Bengali Basic Democrats would vote for Ms Jinnah and if a similar feat could be pulled off among West Pakistan's Basic Democrats, though that appeared difficult under the circumstances, Ms Jinnah would conceivably have a real chance of taking over as Pakistan's new leader.

In the event, tragedy struck the COP. Within days of Ms Jinnah being nominated as its presidential candidate, Khwaja Nazimuddin died of a cardiac arrest in Dhaka. His death was the final straw for many in the Opposition, for they had always pinned their hopes on men like him, Suhrawardy and Huq, to lead the country back to democracy. Now all three were dead and for the first time in years, Pakistan's political Opposition was devoid of a spokesman who could appeal to people across the board and reassure them about a viable alternative to the military regime. It was with a fresh sense of desperation that the COP pressed on. Mujib and his Awami League clearly played a leading role in publicising Ms Jinnah's presidential campaign throughout East Pakistan. Mujib, desperately trying to fill the shoes that would fit a politician of national stature, became the vehicle for the Jinnah candidacy. Paradoxically, it became clear, as the campaign progressed, that while he appreciated the need for the COP to remain united in its defiance of Ayub Khan, he spotted in Ms Jinnah's candidacy the perfect opportunity to take the Awami League closer to the country in the expectation that it would, sooner rather than later, become a household word among the Bengalis. What Mujib was doing was two-pronged. On the one hand, he was trying to generate steam into the anti-Ayub campaign through a meticulous propagation of Ms Jinnah's candidacy. On the other, he was building, in the course of the presidential election campaign, his distinctive constituency in East Pakistan. For all his participation in the campaign, his politics remained focused on East Pakistan. He accompanied Ms Jinnah on her tour of the province as her trusted advisor. Mujib's fiery speeches before the crowds drew attention to the morass Pakistan had fallen into since the death of Mohammad Ali Jinnah. Political expediency prevented him from giving out any hint of his own growing dissatisfaction with Pakistan, for at that stage in his career he was quite willing to go along with Ms Jinnah and the COP, in order to see what, if anything, the state of Pakistan was prepared to offer Bengalis in a Ms Jinnah presidency. His whirlwind tour of the entire stretch of East Pakistan, with Ms Jinnah and without her, was by December 1964 beginning to create good ripples. Even the regime felt a sense of unease at the prospect of a majority among the 40,000 Basic Democrats in the province actually swinging to the COP candidate.

A fortnight before the presidential election, the government took Mujib into police custody, in which state he would remain until the election came and went. The regime had clearly become rattled by what it saw as demagoguery on Mujib's part. It actually made the government panic. Ayub Khan could not afford to lose and did not intend to lose in East Pakistan. Mujib was swiftly charged with making inflammatory speeches and sentenced to a year in prison. Ms Jinnah thus lost the one man whose presence on her team had already begun making a difference.

1965 War and East Pakistan

As 1965 dawned, few people were able to predict that it would be a year which would leave lasting scars on the history of Pakistan. As unfolding events would reveal, it would be a time when careers on the Pakistani political stage would be ruined and made. More ominously, in 1965 there would be all the signs of a state rushing feverishly towards a crisis that would ultimately show up the cracks in its structure. But on 2 January, when President Ayub Khan defeated Ms Jinnah, to win a fresh lease of power, all that was made clear was that the 80,000-member Basic Democrats' electorate had made it possible for the president to strengthen his grip on the country, by a comfortable margin. The grip had never loosened in any case since the October 1958 coup. The president obtained 49,647 votes against Ms Jinnah's 28,345. By winning the election, Ayub Khan thought he could now claim legitimacy as an elected leader even if others considered, and rightly too, the entire electoral system flawed. For the president, the election represented a significant improvement over the referendum his regime had organised in 1960 over its proposals for a new constitution for Pakistan. The results of the referendum had been taken to mean an endorsement of the regime. The 1965 election now gave the president the satisfaction of seeing himself as an elected leader, somewhat in the mould of many others who were then sprouting in the newly independent nations of Asia and Africa.

Even as Ayub Khan savoured his triumph at the elections, conditions began to take unexpected turns. In the spring, Pakistan and India found themselves locked in a dispute over an area known as the Rann of Kutch which straddled the border between the two countries in the Pakistani province of Sind. It would take British Prime Minister Harold Wilson to step in and help resolve the dispute through arbitration that resulted in the two countries claiming chunks of Kutch territory. By August, however, there were clear indications that the Pakistan Army was arming Kashmiri militants, the goal being a reigniting of a conflict that had really not died out. Indeed, claims by both Pakistan and India on Kashmir, whose Hindu ruler had acceded to Delhi in early 1948 when Mohammad Ali Jinnah sent in bands of Pakistani tribals in an apparent effort to take control of the Muslim majority state, had kept diplomacy between them in a stalemate.

Indian Prime Minister Jawaharlal Nehru, who promised in the days immediately after the departure of the British colonial power, a plebiscite to help ascertain the wishes of Kashmiris about their future, swiftly went back on the pledge. The result was that Pakistan, over the years, went on insisting on the plebiscite, while India truly considered the chapter closed. But President Ayub Khan, convinced by the arguments put forward by the army as well as Foreign Minister Bhutto that Kashmiris would rise in revolt against India once they found their Pakistani friends coming to their assistance, agreed to send in his forces into the territory. The result was disaster. Contrary to Pakistani expectations, the Kashmiris did not rise against India and there are in fact stories of how they considered the Pakistani intrusion as an assault aimed at claiming Kashmir for Pakistan. To the government of India, now led by Lal Bahadur Shastri, the only way of checking what it saw as Pakistan's aggression was to hit back. For Shastri and his cabinet colleagues, it was almost a repeat of the situation in 1948, when the fledgling Indian Army had been forced into action against Jinnah's military moves in Kashmir.

The Indian army launched a full-scale assault on Lahore in the pre-dawn hours of 6 September 1965. Led by its chief of staff, General

J.N. Chaudhuri, it aimed at capturing the city and thereby causing a psychological shock in Pakistan's establishment. However, the Pakistani forces were able to hold back the Indian offensive. But elsewhere, and that was largely along the borders in the Punjab and Sind, the Indian forces moved into Pakistan and seized large chunks of territory. The city of Karachi, which had lost its status as Pakistan's capital since Ayub Khan decided to build a new capital in the north known as Islamabad, was bombarded by the Indian Air Force. The war went on for seventeen days and ended on 23 September 1965 in response to a call for a ceasefire by the UN. For its part, the UN was the scene of some pretty dramatic moments, especially when Bhutto went on a broadside against the Indian delegation led by Foreign Minister Sardar Swaran Singh. In his high-pitched voice and melodramatic, liberal use of the English language, Pakistan's young foreign minister undiplomatically flailed away at India and certainly earned good points for his performance back home. For Bhutto, it was one of his finest hours, seeing that he now had an international audience and at the same time an opportunity to demonstrate his ability to speak for his country before his adoring countrymen. The reality on the battlefield was altogether different. The war had reached a stalemate and would soon be called to an end.

The 1965 war between India and Pakistan was a political revelation for Pakistan's Bengali population. The fact that the Indian military chose not to launch an assault on East Pakistan, despite the province's vulnerability, and instead focused on dealing with Pakistan's troops on the western front, was surely a miracle as well as a relief for the Bengalis. But, on a serious note, the defenceless position of East Pakistan during the war convinced large numbers of Bengalis that the state and its political-military establishment were least interested in the fate of East Pakistan. Considering the widening economic disparity between East and West Pakistan since the coup of 1958, the 1965 war served as added proof of the central government's insensitivity to Bengali concerns. The Pakistani establishment had further earned the displeasure of the Bengalis by propagating that the defence of

East Pakistan lay in West Pakistan. They even suggested that had East Pakistan come under Indian attack, Pakistan's friends in the Chinese government would have moved to put a check to Indian designs. None of these explanations satisfied the Bengalis.

For Mujib, it was clear that East Pakistan was being administered more as a colonial territory by President Ayub Khan's government than as an integral part of the country. It hardly mattered that the government had designated Dhaka as the country's second capital, the first and real one being Islamabad, and that a huge parliament structure was already under construction in the East Pakistani capital. Bengali entry into the armed forces and civil service remained low. Compared to West Pakistanis, negligible numbers of Bengalis were in a position to travel abroad for training or higher studies. Life in the rural areas continued to be in the grip of poverty. And Dhaka, despite being the urban centre of the province (a modern railway station was coming up to replace the old British-era facade), still looked every inch a small district town when juxtaposed with such West Pakistani cities as Karachi and Lahore.

The end of the war in September 1965 was therefore an opportunity the Awami League was not willing to miss. For Mujib, the time was at hand when a reassertion of Bengali nationalism was called for. He was now out of jail, where he had been placed before the presidential election of January, thanks to a move by the High Court to order his release. A comprehension of the grim realities East Pakistan could have gone through, had there been an invasion of the province by the Indian military now, spurred him on into building upon the radical political ideas he had already begun to toy with. By early 1965, especially in light of the defeat of Ms Jinnah at the presidential election, Mujib was in touch with liberal, young segments of the Bengali intelligentsia over the future course of his political programme. As would be observed subsequently, these dialogues would result in a sweeping change of strategy on the part of the Awami League and would mark the first time when Pakistan would be jolted into an awareness of the perils it faced unless it opted for a reordering of its politics.

The end of the war, as observed in hindsight, was the precise point when Ayub Khan's grip on power began to weaken. Having ruled Pakistan as its unchallenged strongman for seven years, the president now faced growing criticism for his poor leadership during the military conflict with India. The Rann of Kutch dispute in May of the year had caused a certain dent in his popularity. Now the indecisive war, together with his meek acceptance of a ceasefire, when as a matter of fact his government had all along been dishing out the propaganda of the army's routing the Indians nearly everywhere, caused larger holes in his position. He was badly in need of a way to have the Indians vacate the slices of territory they had occupied in Sind and other areas. The war, the attempt to stir up trouble in Kashmir, all had obviously boomeranged. The resultant discontent among Pakistanis, especially among the military, necessitated a face-saving way out for the president. It was with a sense of relief, therefore, that he accepted an offer by Soviet Prime Minister Alexei Kosygin to negotiations with Indian Prime Minister Shastri in Tashkent in early January of the following year.

President Ayub Khan and Prime Minister Shastri reached a deal on 10 January 1966 in Tashkent after hard and often bitter negotiations over the previous six days. Considered in terms of results, the Tashkent Declaration, as it came to be known, amounted to little more than an agreement by Pakistan and India to withdraw to the positions they occupied before the September 1965 war. Leading them was Foreign Minister Bhutto who, at one point, had been shut out of the talks by Premier Kosygin and Soviet Foreign Minister Gromyko because of the hurdles he was clearly putting up to the negotiations. Bhutto was keen to maintain the image of the tough diplomat he thought he had created for himself by his presence at the UN Security Council debate during the course of the war. In contrast, Ayub Khan was acutely conscious of the need to go back home with some result that would help keep his enemies, who were now increasing in number, at bay. The president was wary about the fallout of the talks. If Pakistanis could not be convinced that their leader had come away from Tashkent with another victory (they had been led to believe that their soldiers had beaten the Indian Army in September, but the establishment knew better, of course), politics would not look comfortable for Ayub. It was from that perspective that the president must have heaved a sigh of relief when, at the eleventh hour, the declaration was initialled with Shastri.

Within a couple of hours of the agreement being reached and having gone to bed before catching the flight back home to Delhi the following morning, Lal Bahadur Shastri succumbed to a heart attack in Tashkent. One of the men pulling the hearse, carrying his coffin to the waiting aircraft, for the sad journey back home was Field Marshal Mohammad Ayub Khan.

PART

3

Six-Point Programme

Pakistan's Opposition parties decided to meet in a convention in Lahore on 6 February 1966. Mujib arrived in the city on 4 February and the very next day caused a stir by declaring a Six-Point proposal for provincial autonomy that he had brought along with him, to be included as part of the agenda of the conference. It was a demand that the other political parties and leaders, all of whom had already reached Lahore, were unwilling to accommodate because they clearly saw the far-reaching implications of the Six Points, as the plan came to be known, on the future of Pakistan's federal structure. In a pretty big and calculated way, Mujib had thrown everything into chaos.

Where the original goal of the Opposition convention had been to shape a strategy against the Ayub Khan government, especially in view of what was increasingly being perceived as capitulation to India, the Six Points struck many as a veiled and yet unmistakable attempt at weaning East Pakistan away from the state that had been cobbled together in 1947. It will not be an exaggeration to suggest that Mujib's programme unnerved many political leaders, who banded together to reject his demand and refused to have it placed on the agenda. Reports of the rejection of the Six Points by the rest of the Opposition filtered out to the media, with the Awami League leader making no effort to deny the facts. It seemed he relished the way it was playing itself out. With newspapers in both East and West Pakistan carrying detailed reports on the Six Points, a storm of protest from Awami League detractors broke out all over the country. The virulence was particularly noted in the west where, for the first time, Mujib was projected publicly as a separatist determined to undermine the ideological and political basis of Pakistan.

Mujib and his colleagues rejected the charge. They suggested that the Six Points had been devised to bring about a balance in relations between the two parts of the country. Mujib could not afford to declare publicly that his party had lost its faith in Pakistan and was therefore keen on moving out of the federation. But those who studied the Six Points, even in those early days, could not fail to read into the subtle nature of the plan. In all the nineteen years that had gone by since the establishment of Pakistan, nothing so far-reaching and sweeping had been attempted by any politician or party in the country. Briefly, the Six Points pointed clearly to a confederal state structure, if not a prospect of outright independence for East Pakistan. The points, as enunciated by Mujib on 5 February 1966, were:

The constitution should provide for a federation of Pakistan on the basis of the Lahore Resolution of March 1940, envisaging a parliamentary form of government elected on the basis of universal adult suffrage;

The federal government, under the scheme envisaged thus, would deal only with the subjects of foreign affairs and defence, all other subjects being placed under the authority of the federating units;

Two separate but freely convertible currencies would be introduced for the two wings of the country, or in the event of such a system not coming into place, a single currency for the whole country, with the proviso that flight of capital from East Pakistan to West Pakistan and vice versa would be constitutionally prevented, would suffice;

The power of taxation and revenue collection would be vested in the federating units, but the federation would be entitled to a share in the revenues, based on the agreement of the federating units, to meet its expenditures;

There would be two separate accounts for foreign exchange earnings of the two wings of the country, with the foreign exchange requirements of the central government being met by the two wings equally or in a ratio to be decided upon; indigenous products would move free of duty between the two wings, with the federating units empowered to establish trade links with countries abroad;

East Pakistan would be empowered to raise and maintain a separate militia or paramilitary force.

The clamour with which his fellow Opposition politicians rejected his demand out of hand forced Mujib to abandon the conference and return to Dhaka. Mujib, more than anyone else, knew that when it came to a question of greater levels of autonomy for East Pakistan, the political classes in West Pakistan—and it did not matter whether or not they were in the government or outside—would band together to prevent upsetting the applecart. The status quo mattered immensely to West Pakistan's politicians. The Bengali leader had thus been under no illusion. The larger aspect of his move was his cool calculation of the defenceless position of East Pakistan during the September 1965 war, followed by the rising chorus of opposition to the Tashkent Declaration, had created an ideal condition for the Awami League to advance its radical politics.

Having been a rebel, one who had been in and out of jail since 1948, Mujib did not underestimate the capacity and intention of the state to hit back—and to hit back hard. But what was enormously satisfying for him was the consternation the Six Points had caused in West Pakistan. The Six Points were in effect a point of departure for the two wings of Pakistan, the first signs of which would be seen in a raging wave of Bengali nationalism, poised to hit hard and without remorse, the old concept of a Muslim state as defined by Mohammad Ali Jinnah in the 1940s.

The onslaught against the Six Points, initiated by middle-ranking leaders of the ruling Convention Muslim League, was soon taken up by individuals at more responsible levels in the corridors of power. Bhutto, yet to run into his own problems with Ayub Khan, publicly challenged Mujib to a debate on the Six Points. For good measure, Bhutto made it clear that he was ready to meet Mujib on the latter's home ground, at the Paltan Maidan in Dhaka. Paltan Maidan had historically been the site of mass rallies since the British colonial days. Clearly speaking on Mujib's instructions, Tajuddin made an announcement that he was ready and willing to represent Mujib at the debate Bhutto had proposed. Bhutto's reply was not forthcoming. Nothing more was heard of the debate.

While public reaction was whipped up in the west by presenting Mujib as a secessionist, in the Bengali east, except for the provincial government of Governor Monem Khan and other Ayub loyalists, there was a good degree of muted support for the Six Points. In West Pakistan, a few quarters like the National Awami Party of the Pathan politician Khan Abdul Wali Khan and the ageing Sindhi nationalist G.M. Syed looked favourably upon Mujib's move. With their nationalist aspirations not quite being able to find open expression, the radicalism of the Bengali politician worked for them as a testing of the waters. Their silent and subtle position did not go unnoticed by the mainstream in West Pakistan.

Since his return from Lahore in early February, Mujib undertook a whirlwind tour of the province to publicise the Six Points. At every public rally he addressed, he made a point of reassuring the country that his programme was not aimed at dismembering Pakistan but rather at strengthening the federation through a decentralisation of political authority. By that point of time, the conviction had grown in the Bengali leader that no amount of democratic liberalisation, unless it came with guarantees of a share of power for Bengalis, would suffice for East Pakistan. The Awami League shared the sentiments of other parties in the political Opposition that the system Ayub Khan and the army had put in place needed to be overturned through a restoration of Westminster-style democracy based on the 1956 constitution.

Observers of Bangladesh's history have generally pointed to 1965, if not earlier, as the period in which a concerted effort was put into devising a clear strategy about Bengali ambitions for the future. Under the 1956 constitution, Bengalis had been compelled to formalise the structure of parity under the One Unit scheme combining the four western provinces into a single West Pakistan entity. That single measure ensured that in terms of political representation, the Bengalis comprising fifty-six per cent of Pakistan's population would share power and everything that flowed from it on a fifty-fifty basis with the forty-four per cent of people who constituted the population of West Pakistan. There have been innumerable arguments presented about Mujib being the progenitor of the Six Points. As early as 1957, with Suhrawardy serving as Pakistan's prime minister, Mujib wondered if Pakistan as it was turning out to be would be where Bengalis wanted to be. It is said that Suhrawardy was shocked to hear this and even reprimanded his young follower, asking him to refrain from entertaining such ideas.

Be as it may, in the earlier part of 1965, Mujib was in contact with a group of young Bengali economists who were able to formulate the policies he already had outlined. Mujib was well aware that the Awami League needed the services of the intellectual class, to become more strategic. Men like Professor Rehman Sobhan, Professor Anisur Rahman, Professor Nurul Islam and Professor Muzaffar Ahmed Chowdhury were acutely aware of the growing nature of the disparity between the two wings of the country. They were also in search of a leader under whose patronage they could shape their perspectives about the future of East Pakistan. The meeting between Mujib and the young Bengali economists, therefore, rapidly turned into a meeting of minds. A good number of months went into giving a concrete shape to what Mujib and his colleagues in the Awami League wished to see as a formal expression of Bengali political intent.

In the period between February and May 1966, the Awami League's programme of publicising the Six Points throughout East Pakistan was beginning to have an effect. The autonomy plan was received enthusiastically by the student community, which in this case largely meant Dhaka University. Since the Language Movement of 1952, the university had gradually and convincingly come to symbolise political dissent in East Pakistan, a condition to which secular political organisations like the Awami League easily related. In 1962, students of

Dhaka University had launched a sustained and eventually successful campaign against a series of controversial academic reforms proposed by the Ayub regime. A convocation ceremony scheduled to be inaugurated by the provincial governor, Abdul Monem Khan, had to be abandoned in the face of student protests in 1964. The governor, a Bengali himself, had become an increasingly unpopular figure in the province because of his kowtowing before the central government, gladly satisfying the regime's desire of seeing nationalist Bengali politicians punished at every conceivable opportunity. Monem Khan's clear incitement of communalism in the same year also brought his reputation down quite a few notches. Finally, there remained the collusion between the governor and the central government in decreeing a ban on the study of the literary works and performance of the songs of the Nobel laureate Rabindranath Tagore, clearly seen as a move to Islamise Pakistan's Bengali populace. Monem Khan, in effect, became a hated figure for Bengalis. He, however, did not quite seem to understand his predicament. He was quite happy in demonstrating a fawning level of loyalty to President Ayub Khan, given particularly the fact that two of his immediate predecessors, Lieutenant General Azam Khan and Ghulam Faruque, West Pakistanis, had both ended up earning the wrath of Ayub Khan and had been eased out of the governor's mansion.

In 1964, student organisations such as the East Pakistan Students League (EPSL) and the left-leaning East Pakistan Students Union (EPSU) found themselves playing a prominent role in promoting the cause of a nascent Bengali nationalism. The pivotal role which these organisations would play in the making of modern Bengali history had been defined by an earlier generation of students who had undertaken the campaign against the education reforms of the regime in 1962. Many of the student leaders involved in the 1962 agitation—K.M. Obaidur Rahman, Shah Moazzam Hossain, Sheikh Fazlul Haq Moni, Rashed Khan Menon, and others would go on to participate in politics on a larger national canvas in subsequent years. But the momentum these young men had injected into university politics would pave the way for their successors to launch a frontal assault on the loyalists of the regime in 1964.

By 1966, the Six Points provided the student community with the ammunition it needed to carry the message of Bengali distinctiveness forward. Of the two organisations mentioned earlier, the EPSU was clearly the more intellectual. Its members had quickly developed a reputation for analytical study of the political conditions in East Pakistan. But it was the EPSL that Mujib identified with. And he had reason to, for it was largely through his efforts and political guidance that the organisation had been founded in 1948. If intellectually the EPSL lagged behind the EPSU, organisationally it more than made up for the gap through the fervour with which it went whipping up campus discontent against the government. As 1966 progressed, the EPSL seized on the Six Points as the perfect reason to launch a fresh offensive against West Pakistani political and economic dominance of the country. For its part, the EPSU, while not quite ready to embrace Mujib's Six Points in its entirety, was nevertheless content to carry on its socialistic-cum-nationalistic programme of autonomy for East Pakistan forward.

Following the announcement of the Six Points in February, events moved at a dizzying speed for Mujib. On 1 March, he was elected president of the Awami League, a clear indication of the overall authority he had begun to wield in the organisation. Taking his place as general secretary of the party was Tajuddin Ahmed. All other senior leaders in the Awami League—Syed Nazrul Islam, Khondokar Moshtaq Ahmed, A.H.M. Quamruzzaman and M. Mansoor Ali—were accommodated in various high level positions in the party. Once he had taken control of the party, Mujib went on an extensive tour of the province. Already, there were the ominous signs of what the Pakistan government had planned to curb his freedom. In the three months after his public declaration of the Six Points in Lahore, he was arrested as many as eight times. In early May, he was taken into police custody for the ninth time, hours after he had delivered an impassioned speech justifying the need for East Pakistan to have a greater say in Pakistan's governance before a gathering of jute-mill workers in the river port town of Narayanganj, outside Dhaka. Mujib was now charged under the Defence of Pakistan Rules, a pointer to the sedition the regime saw building up in the politics of the Bengali leader. It was to prove the beginning of a long ordeal for Mujib and by the time it ended, much of the political landscape of Pakistan would stand transformed.

Mujib's arrest sparked protests all over the province and provoked his party to call a general strike on 7 June. Over the next few days, the government went on a drive against all senior leaders of the Awami League, ostensibly to make sure that no one remained outside prison to organise any effective campaign against it. But the government strategy had quite underestimated the organisational strength of the Awami League. On 7 June, through the efforts of Mizanur Rahman Chowdhury, the young Awami League politician who was at the time a member of the Pakistan National Assembly, and Amena Begum, a respected woman politician who had become a powerful force in the party over the past few years, a total shutdown was observed all over the province. The response of the Bengalis to Mujib's autonomy plan was not in doubt any more, for it had been made patent by the successful strike. The spontaneity of the strike served as a painful blow for the regime and its local supporters. President Ayub Khan was soon issuing dire threats of force to the proponents and supporters of the Six Points. Governor Monem Khan publicly declared his intention of keeping Mujib in jail as long as he was the governor. Pro-government and right-wing political figures in both wings of the country went on a concerted, often shrill campaign to paint Mujib and the Awami League as traitors to the cause of Pakistan, not eligible for pardon.

After May 1966, a clear view developed among the Bengali elite that Pakistani politics called for radical change. The growing measure of acceptance of the Six Points, together with the punishment being meted out to its proponents, began to convince the middle class that if East Pakistan had to find its way out of its predicament, it would surely need the very autonomy which Mujib and his party had enunciated for the province. The six months after the general strike of 7 June was a relatively quiet period, owing to the silence into which the Awami League had lapsed. Its entire leadership, at the senior and middle levels, was in jail. Those who remained outside were not willing, in the face of increasing government repression, to do anything that might bring down a fresh spate of the administration's wrath on them.

The year 1966 would soon reveal quite a few new factors in Pakistan's politics. One would be Bhutto's sense of alienation with the government he served, which grew in leaps and bounds.

Rise of Bhutto

Foreign Minister Zulfikar Ali Bhutto went on leave in June 1966, six months after the Tashkent Declaration was initialed by his president and the prime minister of India. This move was unprecedented as no minister in Pakistan's history had been permitted to go on leave because he did not find it easy to keep working for the government.

Bhutto's growing unhappiness with the government that he was part of created an impression of a rift within the government. The foreign minister clearly did not help matters when he started speaking, at least in private, of a secret clause attached to the Tashkent Declaration. The reality was quite different. There was no secret clause anywhere in the deal Ayub Khan had reached with Shastri. But Bhutto, given to regular bursts of emotion, persisted in peddling the notion that the president had betrayed the country in Tashkent and had in fact frittered away the 'gains' that had been made on the battlefield in September 1965. His position, one of not leaving the government and yet feeling uncomfortable within it, was a source of embarrassment for Ayub Khan.

Bhutto's quandary stemmed from the absence of security in his political future if he left the government. The president, obviously weakened by the war and the talks in Tashkent, was not yet in a position to call the shots. The entire administration, including the provincial governments, did remain beholden to him. The introduction of Basic Democracy had ensured the operation of a system where power flowed from the president and back to him. The national assembly, elected in the same indirect method as the president, remained a toothless body despite the presence of a number of prominent politicians, including the speaker, Abdul Jabbar Khan, a Bengali from East Pakistan. The governors of the provinces, unlike the president and the members of the national and provincial assemblies, were appointed by the president and stayed in office at his pleasure. Ayub Khan realised, despite doffing his army uniform in favour of active politics, that his power base remained the army, now in the hands of his loyalist, General Mohammad Musa, a soldier who had risen through the ranks to reach the top. In the days before the September 1965 war, there had been a change in the air force, with Air Marshal Asghar Khan making way for Air Marshal Nur Khan. The navy was on the watch of Vice Admiral A.R. Khan. In the civil administration, Ayub Khan was served ably and ingratiatingly by the ubiquitous secretary in the ministry of information and broadcasting, Altaf Gauhar. His cabinet was essentially a typical schoolroom, where he was happy to be the headmaster presiding over a group of docile pupils.

For all his ambitions, the foreign minister was also mindful of the consequences, were he to go for a clean break with the president. Ayub Khan was not known to be a forgiving man. Moreover, in the years since his coup in 1958, the military ruler had developed a fondness for the young minister in a way that was more of a father-son relationship. It was to the credit of the president that after removing Iskandar Mirza twenty days into the declaration of martial law, he had seen no reason to throw the young Bhutto out as well. Bhutto had been a Mirza protégé and it was through the ousted president that the young lawyer from Larkana had made his way into the cabinet as minister for commerce. The shrewd Bhutto quickly shifted his loyalty to Ayub Khan immediately after his benefactor's exile. The move turned out to be richly rewarding. Bhutto, over the next few years, rose meteorically in the government. By 1960, he was negotiating gas deals with the Soviet Union as minister for industries and natural resources. He also had charge of Basic Democracy. In 1963, when Ayub Khan commandeered a faction of the old Muslim League to become its leader and so provide a civilian veneer to his government, Bhutto was catapulted into the position of party secretary general. Earlier in 1963, his long-time ambition of shaping Pakistan's foreign policy was realised when Ayub Khan appointed him minister for foreign affairs following the death of Bogra. Built on the earlier opening to China by Suhrawardy, he sought to steer Pakistan away from a complete dependence on the West. There was something of a firebrand in Bhutto that led him into adopting a cynical attitude to Pakistan's position in such regional organisations as CENTO and SEATO. Bhutto, who had grown up in pre-Partition India, had gone to school in Bombay and would not become a citizen of Pakistan until 1949, adopted a shrill anti-India posture as foreign minister, so much so that his arguments in favour of a Pakistani attack on the Rann of Kutch in May 1965 were readily agreed to by Ayub Khan and the military establishment. The consequences were disastrous, as the Indian attack on Lahore only four months later would show.

But if the 1965 war had been a disaster for the country, it was also a reason behind Bhutto's rise to prominence in Pakistan. His spirited defence of the national cause before the UN Security Council quickly earned him the admiration of Pakistanis, who were quite mesmerised by his performance. It was an occasion that Bhutto would have missed had Ayub Khan not sent him to New York. In the initial stages of the UNSC debate, Pakistan's case was argued by Law Minister S.M. Zafar. Within days, however, it was apparent that Zafar's approach was getting nowhere, especially in circumstances where the Indian team was represented by the veteran politician, Foreign Minister Sardar Swaran Singh. Bhutto's appearance before the Security Council was, therefore, a change of tack for Ayub Khan. Speaking in fluent English, a sign of his academic background at Oxford and Berkeley, Bhutto rammed into India in what was clearly a message meant to be heard back home. The Indians were unimpressed, obviously, and so were the representatives of the member-states on the council. The rhetorical

flourishes Bhutto brought to bear on his presentation of the case for
Pakistan lacked substance. But it was enough to make him look like
a heroic figure in Karachi and Lahore. On his part, after he returned
home, Bhutto quite relished the popularity, a condition that nearly
upstaged the public image of his president.

But the UN experience was also the point when his arrogance,
which would later mar his politics and finally his career, began to
display itself. During a December 1965 visit to the White House with
President Ayub Khan, Bhutto riled President Lyndon Johnson so
much that the US president rudely told off the brash foreign minister
when he attempted to interrupt his conversations with Ayub. A
similar situation occurred in Tashkent, forcing Premier Kosygin and
Andrei Gromyko into dealing directly with Ayub, keeping Bhutto
out of the picture altogether. Not even British Prime Minister Harold
Wilson was free of Bhutto-fatigue. He clearly saw a streak of evil
in Pakistan's foreign minister and told his people so. The months
that he was on leave were a time he spent weighing the viability
of a political career, should he strike out on his own. Bhutto, for
all his bravado, was essentially a frightened man in the months of
his estrangement from Ayub. He was aware of the pitfalls, given
Ayub Khan's penchant for punishing detractors. The dilemma for the
foreign minister-on-leave was acute. He was not yet in a position
to branch out on his own and neither did he relish the thought of
suddenly being out of the corridors of power. His stewardship of the
foreign policy establishment was a job he had enjoyed to the hilt and
so he was loath to see it slipping away from him.

The president made it clear, within a month of the minister having
proceeded on leave, that Bhutto had to shape up or ship out. Ayub
Khan held out an implied threat, carried to Bhutto by his emissaries,
that the foreign minister had to resign on his own or face outright
dismissal. Bhutto got the message. He was not ready to be sacked, for
that would damage his political future. Resignation would be seen as
a heroic way out by Pakistanis. And so it was that in the middle of July
1966, Bhutto made his way out of the cabinet. He was with alacrity

replaced by Syed Sharifuddin Pirzada, the attorney general. For the first time in eight years, Bhutto was out on a limb, uncertain of how the regime he had loyally served all this while would treat him. He was still only thirty-eight years old and did not have any desire to walk away into the woods. Politics fascinated him, but till that stage in his career, the only kind of politics he had participated in came by way of his association with the army. Major General Iskandar Mirza had made him a cabinet minister and Field Marshal Ayub Khan had kept him on. In July 1966, the army and the government as a whole seemed to become sudden strangers to him.

Bhutto's predicament was made worse through his inability to reach out to the political opposition. In all his years as a minister, he had presented himself as a diehard loyalist of the military regime. This reputation certainly did not endear him to the politicians who had, for the past eight years, been engaged in a concerted campaign against President Ayub Khan and everything he represented in Pakistan. Bhutto needed time to think about the future. He flew abroad, spending quite some time in London where he spent time reading, meeting old friends and generally pondering over his future. The exiled Iskandar Mirza was in town, but Bhutto did not see or get in touch with him. He needed to be careful and certainly did not intend to give Ayub Khan any reason to think he was in league with the former president. For all his brashness in the ministerial years, once out of power Bhutto felt the need to act rationally in his own interest.

By the time he returned to Pakistan, he had clearly made up his mind. Nothing short of a new approach would do. Over the months he came in contact with some elite sections of West Pakistani society and was soon involved in discussing politics with a band of young men who would eventually be part of the team that would take him back to political office. Most of these men sported a brand of urban socialism that appealed to Bhutto, though he had by no means been attracted to left-wing politics in his career. His class background did not allow him to dabble in politics that even remotely resembled Marxist ideals. Reared in an atmosphere of feudalism, Bhutto was certainly not the man who could build a leftist constituency against the regime and the various class interests in West Pakistan. East Pakistan, of course, was already on a different course with the politics of the imprisoned Mujib gaining in substance with every passing day.

In the end, it was socialism, of a kind, that Bhutto adopted as his bridge to his own future. Most of the young men he collected around him were themselves in need of a figure whose national appeal could carry their socialist theme across. These men—Ghulam Mustafa Khar, Mubashir Hasan, Mairaj Mohammad Khan, Ghulam Mustafa Jatoi, Abdul Hafiz Pirzada, Moulana Kausar Niazi, Rafi Raza—spotted in Bhutto the figure they could utilise to inaugurate a new trend in Pakistan's politics. Bhutto also earned the loyalty and support of J.A. Rahim, an elderly former diplomat, and a Bengali to boot, for his programme. In November 1967, fifteen months after leaving the government of President Ayub Khan, Bhutto launched the Pakistan People's Party (PPP) in Lahore. As a demonstration of his new-found enthusiasm for socialist politics as also his admiration for China's chairman Mao, Bhutto decreed that he would be the chairman of the new party.

The underlying principles of the new party, as Bhutto made clear, were Islam, democracy and socialism, a plank that would soon come under attack from the country's political right on the ground that Islamic faith and socialism did not go together. Bhutto, being the shrewd individual he was, knew that no amount of appeal for public support in Pakistan would mean anything unless he spoke of the place of Islam in the lives of Pakistan's people. Like Mohammad Ali Jinnah, the country's founder, Bhutto lived his life along Western traditions. He was known to have a reputation for drinking and always dressed immaculately in Western attire. His links with ordinary Pakistanis had always been minimal. His feudal background as a Sindhi landlord clearly precluded further the possibility of his identifying with the general masses. But in November 1967, Bhutto clearly foresaw a pretty tenable future for himself through a combination of Islamic principles and socialist philosophy, with a dash of democracy, as the theme upon which he meant to take his new party to the country.

Over the next twelve months, Bhutto successfully transformed himself into a politician by developing links with the grass-roots. He and his party showed clear signs of tapping into the mass discontent that had been welling up among West Pakistan's poor. It was a refreshing change in a social condition where a combination of vested interests had so long dominated politics. While populist politics and dissent had been defining features in East Pakistan, politics in West Pakistan had never really escaped the clutches of the landed aristocracy. With that came the stranglehold of the army and the bureaucracy on the country, a reality that had only become more pronounced in the years of Ayub Khan.

An immediate result of Bhutto's foray into independent politics was the tremendous enthusiasm he aroused in every city and town he travelled to as part of his campaign, to turn the PPP into a household name. The government of President Ayub Khan was clearly rattled by Bhutto's rising popularity and soon unleashed its more rabid elements, such as Ahmad Saeed Kirmani, a minister in the West Pakistani provincial cabinet, to counter Bhutto. One of the means the regime adopted to prevent Bhutto's message from percolating down to the citizen was to blacklist him from the media. Most references to Bhutto and his party, therefore, came through the shrill criticism of him that men like Kirmani periodically made through the newspapers. On state-controlled radio and television, Bhutto, like all other Opposition politicians, was completely ignored.

A little over a month after the PPP came into existence, a whole new drama came into play in the country's politics. The government announced, at the end of December 1967, the arrest of a number of Bengali civilian and military officers on charges of sedition. No names were mentioned and only sketchy reports were made available by the regime on the nature of the crimes the arrested had been accused of. Things became clearer a few days later, on 6 January 1968, when the government of Pakistan charged the jailed Awami League leader Mujib, along with thirty-four Bengali military and civilian officers, in a conspiracy to separate East Pakistan from the rest of the country by force of arms. The regime informed the country that Mujib and his co-accused had indulged in the conspiracy through establishing links with the Indian authorities in Agartala, capital of a union territory in north-eastern India bordering East Pakistan.

Agartala and Resurgent Bengal

The announcement of Mujib's involvement in a conspiracy to destroy the state of Pakistan was greeted with disbelief in the country, particularly in East Pakistan. While Bengalis and a large number of West Pakistanis were aware of the radical nature of Mujib's politics, they were unwilling to look upon him as a conspirator who would seek foreign help to make his province an independent state. Mujib's politics, like that of Suhrawardy, had always pursued a constitutional course. Even when firebrand, elderly politicians like Bhashani had voiced their 'Assalam-o-Alaikum' farewell to Pakistan at Kagmari in 1957, Mujib maintained his faith in the constitution despite his growing disillusionment with the nature of the state. He was every inch an emotional being, but not to the extent where he would lose his grip on reality. The faux pas that Fazlul Huq committed during his visit to Calcutta, soon after taking over as chief minister in 1954— wherein he had waxed eloquent on the traditional bonds of culture uniting Bengalis across the cartographic divide, inviting the wrath of the central government—was a mistake Mujib would never make. His involvement with the Independent Bengal Revolutionary Council in 1961 was certainly a manifestation of his expanding thoughts on Bengali independence, but it was by no means the road he had definitely decided to follow.

A further reason put forward in defence of Mujib's adherence to constitutionalism was the Six-Point programme for regional autonomy which he had presented at an open conference of Pakistan's Opposition political parties in Lahore in early 1966. The Six Points, observers noted, were a clear-cut demonstration of what Mujib and the Awami League wished Pakistan as a state should undertake in the interest of the future of all its constituent units. Obviously, the Six Points would drastically weaken the centre and held out the possibility of the federation being, in time, replaced by a confederal arrangement, leaving disparate units free to opt out as independent states altogether. It could be argued that Mujib was ahead of his time, given that three decades later in Europe, Czechs and Slovaks would find a negotiated way out of a country they had shared for a long time, albeit under communism. More pointedly, Mujib's Six Points came at a time when Pakistan happened to be under the complete dominance of its civil-military bureaucracy, a structure that would brook no challenge to its authority. Ayub Khan, along with his fellow officers as well as vast sections of politicians in West Pakistan, was not willing to entertain any notion of political liberalism in the country. To a considerable extent, the regime succeeded in intimidating the political classes into either falling in line with its views or staying silent altogether. But Mujib and the Awami League, freed from any need for pragmatism of the kind exhibited by Suhrawardy before his death in 1963, were in a class of their own.

The growing sense of political, economic and administrative disparity in the Bengalis, the Awami League reasoned, could only create the conditions for an emergence of extreme, possibly left-wing politics, unless constitutional ways were adopted to resolve the crisis. The Awami League, home to middle class, bourgeois sentiments, was acutely sensitive to criticism of its programmes by the left, especially those Marxists who operated underground. Moreover, the explosion of Naxalite violence in 1967 in the neighbouring Indian state of West Bengal served as a wake-up call to the Awami League. Unless the grievances of East Pakistan were addressed through appropriate political means, the party feared, matters could slip out of its hands and lead to a rise of extremism of the sort the Naxalites had already unleashed in the neighbourhood. The Awami League, under Mujib, was not willing to see itself turning into irrelevance. Hence the Six Points.

The government's move was regarded by the Bengali elite as an attempt to paint Mujib as a traitor before the country and thereby, to set at naught his call for a bigger role for Bengalis in Pakistan's political administration. These fears were not misplaced. Within days of the announcement of the conspiracy, now being referred to as the Agartala Conspiracy case, Bengalis in West Pakistan found themselves targeted as anti-Pakistan elements. There were isolated incidents of Bengalis being humiliated in public. More problems came with the insinuations and innuendos which began to be reflected in the administration. West Pakistani civil administration officials made little secret of their disdain for their Bengali colleagues. In the military, all Bengali officers and lower level soldiers came under careful watch, to the extent where it was being made evident that no Bengali could be trusted to be loyal to Pakistan. The media regularly started carrying statements and commentaries that condemned the Awami League's 'evil design' to break up Pakistan with the help of its enemy, India. Overall, an atmosphere of fear was generated in the country, especially among its Bengali population. The language of force, with which President Ayub Khan had threatened the proponents of the Six Points, was now in full play. Time had come for Mujib and nascent Bengali nationalism to be crushed. To those who watched events unfold in early 1968, it did not appear likely that Mujib would ever emerge free. Everything pointed to his end, possibly by hanging or by a firing squad.

The government of Pakistan constituted a special tribunal to try Mujib and the thirty-four other accused in the case. Headed by Justice S.A. Rahman, chief justice of the Pakistan Supreme Court, the tribunal had two other members, one each from the provincial High Courts of East and West Pakistan. The authorities decided on the Dhaka Cantonment as the venue of the trial, and in what was clearly a state of self-confidence, allowed full access to the media to cover the proceedings. The gamble on the part of the authorities was that an open trial would expose Mujib for the arch conspirator and anti-Pakistan element he was and convince people in Pakistan and elsewhere of the calculated damage that a group of Bengali secessionists had planned on perpetrating. A good number of lawyers, most of them Bengalis, sprang to Mujib's defence. At the same time, with Bengali emotions running high against what was perceived as a policy of repression pursued by the central government against the Bengali leader, expatriate East Pakistanis gathered to organise legal defence for Mujib. In London, Sir Thomas Williams, QC, was engaged by Bengalis largely inhabiting the East End of the city. Sir Thomas duly flew down to Dhaka but soon found himself harassed at every step. Pakistani military intelligence tailed him everywhere, making it obvious that he was not welcome. Eventually, he was compelled to fly back to London. But the point had been made. The trial of Mujib was a spectacle now being observed abroad. For the first time in its twenty-year history, Pakistan stood at a difficult crossroads. Opinion about the nature of the conspiracy, if indeed there was one, was divided. In West Pakistan, where political awareness had never measured up to the serious levels of political behaviour as existed in the east, the tendency was to accept the government's version of events. In East Pakistan, Bengalis saw in the conspiracy case a bigger conspiracy aimed at not only silencing Mujib but also preventing his people from raising the question of autonomy in future. Even as preparations were underway for the special tribunal to open proceedings, the administration zealously rounded up Awami League workers and carted them off to prison. In the universities, however, the first signs of trouble for the government were beginning to develop as students allied to the EPSL went into clandestine action to whip up public sentiment against the trial.

The trial opened on 19 June 1968. The Bengali summer was at its height, with the temperature and humidity adding to the general state of unease all over the province. Mujib and his co-accused were led into the dock in Dhaka Cantonment. Before the accused was a row of journalists gathered from all over Pakistan as well as from Britain and the United States. On taking his place in the courtroom, Mujib noticed among the media representatives a Bengali journalist he knew well. He called out his name, once, twice and then for a third time. It was clear the journalist deliberately avoided making any response, but finally he said, in a whisper and without turning to look at Mujib, 'We cannot talk here. Intelligence men are all around.' The man was afraid. His expression of worry had little effect on the imprisoned politician and in fact was the perfect provocation to an explosion of fury on his part. In a loud voice that surprised even the judges presiding over the trial, Mujib made it clear what he thought of the trial and of the future. 'Anyone who wants to live in Bangladesh,' he said, 'will have to talk to Sheikh Mujibur Rahman.' At one go, he had let everyone present in the courtroom know that he was not intimidated by the charges against him. Additionally, he made it a point to drive a political message home when he referred to 'Bangladesh' rather than 'East Pakistan' in his angry outburst.

His confidence was on full display during the entire period of the trial. Asked by a Western journalist about his view of the case, Mujib told him, 'You know, they can't keep me here for more than six months.' On the opening day of the trial, he made a detailed statement before the tribunal denying all the charges that had been brought against him, making pointed references to his participation in the movement for the creation of Pakistan as a student and subsequently as a political leader. Mujib turned the tables on his accusers, telling the tribunal that the Agartala Conspiracy case was in fact the Rawalpindi conspiracy case, the implication being that the regime had concocted the case in the distant confines of a town in West Pakistan to discredit the Bengali movement for autonomy. Rawalpindi, a garrison town in northern West Pakistan, served at the time as the country's provisional capital as the finishing touches were being given to Islamabad, the new capital.

The government brought in a number of witnesses for the prosecution who largely repeated what had been given out by the authorities in the media all along. There was little question that the procedure adopted by the government was faulty and the arguments against the accused rested on flimsy ground. The general line of argument was that Mujib had secretly travelled to Agartala in 1964 to discuss with Indian officials the details of his plan to take East Pakistan out of the Pakistan federation through instigating an insurrection amongst Bengali armed forces personnel. The allegation that Mujib had secretly travelled to Agartala in 1964 raised eyebrows because of the political realities attached to the year in question. It was a period when Mujib was engaged in reviving and reorganising his party only months into the death of Suhrawardy. That, as well as his direct involvement in the formation of the COP and joining the Ms Jinnah bandwagon against Ayub Khan in the presidential election campaign did not quite tally with the charges the regime brought against the leader of the Awami League. What was, however, also true was that there was hardly any politician, military officer or civil servant in West Pakistan who had any reason to empathise with the Bengali leader. His sustained campaign over the years about the expanding nature of provincial economic disparity and exploitation of East Pakistan had ruffled feathers in the west. Moreover, unlike Suhrawardy, Mujib was blunt about the way he saw politics shaping up or collapsing in Pakistan and had not been averse to pointing at its corruption by the army, in tandem with the civil bureaucracy and political classes that regularly genuflected before the military.

The Agartala Conspiracy trial soon coincided with newer political realities, yet in an embryonic state, in Pakistan. Bhutto's message of 'Islam, socialism, democracy' began to resonate with the poor in West Pakistan, especially in Sind and the Punjab. Alongside the inroads he was making into the world of West Pakistan's poverty-stricken regions, Bhutto was also proving adept in drawing the support of the middle class to his programme. His support in his native Sind was only natural. But it was in the Punjab, a region which clearly dominated recruitment to the military and the civil service, where his rising popularity gave the initial jolt to the Ayub Khan government. The PPP leader barnstormed all the four provinces of West Pakistan attacking his one-time mentor as a dictator who had brought humiliation for Pakistan at Tashkent. President Ayub's difficulty in responding to Bhutto's charges lay in the danger of having to open a pandora's box if he chose to hit back. Both he and Bhutto knew that the war had resulted in a stalemate and not exactly a victory for Pakistan. The president, though he must have been tempted to expose Bhutto's misplaced advice on the war, could not afford to let the country know that on his watch the military had actually suffered a number of reverses, indeed that it had been caught unawares when the Indian Army launched an assault on the city of Lahore.

For Bhutto, everything appeared to be going according to plan. At every railway station, airport and town centre, he repeated his allegations about a secret clause to the Tashkent Declaration. Much as the supporters of the president denied the allegations, the belief taking hold of the public imagination in West Pakistan was that the former foreign minister might well have been telling the truth in contrast to the feeble fiction dished out by the regime. Bhutto's party based its policy on populist politics and in furtherance of its goals began to launch sustained attacks on the rich. The PPP, along with a number of leftist and left-of-centre parties (and that included the Awami League), developed the notion, with a good deal of justification, that Pakistan's economy had come to be concentrated in the hands of twenty-two industrial families. In the two decades since the emergence of the country, these families had cast their increasingly long shadows over national resources even as economic conditions for the 100 million people of the country deteriorated steadily. For years, Mujib had complained about the increasing dominance of the twenty-two families, and its ramifications felt in East Pakistan, where a big business such as jute was in the hands of entrepreneurs based in the west. Now Bhutto was taking up the same theme.

In mid-1968, as East Pakistan turned restive by the day with the Agartala case proceedings holding the attention of the Bengalis, and West Pakistan providing political space to Bhutto, the government of President Ayub Khan went on a spree of celebrations to commemorate a decade in power. The regime chose to highlight the remarkable industrial progress and social discipline achieved in the ten years since Ayub had taken over. And yet, there was a bizarre irony in the situation, with the reality of the widening economic gap between the two regions of the country, and the high levels of poverty not just among the Bengalis but also in the relatively poor regions of Sind, Baluchistan and North West Frontier Province (NWFP). Ayub Khan's loyalists trumpeted the period as a decade of progress, a definition that failed to match ground realities. The media, in the absolute control of the regime, went into overdrive in projecting the achievements made by the president and his team. Fawning commentaries were carried by many newspapers, if not all, placing Ayub Khan on a pedestal with Egypt's Gamal Abdel Nasser and France's Charles de Gaulle. The president had already given the country his memoirs, allegedly ghost written, and appeared ready to go into a fresh term in office through the presidential elections of 1970. But 1968 was also the year in which Ayub Khan fell ill and remained bedridden for several months. Rumours went around of his having come close to dying. But no public announcement of his condition, or even the fact that he was ailing, was given out. It would emerge only later how grave his illness had been and how affairs of state had been handled by the army chief, General Agha Mohammad Yahya Khan.

It was in the summer of 1968 that Bhutto declared his intention to seek the presidency of Pakistan at the next election. Clearly, he was telling the country that he would take the president on at the polls in the expectation that he would win. Bhutto had come to the conclusion that Pakistan's people were in a mood for change in leadership and that he was destined to be the vehicle of such change. He thereby fully ignored the nature of the struggle waged over the years by Pakistan's mainstream Opposition, which insisted that any political change would need to be based on a return to parliamentary democracy on the basis of the abrogated constitution of 1956. The problem for Bhutto, even as he sought to identify himself with the opposition to Ayub Khan, was his feeling that he, rather than anyone else, represented a credible challenge to the government. Despite his break with Ayub Khan and the formation of the PPP, Bhutto was not yet ready to comprehend the bigger issue of the large scale political changes the country would need for politics to proceed on a smooth plane in a post-Ayub situation.

For their part, the politicians in the traditional Opposition camp were yet to trust Bhutto, considering that he had been part of the regime for eight years. But they were willing just the same to utilise his growing stature in the gathering movement against the government because it would lend greater substance to their struggle. But they remained wary of Bhutto, nevertheless, and clearly served the caveat that any movement against the regime had to be based on the principles they had already enunciated. In other words, in autumn 1968, three clear strands of Opposition thinking were at work. In the first place, the Opposition (minus the Awami League) was insistent that the country be returned to the conditions as they had existed prior to the declaration of martial law in October 1958. In the second, the Awami League was clearly too deep into its Six Points for it to retreat to any soft measures against the government. Finally, there was Bhutto with his own programme, one that he based on the personality cult fast developing around him, that he thought could be implemented through making use of the political system as it existed.

Politics took a dramatic shape in early November. As President Ayub Khan addressed a public rally in the north-western city of Peshawar, a young student took a few potshots at him. The bullets, fired from a great distance, predictably missed their mark. But the incident was enough to create commotion in the president's inner circles. Outside these circles, a palpable sense of the ominous developed all over the country, especially since it was the first time that an attempt had been made on the life of Ayub Khan. The Peshawar incident was strong proof that the state of discontent which had set in earlier in East Pakistan had now managed to reach all the way to the neighbourhood of the president in West Pakistan. The president and his advisors were not ready or willing to take any of it lying down.

Ayub Khan, still dependent on the army rather than his civilian government for advice, agreed with those who suggested harsh measures against the Opposition. In the east, the case against Mujib was going badly but that in no way signified the weakness of the arguments the government's lawyers were making against the Bengali leader. There was as yet no one in the presidential circles who even remotely considered the thought of the Agartala case backfiring on the administration. As far as the regime was concerned, Mujib and the Awami League were a spent force and the trial in the Dhaka cantonment was only the grand finale in a drama that would soon see Mujib out of the way. It was in West Pakistan, though, that the gathering pace of political unrest with its increasing levels of violence that worried Ayub Khan. He saw his authority eroding and one way of preventing the slide was to go for tough action against the Opposition. Bhutto, more than any other West Pakistani politician, was a threat as well as an irritant the president needed to push aside if he meant to reassert his authority.

On 13 November, the government placed Bhutto, Khan Abdul Wali Khan, the leader of the National Awami Party, and eleven other political personalities under arrest. The charge against these politicians was the hatred and contempt they disseminated against the president before the country. If Ayub Khan thought he now had everything under the lid, he was to be proved wrong. Only days after Bhutto was carted off to prison, Air Marshal Asghar Khan, the former commander-in-chief of the air force, announced his entry into national politics. The newspapers carried the news of Khan's foray into politics in a brief item on the back pages. No one was left in any doubt, judging by the treatment of the news, that the former air force chief had opted to be in the Opposition camp. The retired air marshal's move left the regime stunned. It had not been prepared for the eventuality of a military man taking a plunge into politics. Worse, Asghar Khan's move increased fears in the government of the Opposition taking fresh impetus from a man respected for his professionalism and decency joining its ranks.

The only other time Ayub Khan had feared any threat from a military figure was in the early 1960s, when as governor of East Pakistan,

Lieutenant General Azam Khan acquired a degree of popularity. He had stripped Azam Khan of his responsibilities as governor of East Pakistan in 1962. But Asghar Khan was a different kettle of fish. Besides, he had walked into politics at a moment when things were going badly for the president. Any move that remotely seemed to suppress him would not go down well with significant sections of the armed forces. And just as the regime wondered how to deal with the change in the equation, it was faced with a new threat to its stability. Within days Justice Syed Mahbub Murshed, former chief justice of the East Pakistan High Court and prime mover behind the Tagore centenary celebrations of 1961, declared that he too was going into politics. The arrival of the jurist, universally respected for his integrity and ability to identify with the right causes, was greeted with a sigh of relief by a beleaguered Opposition. With Mujib on trial in East Pakistan and Bhutto, Wali Khan and others in detention in West Pakistan, the emergence of Asghar Khan and S.M. Murshed made a huge difference. It boosted morale in the anti-Ayub camp to a considerable extent and injected fresh energy into the movement. The two men made it clear that the government of Ayub Khan was in need of a rethink on its programmes. They demanded the release of all political prisoners as a way of stemming the slide to disorder.

In Dhaka, students and other sections of the province were getting restive and violent. The peripatetic Bhashani, the one senior political figure who had managed to stay out of jail, now took over the leadership of the protest movement in East Pakistan. Despite his advancing years, the moulana still commanded support among broad swathes of Bengali public opinion, a fact borne out by the large crowds that gathered to hear him all over the province. Loved by Bengalis for his pro-people, anti-establishment stand, the parting of ways between the Awami League and him in Kagmari in 1957 had not however, completely severed or loosened Bhashani's bonds with the old party. The level of personal affection with which Bhashani saw Mujib had never been disturbed by the serious differences the two men demonstrated on matters of public policy.

By December of the year, Bhashani had begun demanding the withdrawal of the Agartala case and the freeing of Mujib and others accused of treason. In repeated emotional outbursts, he exhorted the masses to set fire to the government and burn it to cinders, a political programme that would be more commonly known by its Bengali terminology *jalao-gherao*. Roughly translated in English, it meant 'burn and besiege'. He was unabashedly speaking the language of violence, prompting fears in the government of a total slide to anarchy. But even if the regime were disposed to hauling Bhashani away to prison, it was wary about the repercussions of such a move.

Mujib was already giving the special tribunal in Dhaka a hard time. In Lahore, Bhutto's lawyers had filed a writ petition challenging his detention and the hearings could begin any day. In other words, the government had achieved little by its actions against the Opposition. By the end of December, what should have been a happy conclusion to celebrations of his decade in power, President Ayub Khan was in a state of psychological as well as physical exhaustion. The country, for the first time in ten years, was defying him in an unprecedented way. With every passing day, the streets were getting out of control. But, ironically, the president did not see it as having to do anything with his government's policies. Instead, he spotted a huge conspiracy by the Opposition to destabilise Pakistan. As president, it was his constitutional and moral responsibility to reclaim the country from the anarchists. For the moment, therefore, he was convinced that he could yank the country away from the brink and clamp order on it. Neither he nor his administration saw the writing on the wall.

By January 1969, Pakistan and its president were in deeper trouble. In Dhaka and other places of East Pakistan, the gradual and steady resistance to the regime had now snowballed into a mass upsurge. The government responded, in the only way it could, by ordering the police to fire into the crowds. In the northern city of Rajshahi, Professor Zoha, a teacher at the university, was shot dead by the police. In Dhaka, a young man named Asaduzzaman was killed in police firing. His fellow protesters quickly made a banner of resistance out of his bloodied shirt, and so injected a new spirit into the anti-Ayub movement. In Dhaka's Mohammadpur residential zone, Ayub Gate, the entry to the locality and named after the president, was swiftly renamed Asad Gate by the agitating students. A school student, Matiur Rahman, who had joined an anti-government procession, died when police fired into the protestors. For an angry Bengali populace, each new death turned into a symbol of renewed defiance.

On 5 January, student political activists at Dhaka University set up the *Kendriyo Chhatra Sangram Parishad* or Central Students Action Council (CSAC), ostensibly as an adjunct to the Awami League and the broader political movement to force the government into withdrawing the Agartala Conspiracy case and freeing Mujib. The council, spearheaded by the charismatic student leader Tofail Ahmed, announced its own eleven-point programme which was essentially a fleshing out of the Awami League's Six Points. The intention was to send out a message to the authorities that the student community was now officially part of the anti-Ayub movement and, more pointedly, considered itself a complement to the Awami League in raising the demand for sweeping autonomy for the province. The frenetic pace of activities the CSAC set for itself expanded to include wider areas in the province. In Rajshahi and Chittagong, university students lost little time in joining the struggle. Shortly thereafter, even college students, especially in the capital, began to join up with the university students, thus opening a new front of violent dissent which the government was unable to roll back.

The authorities responded, typically, through an imposition of curfews and regulations such as Section 144 of the Criminal Procedure Code, promulgated by the British colonial authorities, to restrict any gathering of people that could threaten the stability of the state. But these measures proved ineffective as Bengalis throughout the province started demonstrating a readiness to violate both curfews and Section 144. A desperate police force then resorted to firing into the crowds, which only exacerbated tension all over again. In the gathering crisis, Bhashani proved pivotal in his leadership of the movement. Day after day he exhorted the masses to rise in rebellion against the regime. His voice was heard through an unprecedented display of violence on the streets. Bhashani's calls for the release of Mujib resonated with the sentiments of a nation which now evidently saw little reason to identify any longer with the rest of Pakistan.

The government panicked, as its actions showed all too well. Publicly, its leading figures, including the president, continued to warn of severe action against the troublemakers. That did not help a situation which called for some conciliatory moves. As every day went by, East Pakistan seethed in growing anger. Every grievance of the Bengalis now appeared to be coalescing around the demand for the withdrawal of the Agartala case and the release of Mujib from imprisonment. Popular determination to free Mujib was heard for the first time, in loud slogans at the numerous public rallies taking place all over the province. 'We will break the locks of the prison. We will free Sheikh Mujib' were some of the more incendiary sentiments that Bhashani and the students encouraged. Matters took a truly serious turn when the moulana began to make ominous threats of leading demonstrators, which in East Pakistan meant thousands of people, perhaps more, marching down the streets to the cantonment, to free the Awami League leader. The officers and servicemen in the cantonment, most of whom were from West Pakistan, were not amused. Over the weeks, the local population had been getting increasingly restive, to a point where it had become impossible to persuade them to return home without seeing Mujib freed. West Pakistani central government officials posted in Dhaka and elsewhere, as well as their families, stayed well out of sight of Bengalis. The situation for Governor Monem Khan and his provincial administration, which had earned the wrath of the populace in a way that was unprecedented, was worse.

Towards mid-January, the government of Ayub Khan was plainly shaky despite its earlier rhetoric about restoring order in the country. In West Pakistan, students, taking a cue from their counterparts in the east, but surely for reasons of a different nature, went on a rampage in

Karachi, Lahore, Rawalpindi and Peshawar. Even Quetta, a normally quiet garrison town that served as the capital of Baluchistan, went through its own share of political disturbances in that season of fury. But it was East Pakistan that every day was making Ayub Khan's hold on power steadily weaker. He could either decide to quit by handing over power to the speaker of the national assembly or could go for an eventual show of strength. The latter course was fraught with risks, since there was little proof or guarantee that a last-ditch effort by the president, to bring the Bengalis to their heels, would succeed. But here was the dilemma for Ayub. If he used the army, he would be undermining his own role. If he did not, there was no way in which he could avert his government's collapse, since the system he had set up was not equipped to continue without him. There was no vice president. In the president's travels outside the country, it was the speaker who took charge as acting head of state. But that was a nominal affair and left unanswered the question of who would take over if the president resigned or was removed or was incapacitated. Constitutionally, the speaker could take over as acting president, but somewhere down the line there would need to be a more effective way of doing things. Ayub Khan's illness in early 1968 had demonstrated how tenuous the system was when nearly all his powers were exercised by the army chief, General Yahya Khan. Abdul Jabbar Khan, the speaker of the national assembly and a Bengali, was ignored.

As the violence raged in East Pakistan, the country's Opposition happily smelled a change in the atmosphere. In the virulence of the civil disorder in the country there was now a chance to remove Ayub Khan from power. No opportunity could be greater, they reasoned, for a return to the constitution of 1956. These politicians came together to form the Democratic Action Committee (DAC), the chief objective of which was to shape a coordinated strategy on the part of the Opposition as a way of offering the country a democratic alternative. The Awami League, along with other parties like the Council Muslim League, National Awami Party (Wali), National Democratic Party, *Nizam-e-Islam*, Jamaat-e-Islami, joined the DAC. Also associated with the front were Asghar Khan and Justice S.M. Murshed. Significantly, Bhutto's PPP and Bhashani's NAP stayed out of the DAC.

Much, against his wishes, much as he detested the Opposition, by the latter part of January Ayub Khan realised that there was little alternative to talking to the Opposition. He sent off a letter to Nawabzada Nasrullah Khan in the second week of February inviting the Opposition to a round table conference (RTC) with the government in Rawalpindi as a way of finding a solution to the crisis. For the Opposition, the invitation to an RTC was a significant victory and was further proof of how much ground the president had lost. The letter to Nawabzada Nasrullah Khan was not replicated to other politicians, the assumption being that as convenor of the DAC, he would be selecting the opposition representatives to the conference. The nawabzada, in his turn, intimated the presidential intentions to politicians such as Nurul Amin, Hamidul Haq Chowdhury, Moulvi Farid Ahmed, Chaudhri Mohammad Ali, General Azam Khan, Asghar Khan, S.M. Murshed, Zulfikar Ali Bhutto, Moulana Bhashani, Khan Abdul Wali Khan, Moulana Abul A'la Moududi, Sardar Bahadur Khan and, through intermediaries, also Sheikh Mujibur Rahman.

Almost immediately, questions began to be asked about the modalities of ensuring Mujib's participation in the RTC. It struck people as rather strange that a politician who was on trial for treason could now command enough importance to be invited to a meeting with the government. Nawabzada Nasrullah Khan, it was fairly obvious, could not have sent out the invitation to the Awami League leader had he not had a nod from the president. But now that Mujib had been invited to the conference, ways and means had to be found to ensure his attendance. The conspiracy trial in Dhaka was already running into problems, with the prosecution yet engaged in producing its witnesses six months into the proceedings. Mujib's defence team was yet to initiate its own examination of witnesses. With civil unrest demanding the withdrawal of the case spreading throughout the province, grave doubts were already being expressed about the ability of the government being able to sustain its position.

As January wore on, the government received repeated body blows at the hands of its Bengali population.

In the west, Bhutto went into his usual mode of introducing the usual element of drama he had become famous for, at the hearings of his case in Lahore. He lost little time in playing to the gallery, at one point even producing in court a piece of meat left over from the previous night's dinner in prison. Holding up the piece, Bhutto let the court know that this was one of the two bits of meat he, a former foreign minister and now chairman of the PPP, had been given for dinner. He had the sure sense that the country was turning against Ayub Khan, which probably meant that it could turn out well for him. He declaimed before the judge: 'In the fullness of time, the wheel of fortune will turn and in the revolution of this turn a better tomorrow will dawn.' In contrast, down in Dhaka, Mujib was taking recourse to no such gimmickry. He was aware from the daily prison visits of his wife that East Pakistan was in a state of uproar over his trial. It was one of those moments when the Awami League leader actually felt cheered over the course of events in the country. The time he had looked forward to, that of Ayub Khan capitulating, was at hand. Behind all such sentiments though, he could not reasonably say when he would walk out free from prison. He had realised from day one of the conspiracy trial that the charges against him were no trifling matter, and that indeed he required a strong defence to be put up in order for him to debunk the idea that he was a secessionist, out to undermine Pakistan.

As February progressed, there were all the unmistakable signs of the government going through a rethink on the crisis around it. A direct consequence of such a rethink was the release on 17 February of Bhutto, Wali Khan and everyone else who had been arrested the previous November. In political terms, the move represented stage two of the government's weakening position. But the enthusiasm that should have greeted Bhutto's release from jail was overshadowed by the larger presence of Mujib in Dhaka and in the rest of the country. The media in both wings of Pakistan now openly began to speculate on the political status of the Awami League chief, notably the probability or otherwise of his being able to take part at the projected RTC. Nawabzada Nasrullah Khan was going nowhere with the idea and the government was clearly not helping him break through the conundrum. There was resistance yet from the government to any thoughts of freedom for Mujib. Indeed, the president publicly made it clear that the Bengali leader could not be released and the Agartala Conspiracy case could not be withdrawn because it involved national security. The ground reality, of course, was different. By having Mujib invited to the RTC, the government had weakened its own case against him. One face-saving way out of the imbroglio was an exploring of the possibility of Mujib being brought to the conference, which would be held in Rawalpindi, on parole. The idea was quickly shot down by the Awami League, which preferred to wait till developing events forced the regime to free its leader without any conditions. In his incarceration, however, Mujib proved quite amenable to the idea of being freed on parole, and appeared to have encouraged the authorities in the belief that he was ready to agree to such a deal. Bhashani soon got wind of Mujib's train of thought and so did the student community now in the vanguard of the mass uprising.

For the first time, a terrible sense of worry enveloped the Awami League and Mujib's fans across the province. If he agreed to be released on parole, the entire edifice of the movement that had been built around the demand for his freedom and by extension around his Six-Point programme would collapse and clearly make it possible for Ayub Khan to regain the ground he had already lost. Mujib's wife Begum Fazilatunnesa, who had fairly regular access to her husband in the cantonment, was confronted by Mujib's colleagues in the Awami League, who explained the nature of the parole politics the government was trying to promote. She passed on the message to Mujib, along with the fact that she agreed with the assessment made by his party colleagues. The bottom line for Mujib was made unambiguously clear: parole was out of the question and unconditional freedom was only a question of time. Mujib listened to his wife. He did not give any thought to freedom on parole any more.

On 15 February, one of the accused in the conspiracy trial, Sergeant Zahurul Huq, was shot inside Dhaka cantonment by his army guards. The government explanation of the tragedy was clearly untenable and therefore was rejected out of hand by nearly everyone. Huq, it was said in a government press note, had been shot while he was trying to escape his maximum security cell in the cantonment. News of Zahurul Huq's killing ignited new fires in a condition already beginning to give the appearance of a political wasteland for the government. Pressure mounted on the government for a withdrawal of the case. In Dhaka, furious demonstrators attacked the guest house where Justice S.A. Rahman, chief presiding judge at the conspiracy trial, had been lodged. The angry Bengalis soon set fire to the building, compelling security forces to whisk Rahman out of the premises. He did not stay in Dhaka after that. To all intents and purposes, the Agartala Conspiracy case had collapsed. Only an official announcement remained to formalise that reality. On 21 February, spontaneous rallies marking the anniversary of the Bengali Language Movement of 1952 were organised in Dhaka and other towns in East Pakistan. As further proof of defiance of the authorities, Bengali men and women openly sang the songs of Rabindranath Tagore, the globally acclaimed poet, proscribed by Ayub Khan's government in 1967, in the interest of promoting the ideology of Pakistan.

—◦◦◦—

A young Mujib, 1948

Mentor and pupil: Sheikh Mujib with Huseyn Shaheed Suhrawardy

Opposition politicians, Mujib among them, in the early 1960s

United Front leader A.K. Fazlul Huq with Sheikh Mujib on the campaign trail in 1953 With them is Tofazzal Hossain Manik Mia, later to be editor of the Bengali daily newspaper Ittefaq

Sheikh Mujibur Rahman meets Chairman Mao Zedong in Beijing, 1953

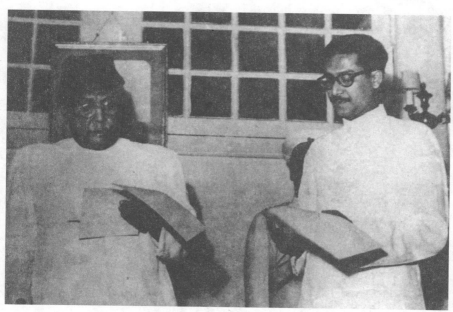

Mujib is sworn as minister in the United Front government, 1954

Mujib among his party men

Three influential Bengali politicians ---- Bhashani, Suhrawardy and Mujib

Mujib reads out an address of welcome to visiting Chinese
Premier Chou En-lai, 1956. Pakistan Prime Minister Suhrawardy
looks on

Sheikh Mujib in the **1960s**

Ayub Khan and Yahya Khan, Pakistan's first and second military rulers

Tajuddin Ahmed, later to be prime minister of the Bangladesh government-in-exile, speaks on the Awami League's Six Point plan in Dhaka

Sheikh Mujib on his way to court in the Agartala
conspiracy case, June 1968

Mujib emerges free after the Agartala conspiracy case is withdrawn by the government,
February 1969

Freed from jail, Mujib joins Pakistan's opposition leaders at round table conference with
President Ayub Khan, Rawalpindi, February 1969

The left wing mass leader Moulana Abdul Hamid Khan Bhashani at a public rally
in Dhaka, 1969

With Bhashani, whose firm leadership compelled the Ayub regime into a retreat,
February 1969

Awami League politician Mizanur Rahman Chowdhury (in suit) at the height of
the anti-Ayub Khan mass movement in January 1969

His moment --- Sheikh Mujibur Rahman lost in thought

Sheikh Mujib, with party colleagues, on election night, December 1970

A cheerful Sheikh Mujibur Rahman after his party's
triumph at elections, December 1970

President Yahya Khan arrives in Dhaka, December 1970. He described Sheikh Mujibur
Rahman as Pakistan's future prime minister

'The struggle this time is for emancipation. The struggle this time is for independence'.
Bangabandhu Sheikh Mujibur Rahman speaks at a million-strong rally, Dhaka, 7 March 1971

Sheikh Mujib, mid 1960s

Mujib, lost in thought, moments before delivering ground-breaking speech, 7 March 1971

The leader among his people

Bangabandhu addresses mass rally, Dhaka, 7 March 1971

A copy of the Koran, burnt by Pakistan's soldiers in Dhaka, March 1971

Collaborationist Bengali political leaders Ghulam Azam and Nurul Amin meet General
Tikka Khan after the army crackdown on 25 March 1971

Mujib in detention at Karachi airport, end March 1971

Pakistan's Major General Rao Farman Ali, left, in Dhaka, in 1971.

The consequences of genocide

The Mujibnagar government, April 1971

Pakistani military commander A.A.K. Niazi walks to surrender ceremony, The man in the dark jacket is Major Haider, a leading Bangladeshi guerilla.

Acting President Syed Nazrul Islam during the War of Liberation

The Bangladesh flag rises

A well known cartoon of Pakistan's military
leader Yahya Khan, used to good effect in the
propaganda against Pakistan in 1971

Justice Abu Sayeed Chowdhury speaks at a rally of Bengalis in London, 1971. He would
later become president of an independent Bangladesh

Leaders of the Bangladesh government-in-exile return home, December 1971

Edward Heath visits a recuperating Sheikh Mujib at a London hospital, July 1972

A free Mujib meets British Prime Minister Edward Heath at 10
Downing Street, London, 8 January 1972

With Indian Prime Minister Indira Gandhi, March 1972

Mujib and renowned Indian playback singer Hemant Mukherjee with the former's grandson Joy

A free Mujib returns home to a free Bangladesh, 10 January 1972

The homecoming: Bangladesh's founding father returns home after nine months of imprisonment in Pakistan, 10 January 1972

Mujib breaks down at Dhaka rally, 10 January 1972

Mujib with the poet Jasimuddin, revered as palli kobi

The rebel meets the rebel: Bangladesh's leader with the poet Kazi Nazrul Islam, Dhaka,
May 1972

At a ruling Awami League meeting, with Syed Nazrul Islam beside him

Sheikh Mujibur Rahman is sworn in as Bangladesh's prime minister by President Abu Sayeed Chowdhury, 12 January 1972

Sheikh Mujib affixes his signature to Bangladesh's
constitution, November 1972

Mujib and his chief lieutenant Tajuddin Ahmed. The two men would fall out in 1974

The prime minister with the three services chiefs

Mujib addresses soldiers in Comilla cantonment. Behind him, on the left, is army chief
K.M. Safiullah and, on the right, deputy army chief Ziaur Rahman. Zia would subsequently
emerge as Bangladesh's first military ruler

On a state visit to Moscow in March 1972, Prime Minister Sheikh
Mujibur Rahman meets Soviet leader Leonid Brezhnev

With Soviet Premier Alexei Kosygin

The prime minister speaks in parliament

With schoolgirls in Rajshahi, 1973

With Egyptian President Anwar Sadat

With Saudi Arabia's King Faisal

A sombre Sheikh Mujibur Rahman

In conversation with the French philosopher-politician Andre Malraux, Dhaka, 1973

With Burma's General Ne Win

Sheikh Mujibur Rahman with Cambodia's Prince Norodom Sihanouk

Cuban leader Fidel Castro calls on Bangladesh's prime minister, Algiers 1973

Libya's Muammar Gaddafi, Pakistan's fervent supporter, meets Mujib, in Algiers 1973

Mujib's home in Dhanmondi, Dhaka

Mujib with his parents

In his library

In the company of his pet pigeons at home

Sheikh Mujibur Rahman is welcomed by Queen Elizabeth II at Buckingham Palace, 1973

Sheikh Mujibur Rahman with Yugoslavia's President Josip Broz Tito, 1973

With visiting UN Secretary General Kurt Waldheim, Dhaka 1973

With Zambian leader Kenneth Kaunda

Mujib, with daughter Hasina behind him

The Bengali in his element: Mujib among his family at home

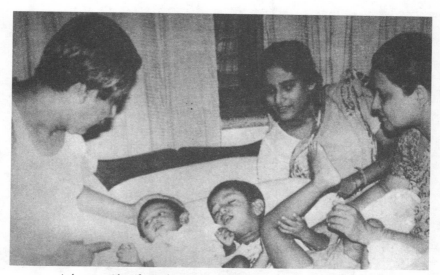

At home, with wife Fazilatunnessa, daughter Hasina and grandchildren

A Bengali to his core: a relaxed Mujib at home

With Senegalese poet-president Leopold Sedar Senghor

Bangabandhu Sheikh Mujibur Rahman addresses the UN General Assembly, New York, September 1974. His speech was delivered in the Bengali language

Flanked by (left) Algerian President Houari Boumeddiene and (right) Pakistan's Prime Minister Zulfikar Ali Bhutto, Islamic Conference, Lahore, February 1974

The Mujibnagar leaders—Syed Nazrul Islam, Tajuddin Ahmed, M. Mansoor Ali, A.H.M Quamruzzaman—all of whom were killed by soldiers in November 1975

The boat---symbolic of Sheikh Mujib's politics

15 August 1975: Bangladesh's founder Sheikh Mujibur Rahman gunned down at his residence in a coup

২০০ বিজয় পতাকা, ১৬ ডিসেম্বর, ১৯৭১
200 Victory Flag, 16 December, 1971

Liberation: the Bangladesh flag is held high on 16 December 1971

PART

4

Bangabandhu, Bengal's Spokesman

At noon on 22 February 1969, Vice Admiral A.R. Khan, Pakistan's defence minister, made a terse announcement in Dhaka. The government of Pakistan, he informed the media at a news conference, had decided to withdraw the Agartala Conspiracy case and release all thirty-five individuals accused in the case without conditions. It was thus that Mujib came to score, till that point in time, the biggest triumph of his political career. By the time he arrived home in Dhaka's Dhanmondi residential area, huge crowds had gathered along the roads leading to his residence. It had been nearly three years since he had last been home, except for a few hours in 1968 when he had been escorted to his village Tungipara in Faridpur to see his ailing mother. On this day, however, the manner of his release from captivity and the cult status that he clearly enjoyed was evidence of the veneration in which Bengalis now held him.

Awami League politicians, students, journalists, rickshaw pullers, in fact nearly every Bengali seemed to be taking the road to Dhanmondi on that day. Earlier, as soon as he had entered his home, his elder daughter Hasina ran into his arms, an image that was captured on the front pages of the following day's newspapers. Mujib was clearly exhausted after his ordeal, but that did not appear to dampen his spirits. He was enjoying his freedom. But more important than that was the knowledge that he was now the de facto leader of the Bengali people. His elevation from the position of president of the Awami

League to that of undisputed spokesman for his nation had been in the making over the past many months. Now that elevation was clearly being confirmed. He shook hands with many, gathered his political associates and student leaders in repeated embrace and expressed his gratitude to the people for speaking up in his defence.

As he stepped on to the second floor balcony overlooking the street, he reminded the crowd that the struggle was not yet over. The Six Points, he told his audience as also the rest of Pakistan, had now turned into what he called the property of the people. The mass uprising that had forced the regime to free him had convinced him that his sweeping programme of provincial autonomy had found acceptance among the Bengalis. He would not, said he, let his people, the Bengalis, down. There was little in Mujib's remarks on that day and later, to say that he spoke for the whole of Pakistan. He was not willing, at that stage, to turn his back on the politics he had assiduously built around the economic and political future of Pakistan's Bengalis. If anything, the Agartala case had reinforced his conviction that no political settlement in the country could prove durable unless his programme for autonomy was accepted across Pakistan.

The next day, 23 February, Mujib addressed a huge rally in Dhaka. An unprecedented million people turned out to hear their leader. No other Bengali politician, not Suhrawardy, not Huq, not Bhashani, had achieved the kind of popularity that Mujib now enjoyed. He had been the long-suffering leader who had never compromised in his opposition to various levels of West Pakistani exploitation of Bengalis for more than two decades. What added to his charisma was the courage he had demonstrated since his entry into politics at a young age. Now, a month short of his forty-ninth birthday, a six-foot figure sporting a moustache that accentuated his presence, Mujib was ready to play the role he had always sought in life. He would lead his people to a better future, which for him meant political liberty. For the moment, the Six Points would be a test of whether the state of Pakistan was ready to listen to him or, as hithertofore, ignore Bengali aspirations. One satisfaction for Mujib and the Awami League was that the overwhelming adulation in which East Pakistan held him would make the authorities think twice before they tried any new repressive measures against the Bengalis. At the rally, Mujib told his charmed audience that he would be taking part at the RTC in Rawalpindi where he intended to present the Six Points as the template on which the constitutional future of Pakistan would have to be decided.

The rally in Dhaka was effectively a recognition of Mujib as the authentic and sole voice of the Bengalis. In a rousing speech before the crowds, student leader Tofail Ahmed left no doubt as to the degree of loyalty Mujib commanded in the country and called him Bangabandhu, friend of Bengal, for his relentless pursuit of Bengali aspirations and for his uncomplaining suffering at the hands of his tormentors. Mujib was thus placed on the same pedestal as Chittaranjan Das, the Bengali political figure who died in 1925, and Subhas Chandra Bose, Mujib's hero Mohammad Ali Jinnah, and Mahatma Gandhi. The honorific Bangabandhu would henceforth be the way Mujib would be addressed by his people. For those of his generation, he was now being referred to respectfully as *Sheikh Shaheb*.

On 24 February, two days after his release from prison, Mujib arrived in Rawalpindi with his team comprising senior party leaders Khondokar Moshtaq Ahmed, Syed Nazrul Islam and Tajuddin Ahmed and others. Arriving in Pakistan's provisional capital, Mujib found himself besieged by newsmen. He was asked a number of questions, all of which were respectful and most of which he chose not to answer. He, however, did quip that he who had been treated as a traitor only the other day was now being honoured as a patriot. In the countdown to the RTC the next day, a moment of supreme irony could not missed by the national media when President Ayub Khan welcomed Mujib into the conference hall. There had been little love lost between the two men. For more than a decade, Ayub had distrusted the Bengali leader who always taxed his patience with his radicalism. On his part, Mujib had all along considered the president as the epitome of everything that was wrong for the Bengalis of Pakistan. Mujib certainly could not erase the feeling that had it not been for the virtual uprising that had shaken the regime, Ayub Khan would now be preparing to send him to the gallows. More than anything else, the pictures the media carried on the front pages of the two men shaking hands told a simple story: Ayub Khan's career was on the wane and Mujib's star was in the ascendant.

The RTC, conceived along the model of the RTCs convened by the British Government in London in the early 1930s to discuss the question of self-rule for India (with Gandhi, Nehru and Jinnah being the more important politicians to be present), did not get off to an auspicious start. For one thing, it was boycotted by Bhutto and Bhashani, who were then meeting in Dhaka to strike a deal between their parties on how best to push the regime from power. For quite another, differences of opinion within the DAC brought out in the open the deep fissures that could wreck Opposition unity. While a large number of Opposition representatives favoured a simple deal with the president envisaging a return to parliamentary government on the basis of the 1956 constitution, the Awami League made its position clear that nothing short of an agreement based on its Six Points would satisfy East Pakistan. In his opening address at the RTC, Mujib lost no time in reminding his Opposition allies as well as the government team, which was led by Ayub Khan, that any deliberations on Pakistan's constitutional future rested on a decentralisation of power, based on a draft of autonomy measures with the adoption of the Six Points scheme. The president pointed out to him the risks that the Six Points posed to the federation. In his response, Mujib went into a recapitulation of the history of political and economic exploitation East Pakistan had been subjected to for twenty-two years.

The RTC was adjourned until early March, by which time it was hoped that the politicians, including those on the government team, would be able to examine the various options towards a settlement of the crisis. Aware that without the Awami League it would lose meaning, the DAC tried to convince Mujib that the immediate task before the country was the removal of Ayub Khan by returning to a Westminster-style government. The Awami League leader gave no ground, insisting to his colleagues that the people of East Pakistan had voiced their support for the Six Points overwhelmingly through the mass movement of the previous few months. It was no surprise that when the RTC reconvened on 10 March, Mujib found himself alone. Both the government and the other components of the DAC rejected any constitutional formula based on the Six Points, with the consequence that when the conference ended, little had been achieved. President Ayub Khan agreed to return the country to parliamentary government elected on the basis of universal suffrage. It was the final nail in the coffin, that he more than anyone else, had built for his government. The DAC's Nawabzada Nasrullah Khan was in an ebullient form in the assumption that under his stewardship the Opposition had pulled off a coup. It had not yet occurred to him that with the Awami League seething in anger at what it considered betrayal on the part of its partners, the uncertainty which had crept into national politics was far from resolved. Soon enough, the government and the DAC were both upstaged by Mujib's announcement in Rawalpindi that he was taking the Awami League out of the Opposition alliance over its failure to address the Six-Point formula in the negotiations with the government. Mujib did not waste any more time in Rawalpindi, preferring to take the earliest available flight back home. For him and for a vast majority of Bengalis, men like Nurul Amin and Hamidul Haq Chowdhury had disappointed their fellow Bengalis. Mujib would henceforth make sure that they were marginalised in politics.

If there had been any feeling that the end of the RTC, in however divisive a manner, would lead to a restoration of calm in Pakistan, it was misplaced. For the Bengalis, the conference had resolved nothing. There are reasons to assume that President Ayub Khan and Mujib had at least one, if not more, exclusive meeting at the initiative of the former. The president had offered Mujib the prime minister's post in what might have been a calculated strategy of either doing his last bit to douse the flames or putting the Awami League chief in a position where he could only self-destruct. Mujib showed little interest in the proposal. He had never trusted Ayub Khan and he was not about to change his opinion now. That is why he agreed with his party and broad Bengali opinion that no political settlement could prove viable without the Six Points.

The country remained in turmoil. Bhashani, who had earlier tried to coax Mujib into staying away from the RTC because of his conviction that it would turn up nothing, now felt vindicated. In West Pakistan, Bhutto too relished the inconsequential results of the RTC, exhorting the crowds that came to hear him that nothing less than the programme set forth by PPP could put the country back on the rails. For Mujib, however, politics now began to take a new, ominous turn. He and his party began to worry about the real possibility of an unconstitutional change of government that could set the country back once more. In the weeks before the RTC, there had been a fair degree of speculation about Ayub Khan's stepping down in favour of an interim administration led by Justice S.M. Murshed. But the president and the opportunism of Mujib's colleagues in the DAC had put paid to that chance. With continuing political violence, and Bhashani still calling for jalao-gherao in East Pakistan, Mujib sensed that conditions were on a slide. In the event of the president's resignation, under the terms of the 1962 constitution, power would normally pass into the hands of Speaker Abdul Jabbar Khan. But there was little sign of the president moving in that direction. More tellingly, reports that he had been consulting the army and ignoring the speaker and his ministers altogether reinforced Mujib's fears that drastic action was in the offing. Just how menacing the threat was or when it would come to pass, he and his party colleagues were unable to say.

Rumours of a more frightening nature began to circulate in Rawalpindi around that time. The president was clearly not in a mood to give up authority and explored the possibility of placing the country under martial law once again, as the supreme commander of the armed forces, a position he thought still allowed him a huge say over the military. But he had quite overestimated his political clout. As for the army itself, it was well prepared to strike again, but without the president. The commander-in-chief, General Yahya Khan, was absolutely willing to impose martial law but only as long as he called the shots. In effect, the president would have to go in the event of a new military takeover. While Ayub wrestled with the dilemma, he also felt that some desperate measures to claw back to a reasonable level of power were called for. He replaced the governors of East and West Pakistan. General Musa, who had been governor of the western province since his retirement from the army, made way for Yusuf Haroon, member of a leading industrial family and owner of *Dawn*, the country's leading English language newspaper. In East Pakistan, the despised Abdul Monem Khan was replaced by his finance minister, the academic Dr M.N. Huda. The changes were announced on 24 March.

Early in the evening of 25 March 1969, President Ayub Khan addressed the country over radio and television to announce his resignation from office. He could not, he said, 'preside over the destruction of my country.' He informed Pakistanis that General Yahya Khan was taking over power. The next morning, Yahya Khan spoke to the country to let it know that his task would be to promote conditions conducive to the holding of general elections, with the objective of transferring power to the elected representatives of the people. Unlike the earlier coup of October 1958, the army did not go looking for politicians to arrest. Neither were the soldiers to demonstrate a heavy presence on the streets. What was nevertheless clear was that Pakistan needed to begin from scratch once more and Yahya Khan, who combined in his person the positions of president and chief martial-law administrator, appeared ready to act as a cementing force in the field of fissiparous national politics. Within a month of taking over, he undertook a programme of meeting the leading politicians of the country, including Mujib and Bhutto. The new military ruler conveyed the public impression that his was a transitional administration which would leave as soon as a constitutional structure was in place. In July, he welcomed the newly elected US President Richard Nixon to Lahore.

Politics, under the weight of martial law regulations, remained in a state of suspension. But that did not prevent the politicians from liaising with one another or with their natural allies informally. The

Awami League, encouraged by the right noises General Yahya was making, went into internal meetings to finalise an election strategy. It appeared that the president was going out of his way to gain Mujib's support for his government's programmes. On one of his visits to Dhaka, Yahya Khan played host to the visiting Shah of Iran. At a reception for the monarch on the lawns of the president's house in the lush green surroundings of Ramna, the president introduced the Bengali leader to the visiting dignitary.

In late October, Mujib travelled to London, his first in many years, primarily to express his gratitude to the expatriate Bengali community in the United Kingdom for the efforts it had taken in putting up a legal defence for him in the Agartala Conspiracy case. Returning to Dhaka, about three weeks later, he told a meeting on the occasion of the sixth anniversary of the death of Suhrawardy that henceforth the province of East Pakistan would be known as Bangladesh. He had particular reason to insist on the new definition. In his view, the Bengali identity that had been part of heritage in the region could not be found anywhere except in reference to the Bay of Bengal. Further, he argued that if the four provinces comprising West Pakistan could maintain their distinctive linguistic and cultural identities, there was hardly any reason why Bengalis could not do the same. Besides, the term 'Bangladesh' had always been generic. In everyday Bengali conversation and literature it was always referred to as 'Bangladesh' and hardly ever as 'East Pakistan'. The works of Tagore and other Bengali men of letters never ceased to speak of Bangladesh. Similar terms such as *Bangla* and *Banga* were also used, which was the assertion of a distinctive cultural identity for the people. It did not matter that the Bengalis on the Indian side of the frontier were citizens of a different country. For Bengalis across the divide, sentiments of commonality had always been more important than the cartographic chasm created by the communal politics of the 1940s.

—◦◦◦◦—

Pakistan's Prime Minister in Waiting

The ban clamped on political activities when martial law was imposed, was lifted on New Year's Day 1970. Earlier, in November 1969, President Yahya Khan had announced his government's intention of holding general elections to the national and provincial assemblies in Pakistan by October 1970. That news had come as a pleasant surprise for politicians across the spectrum. Yahya did not appear to be obsessed by a need to hold on to power. Since taking over, he had been going out of his way to hear out the politicians across the spectrum, thus convincing many of his sincerity about inaugurating a new era in the country's politics.

General Yahya Khan and the band of officers who were with him in the regime fully comprehended their difficulties. The kind of fearful silence that had greeted Ayub Khan's takeover in 1958 was almost absent in 1969. There were loaded reasons behind such unwillingness to take the new martial law lying down. In the first place, the country's political classes in both the provinces were better organised and focused than they had been a decade earlier. Second, the Ayub era had spawned populist politics of the kind never experienced before in the country. The strong presence of Mujib, Bhashani and Bhutto testified to the choices Pakistanis had before them when it came to choosing their political leadership. On a slightly less elevated level, Asghar Khan, Justice S.M. Murshed, Khan Abdul Wali Khan and Professor Muzaffar Ahmed provided a second tier of leadership the country could fall back on.

In other words, by the time Yahya Khan replaced Ayub Khan, the process of public political consciousness had become irreversible in the country. The Yahya regime understood that it could not afford the luxury of hanging on to power like the previous regime. Besides, there was hardly any reason to have the army lose any more respect than it already had lost in the dying days of the Ayub junta. The former president had not hesitated in deploying soldiers to quell civil disturbances in both East and West Pakistan, which had eroded the standing of the military. Especially in the east, owing to the role of the military in the arrest and trial of Mujib in Dhaka Cantonment, the army had lost considerable face. Yahya Khan was therefore not inclined to see the military coming into fresh disrepute by appropriating power to itself, for an indefinite period of time.

The Awami League officially launched its election campaign at a public meeting organised at the Paltan Maidan in Dhaka. Mujib made it clear that his priorities lay within the parameters of the Six-Point programme. He told the huge crowd gathered to hear him that the elections of October would be a referendum on the Six Points. It was, as many saw it, a throwing down of the gauntlet to West Pakistan. While most other political parties plunged into the campaign on the simpler premise of seeing parliamentary government restored through the elections, Mujib and the Awami League pushed for more than that. For the party, a restoration of elected civil, Westminster-style government was not the issue anymore. What mattered was a wholesale recasting of Pakistan's federalism, that could in time be whittled down to a confederal system. But such a process of initiating change implied capturing a majority of seats in the national assembly.

The basis on which the elections were to be held, and indeed power was eventually to be transferred by the army to a representative government was contained in the Legal Framework Order (LFO). Made public by the government on 30 March 1970, the LFO was, in the absence of a constitutional structure, the document that would determine the nature of Pakistan's transition to an elected government. It envisaged a national assembly comprising 313 members to be elected on a system of proportional representation. The calculation thus had 162 seats reserved for East Pakistan, with 138 going to West Pakistan. The remaining 13 were seats reserved for women, on a division of 7:6 in favour of East Pakistan. In West Pakistan, which was scheduled to revert to the pre-One Unit arrangement of four separate provinces on 1 July 1970, the 138 national assembly seats were fixed in proportion to the population of the four units of the province, with the result that the Punjab was guaranteed 82 seats, Sind 27, the NWFP 18, and Baluchistan 4. The final seven seats went to the central government administered tribal areas in West Pakistan.

The more noteworthy features of the LFO related to the constitution-making provisions enshrined in it. The national assembly elected in the October elections would be required to frame a new constitution for Pakistan within a stipulated time frame of 120 days, failing which it would stand dissolved. No one in the regime could quite explain what course politics would take should the national assembly, failing to stick to the 120-day deadline, be decreed out of existence. Another point that hinted at future complications was the right of the president, in this case Yahya Khan, to reject the constitution framed by the elected representatives of the people should such a constitution militate against the principles of Islam, the Holy Quran and other relevant Muslim practices. It was the regime's way of appeasing the religious right, particularly in West Pakistan, but it simply did not impress the centre and left in national politics. The LFO also made it clear that the constitution would uphold the Islamic Republic of Pakistan, a provision that faced no difficulties in West Pakistan, but ran counter to feelings in East Pakistan where secular politics had increasingly become the pattern. Besides, the Awami League's programme studiously stayed away from making any mention of Islam, the Quran or Sharia laws. While it was obvious to the party that its goals contradicted the guidelines set forth in the LFO, Mujib was content not to raise any unnecessary controversy on the issue. Of course, party leaders did make it a point at their rallies and especially when the religious right, particularly in the west, raised the issue, that they would not incorporate anything in the constitution that was repugnant to Islamic rules and practices. But that was more in the nature of an anodyne than any serious attempts at upholding Islam as an electoral strategy. The larger truth, which President Yahya Khan and the other political parties made note of, was Mujib's preoccupation, despite the LFO, with the Six Points. He appeared to have no time for the LFO, or thought of it as a nuisance best ignored.

Throughout the election campaign, the mass appeal of the Awami League was evident. It was in essence the near superhuman popularity of Mujib that defined the party. He drew huge crowds everywhere he went and the glory rubbed off on his party leaders and workers throughout the province. His strategy, as also that of his colleagues, at the hustings, relied on a simple premise of drawing attention to Bengali grievances of the previous twenty-three years and making promises of such grievances being rolled back through an implementation of the Six-Point plan. The emphasis was constant and insistent on autonomy for East Pakistan. The Awami League promised a revival of *Shonar Bangla* or Golden Bengal, with its resources remaining in the hands of the province. To his critics, Mujib clearly appealed to Bengali provincial instincts, to the detriment of Pakistani unity. He of course did not see things that way. What was happening was a rise of Bengali nationalism, which was not quite the same as provincialism. The sweeping plan for autonomy was, in the view of the Awami League, only laying the groundwork for eventual political freedom for the Bengalis. Mujib had since the early 1960s been referring to his people as a nation, which was a good indication of the way he thought politics should develop. On the campaign trail, which took him to some of the remotest parts of East Pakistan, he spoke of Bangladesh. Not once, not even by mistake, did he speak of East Pakistan. If it was not Bangladesh, it was East Bengal he referred to, something the rest of Pakistan did not comprehend or was reluctant to remember. The Awami League chief had said the polls would be a referendum on his autonomy plan. And referendum it would be if the mathematics were done right.

As the campaign gathered pace in both wings of the country, Mujib's disinclination to visit West Pakistan became noticeable. The impression grew, and there was little that was ambiguous about the fact that he had deliberately made a point of not seeking votes in the western part of the country. A few factors were at work here. One of those was Mujib's belief that the Awami League was in an extremely weak position in West Pakistan, which was quite true. Indeed, from a historical point of view, the party had never quite overcome the public perception that it was essentially a Bengali-led and Bengali-oriented party. Even in the times of Suhrawardy, who went out of his way to demonstrate his all-Pakistan credentials, the Awami League remained pinned down to East Pakistan. This position was all the more reinforced when Mujib came forth with the Six Points, which was practically a turning point in the rising popular belief that the party had consciously taken the decision to uphold Bengali interests in the federation of Pakistan. Mujib had never shown interest, back in the pre-martial-law times of the 1950s, in serving in the central government even when his mentor Suhrawardy became prime minister. In 1969, he appeared to have rebuffed Ayub Khan's offer of joining him in stabilising politics in the country. It was only too obvious that when the time came for the election campaign, he would not be tempted to go seeking votes in the west. To be sure, branches of the Awami League operated in the four provinces of West Pakistan. But they were more fish out of water than assertive organisations promoting the Six Points. Mujib's reluctance to visit West Pakistan was therefore based on some pretty cogent reasons.

Yet the Bengali leader was required to provide proof of his readiness to be a politician at the national level. With all the allegations of provincialism being hurled at him and his party by other parties, largely the smaller ones, he knew that a visit to West Pakistan would need to be undertaken at some stage during the campaign. Besides, there were all the channels he needed to keep open should the election results leave him in a situation where he was forced to be the leader of the Opposition. Mujib surely had in mind those West Pakistani politicians who were more his kind, such as Wali Khan, G.M. Syed and Baluchistan's Abdus Samad Achakzai. In late June, accompanied by senior Awami League politician Zahiruddin and the student leader Tofail Ahmed among others, he arrived in Karachi. In the course of the next couple of weeks, he travelled to Lahore, Peshawar and Quetta, where West Pakistani crowds milled around him largely out of the curiosity of seeing a Bengali politician who had become symbolic of Bengal. Mujib made valiant efforts to address the crowds in Urdu, but all too often brought into his speeches the terms and phrases he normally employed in his Bengali oratory. Despite his Urdu-related problems, Mujib was surprised to see the West Pakistanis applauding him even as he struggled to make a point. When he finished, it was the turn of Zahiruddin, fluent in Urdu, to explain the Six Points to the non-Bengali crowds in a way no one could have equalled.

On that trip, Mujib made little effort to establish contact with politicians like Bhutto, Khan Abdul Qayyum Khan and Mian Mumtaz Daultana. He did not appear interested in going to Rawalpindi for a courtesy call on President Yahya Khan. At a dinner arranged in his honour in Quetta, the capital of Baluchistan, he was thrilled to meet the tribal politician Abdus Samad Achakzai. The Baluch politician, like Mujib, had spent a number of years in prison during the Ayub Khan era. As they greeted each other, Achakzai remarked how aged the Bengali leader appeared to be. Mujib retorted, 'Ayub Khan has turned you and me into old men.' When Yahya Bakhtiar, a prominent lawyer who would in future serve as attorney general under Bhutto, politely remarked that the Six Points might lead to the break-up of the country, Mujib nearly exploded. He loudly exclaimed, 'You have sucked our blood for the last twenty-two years. How do you expect us to behave now?' Bakhtiar of course, did not respond.

It was with some impatience that Mujib returned to Dhaka from West Pakistan. He felt good at the way support for the Six Points seemed to be growing in the province. He was clearly convinced that the Awami League would sweep East Pakistan when the elections took place in October, though whether he would have an overall majority in the national assembly was hard to predict. The arithmetic pointed to a 60-70 per cent lead for the party in East Pakistan, and that was certainly not enough for it to contemplate power at the national level. All signs, therefore, pointed to Mujib taking charge of East Pakistan and thereafter pushing for the Six Points to be conceded to by the central government.

The annual floods that left the alluvial plains of East Pakistan under water for weeks, even months, struck in August. For nearly two months in August and September, the province was rendered immobile by the surging waters of the innumerable rivers that were a feature of the Bengali landscape. The mounting difficulties related to movement quickly persuaded Yahya Khan that the election would have to be deferred. A new date was set for December of the year. It was a decision that did not please Mujib, though it did make his political rivals in the other parties happy. They obviously saw in the two-month postponement of the polling a new opportunity to recharge the batteries of their faltering campaign in circumstances that still predicted an Awami League sweep. Many in the Awami League were suspicious that the floods had little to do with the postponement.

There was little the Awami League could do. It could not afford to grumble too loudly about the postponement lest that gave the impression of its insensitivity to the sufferings of flood-stricken East Pakistanis. The party was soon organising relief operations to help the marooned in nearly all parts of the province, a task it accomplished far better than any other political organisation owing to its enormity of resources. The coffers of the Awami League, to which business groups had regularly contributed even in the dangerous times of Ayub Khan, positively creaked with the weight of the funds that began to flow during the post-Agartala Conspiracy period. A crucial factor in the fledgling Bengali business class's willingness to contribute financially to the Awami League was its belief that with the party coming to power in future, the interests of Bengali businessmen would take precedence. After all, had Mujib not already warned that he and his party would ensure that East Pakistan's resources from its leading industries, jute and tea, would in future not be exploited to promote the economic development of West Pakistan?

By the end of October, despite its earlier sulking about the elections being deferred, the Awami League was feeling good with itself. Its own projections showed that the other parties had not been able to strip away at the support it had enjoyed prior to the postponement. There was little question that it was poised to capture political power in East Pakistan. But soon, nature would come in once again to push politics aside. On 12 November, the coast of East Pakistan would be hit by a cyclone that would eventually leave a million Bengalis dead. In Chittagong, Cox's Bazar and on the offshore islands of Hatiya and Sandwip, the cyclone left a trail of devastation that had the province reeling. Houses were blown away and cattle disappeared. The maimed, battered bodies of adults and children were discovered in conditions reminiscent of fictional horror. And yet it was a time when the government of General Yahya Khan failed to rise to the occasion.

For days the magnitude of the disaster was scandalously ignored by the regime. Even as the outside world woke up to the reality of the terrible affliction, the government seemed not to give any importance to the crisis. Cyclones and tidal bores were a normal feature along the East Pakistani coast bordering the Bay of Bengal, which was a plain reason why the regime did not appear to be too rattled. But when the Western media began to disseminate news of the tragedy and relief materials and personnel began to arrive in the province did the generals realise the enormity of the blunder they had committed. When the regime moved to act, it was rather late in the day. Mujib, Bhashani and a host of other Bengali politicians had already begun to accuse the central government of sheer callousness to the plight of the poorer eastern province. For Mujib it was another gross instance of the colonial attitude towards Bengalis on the part of the ruling circles. For him and the Awami League, the death of the one million Bengalis in the cyclone was one more reason why the Six Points mattered.

The tragedy, in hindsight, injected a little more of radicalism in Bengali politics and improved further the chances of the Awami

League sweeping the elections in a way no one could have imagined. While Mujib looked forward to a convincing victory, there was also the NAP of Bhashani to consider. The NAP, which had grown into a factionalised organisation since its founding at the Kagmari conference of 1957, was hardly any threat to the Awami League. But given that Bhashani often appeared to be expressing views more to the left of the Awami League chief, there remained a possibility of his party making dents in the triumph of the league. But even as Mujib and his friends calculated their electoral mathematics with the NAP in the picture, Bhashani once again demonstrated his ability to spring surprises. He made a public announcement that his party would not be taking part in the elections. That move could signify only one thing, that the Awami League would now be unstoppable. And then Bhashani sprung a second surprise when, outraged by the failure of the government to come promptly to the assistance of cyclone battered Bengalis in the coastal areas, he declared the 'independence' of East Pakistan on 4 December 1970, a mere three days before the election. Bhashani's 'independence' move was aimed at increasing the pressure on Mujib to go for meaningful action towards taking Bangladesh out of Pakistan. For his part Mujib was not willing to take the bait. Ever the constitutionalist, Mujib preferred events to be shaped by popular mandate. Such a mandate, he reasoned, could only emerge through an exercise of the ballot.

The ballot, when it was finally exercised on 7 December, left Pakistan stunned and Bengalis jubilant. A total of twenty-four political parties contested the election, the more important of them being the Awami League, Bhutto's PPP, Moududi's Jamaat-e-Islami and the three factions of the Muslim League. The Awami League took East Pakistan by storm when it won 160 of the 162 seats reserved for East Pakistan in the national assembly. The PPP dominated the show in the Punjab and Sind, where it garnered altogether 81 seats. In contrast, the right-wing political parties did rather poorly. The combined number of seats gained by the three factions of the Muslim League, Jamaat-e-Islami, Jamiat-e-Ulema-e-Pakistan and Jamiat-e-Ulema-e-

Islam came to a mere 37, while in the NWFP and Baluchistan it was the National Awami Party of Khan Abdul Wali Khan that dominated.

The Awami League was in a commanding position with altogether 167 seats in a national assembly of 313 members. In the 300-member provincial assembly in East Pakistan, the party was in control of 288 seats. Almost immediately after the election, talk in Pakistan focused on how soon Mujib would enter upon office as Pakistan's first elected prime minister. But before that necessary transfer of power could be effected, there was the difficult job of drafting a new constitution for the country, a task the Awami League thought it was ready to do given that it had the simple majority needed to adopt a constitution. As for Mujib, his position in the post-election period assumed a predictable hardening when he noted that Bengalis had, in line with his arguments, actually considered the election as a referendum on his Six Points. Now that the programme had been so overwhelmingly endorsed by the electorate in East Pakistan, it became easier for the Awami League to claim loudly that there could no compromise on it. The future constitution for Pakistan could not but be framed on the basis of the Six Points.

The elections had certainly created a huge opportunity for the people of Pakistan to be governed by politicians with legitimate claims to authority. In conventional terms, the future promised a government led by Mujib, with Bhutto providing leadership to the parliamentary Opposition. But that was a simplistic take on the situation. More complicated and ominous was the fact that the elections had thrown up parties with disparate constituencies. The Awami League, despite having put up a handful of candidates in West Pakistan, had come by no seat there. Bhutto's PPP had not even put up a token fight in East Pakistan. It was quite credible to suggest, in light of the electoral outcome, that the two wings of Pakistan stood poised on the brink of a crisis. The expectation among many in the West that Mujib would travel to Rawalpindi in his capacity as majority leader and therefore future prime minister was belied by the Bengali leader's reluctance to undertake any such move.

In the latter part of December, President Yahya Khan travelled to Dhaka for the first time since the elections. The talks which ensued between him and Mujib at the president's house in the East Pakistani capital left him in little doubt about the Awami League's determination to stick to the Six Points as it approached the constitution-making process. The regime faced the onerous job of preserving the federation in its existing form with Mujib and his colleagues in an upbeat mood about a restructuring of relations between the two wings. The president tried, nevertheless, to keep up appearances. Prior to his departure for Karachi at the end of his talks with the Awami League leader, he told the media that Sheikh Mujibur Rahman was Pakistan's future prime minister and therefore it was only right that all questions relating to the economy, etc. would be dealt by him. Unbeknownst to General Yahya Khan, that statement would soon set sparks flying in West Pakistan.

PART
5

Road to Bangladesh

The first formal declaration of Awami League intent was made on 3 January 1971. The party chose the Dhaka Race Course, a much more expansive area than Paltan Maidan, to convey its action plan to the people of East Pakistan. At the same time it served notice on West Pakistan that it had arrived. Mujib, after the decades spent spreading the message of autonomy in the villages and small towns of the province, coupled with the years lost in Pakistani prisons, had finally achieved the stature of a recognised national leader. To his fellow Bengalis, he had metamorphosed from a pre-eminent politician to the greatest political leader in their history. To other Pakistanis in the west, he had finally and miraculously emerged from being a conspirator against Pakistan to its prospective prime minister. In early January therefore, it was a season of irony in full blossom. Mujib, as the days went by, would only add to the irony. In a different manner, Bhutto would do the same. The conflict of interests that separated the two men would eventually create the perfect opportunity for the army to adopt its own fatal measures. But in those early days after the election, Mujib was the individual from whom power flowed, to flow back to him. Bengalis saw in him the law. He was not a dictator, as the election results had so clearly demonstrated. But there were shades of a Julius Caesar in him.

It was a rather confident Mujib, with all 167 members of the national assembly elected on his party's platform and all 288 members of the East Pakistan Provincial Assembly in tow, who mounted the dais at the Race Course on that January day. In his address following the oath-taking by elected members of the national assembly (MNAs) and members of the provincial assembly (MPAs), Mujib was emphatic about his plans. He solemnly promised the crowds gathered before him that the Awami League, recognising the fact that the Six Points had now been endorsed by the people, would frame a constitution for Pakistan based on the programme. At no point during his address did he raise the issue of a transfer of power or negotiations towards an assumption of central authority by his party. And then, in a dramatic flourish, he told Bengalis that should any member of the Awami League elected to the national and provincial assemblies betray the Six Points, the people would have every right to bury him alive. And the rule applied to Mujib as well, he pointed out in the third person. It was by far the most unambiguous message on his part about his unyielding attitude over the issue of provincial autonomy.

Two days later, Bhutto threw a spanner in the works when he suggested in public that the keys to power lay in the Punjab and Sind. He was clearly hinting at his own desire to be part of the power sharing structure, but it also smacked of the old conspiracies which had since 1947 kept the Bengalis out of the power circles. The Awami League, it was pointed out to Bhutto, possessed enough parliamentary strength not only to frame a constitution for the country but also to form its central government. Bhutto, despite his resounding success in West Pakistan, was still only the second largest in the national assembly. As a man who had of late entertained ambitions of attaining political power (a presidential candidate in 1968), the prospects of Mujib becoming prime minister and his being left out in the cold was a trifle too distressing. It was from such a perspective that he reasoned out what he thought would be a credible approach to the foremost political issue of the day. He took the grand coalition between the Christian Democrats and Social Democrats in West Germany as his point of reference to explain why Pakistan would be better off with a similar structure in place. For him, a Mujib-Bhutto combination would be as good, if not better than the Kiesinger-Brandt formation in Bonn. The trouble was the Awami League saw through his plans. It was actually his close links with the Punjabi military and the bureaucratic class that backed Bhutto in his bid to strike a deal with Mujib.

On 27 January, Bhutto turned up in Dhaka with a large PPP delegation, the obvious goal being a testing of the waters with the Awami League. Over a period of three days, the leaders of the majority and minority parties conferred one-on-one as well as with their delegations in attendance over the future of Pakistan's democracy. The Awami League, while politely paying attention to the points Bhutto and his team raised about the central government being cast in a national image, made it clear that it saw no role for Bhutto other than that as part of the Opposition in the national assembly. For his part, Bhutto did not pretend to camouflage his desires. He made it plain to Mujib that while the Awami League would of course be the leading force in the country, with its leader as prime minister, the PPP with Bhutto in a role, such as that of foreign minister could effectively make the government look like one formed on an all-Pakistan basis. And then, naturally, there were the Six Points. It was plain to the Awami League leaders that while on the one hand Bhutto argued that the Six Points needed to be watered down if Mujib expected West Pakistani support on the framing of the constitution, on the other he was quite willing to take back much of his opposition to the autonomy plan if his party were accommodated in government. Mujib upheld the principle that since parliamentary democracy was a matter of the majority versus the minority, with no regional configurations coming into the picture, the Awami League was entitled to form the next government for Pakistan. Bhutto and his team left Dhaka on 29 January, deeply frustrated at their failure to make the Awami League budge from what they saw as intransigence on its part.

Meanwhile, drama of a different kind was being enacted in West Pakistan as Bhutto made his way back to Lahore. A couple of young Indian Kashmiri Muslims, having hijacked an Indian aeroplane on a domestic flight, forced the pilot to land in Lahore. Their demand was freedom for the state, which since Partition had stayed uncertainly divided between India and Pakistan. Unless their demands were met, said the hijackers, the aircraft would be blown up. The Indian government, expecting the Pakistani authorities to arrest the hijackers and return the plane to it, turned increasingly exasperated when it became obvious that the Pakistanis were in fact treating the men as Kashmiri freedom fighters who deserved the support of all Pakistanis.

It was into this situation that Bhutto stepped right after his return from his abortive talks with Mujib in Dhaka. The chairman of the PPP, depressed after Dhaka, now discovered a condition that could not but be put to advantage. He made a public show of walking up to the hijackers on the tarmac, congratulating them on their act of bravery and posing for photographs with them. Bhutto's actions were in sharp contrast to the reaction from Mujib, who issued a statement in Dhaka condemning the hijacking and demanding that the authorities return the plane to India and deal with the hijackers firmly. It was one more classic instance of the wide chasm which separated the two wings of Pakistan in temperament and political attitudes.

The Kashmir problem had never been an issue with the Bengalis, even though it was the sole subject West Pakistanis raised in almost every discussion about relations between India and Pakistan. In the aftermath of the hijacking, it was the very different approaches to what was now a major crisis that were revealed by the two men in whose hands the future of Pakistan rested. Bhutto, having shaped his fortunes on hatred for India, was now being countered by Mujib, who had never had cause to forget the distinctive cultural traditions his Bengalis were heir to as part of the old Bengal before Partition.

A day after their meeting with Bhutto, the 'heroic' Kashmiri hijackers blew up the Indian Airlines plane at Lahore Airport. The Indian government of Prime Minister Indira Gandhi promptly retaliated by banning overflights across its skies by Pakistani aircraft. An immediate impact of the ban was the inability of Pakistan International Airlines (PIA) to fly between East and West Pakistan directly over India. The failure of the military regime of General

Yahya Khan to deal with the hijackers under the law and prevent the blowing up of the aircraft had thus created a situation where PIA was compelled to reroute its flights to and from East Pakistan via the Ceylonese (now Sri Lankan) capital of Colombo. The detour took six hours for a one-way journey between Karachi and Dhaka, where the earlier flight path across India had taken only three hours.

Thereafter, politics in the country went into a spiral of increasing gloom. By February, questions were being asked about the delay in calling the national assembly to session. The awareness that the Mujib-Bhutto talks in Dhaka had failed to produce results and that there was no possibility of cooperation between the Awami League and the PPP in the future was quite overpowering. In East Pakistan, Mujib was already being looked upon as the spokesman for the Bengalis if not yet for the whole of Pakistan. The provincial martial law administration operated more as a transitional arrangement than as the governing institution.

At that point in time, the governor, Vice Admiral S.M. Ahsan, and the zonal martial law administrator, Lieutenant General Sahibzada Yaqub Khan, appeared to be concerned with an orderly transfer of power to the politicians. Both men being from West Pakistan, Ahsan and Yaqub Khan were decent individuals, not tainted by the ill reputation that characterised many of their peers in the military. The governor had been aide-de-camp to Mohammad Ali Jinnah in the formative years of Pakistan. Yaqub Khan, a young officer in the Indian Army before Partition, had opted for Pakistan in 1947, leaving his clan back in India. He had then risen in the service of his country and along the way had developed a reputation as an aesthete in a force that otherwise placed much faith in sheer physical prowess. The two men were in regular contact with Mujib and apparently shared his conviction that an early convening of the national assembly was essential to the framing of a constitution and a subsequent transfer of power to the elected representatives of the nation.

Such thoughts were clearly not being shared in distant Rawalpindi, where the collapse of Bhutto's talks with Mujib seemed to be used by the hardliners in the army as an excuse for a delay in calling parliament into session. The Pakistan military had never been favourably disposed towards the Awami League and the antagonism between the army and the Awami League was deep enough where each regarded the other with suspicion. The soldiers had not been able to get over their feeling, despite the results of the election, that Mujib was an anti-Pakistan politician from whose hands it might become necessary for the state to be saved. In the Awami League, the sentiment persisted that the Pakistan Army, having been a prime instrument for Bengali exploitation over the years, would need to have its powers trimmed to the point of its being unable to seize the state in future, as it had already done on two occasions. The party, of course, had its own plans about what it meant to do with the army in future. Within the parameters of its Six-Point programme lay the provision for the creation of a paramilitary force for East Pakistan. As Mujib and his colleagues saw it, such a force, manned by Bengalis and stationed in the province, would effectively preclude the requirement of the Pakistan Army, comprising overwhelmingly officers and soldiers from West Pakistan, in East Pakistan.

President Yahya Khan finally summoned the national assembly to meet in Dhaka on 3 March. There was a palpable sigh of relief when he did so, though at the time he made the announcement there was little way of knowing what was about to descend on the country. When trouble did come, it came from Bhutto. Only two days after the presidential announcement, he publicly stated his position. The PPP, he said in extremely unambiguous terms, would not be attending the national assembly session unless it was reasonably reassured that the Awami League would not impose a constitution on the country unilaterally. He warned that his lawmakers could not afford to place themselves in the position of double hostages, by which he clearly referred to what he saw as a physical threat to him and other West Pakistani MNAs in Dhaka. Bhutto made matters worse when he cautioned all West Pakistani MPAs, and not just those belonging to the PPP, that they would have their legs broken if they travelled to Dhaka.

It was typical Bhutto at work, threatening violence where persuasion should have sufficed. Almost immediately after he announced his boycott of the assembly, Bhutto ran into heavy-handed criticism from other politicians in his native West Pakistan. Wali Khan and Asghar Khan did not fail to notice the selfish motives involved in his declaration. In East Pakistan, the Awami League condemned Bhutto and was able to point to his remarks as one more sign of the western power elite refusing to let go of privilege and influence, even when the country had voted for a democratic order. An unfazed Tajuddin Ahmed told the media that despite the tantrums Bhutto was throwing, his party was going ahead with its own drafting of the constitution.

Over the next few days, as Bengali anger over what was considered as Bhutto's perfidy rose steadily, the first tentative demands for East Pakistan to break away from the rest of the country began to be heard. At Dhaka University, the Central Students Union, now under the control of radical Bengali young men such as A.S.M. Abdur Rab, Nur-e-Alam Siddiqui, Abdul Kuddus Makhan and Shahjahan Siraj, went to work contemplating the political dimensions of an independent Bengali state. Close to Mujib, these young men saw in the developing crisis an opportunity for the Bengali leader to strike out on his independent course. Indeed as time went briskly by, they would increase the pressure on the Awami League chief to repudiate Pakistan and take the people of East Pakistan along their separate way. But Mujib had other, more pressing concerns at that stage. In the first place, the silence of the military authorities in the face of Bhutto's threat to boycott the national assembly session was baffling. Second, when word came through of General Yahya Khan's turning up as Bhutto's guest in Larkana, Mujib and other Awami League leaders felt truly concerned at the way things could be shaping up. The president spent three days hunting on Bhutto's vast property. But no one missed the fact that he and the chairman of the PPP were busy dealing with issues of dimensions infinitely bigger than hunting. For Mujib, it could not but have rankled that while Yahya Khan was cheerfully spending time on Bhutto's ranch, he had carefully avoided paying a visit to the Bengali leader's more modest residence in Dhaka during his December trip to East Pakistan.

Mujib's fears that the Larkana parleys between Yahya Khan and Bhutto would further compound the political crisis in the country were proved correct when, on 1 March, the president announced a postponement of the national assembly session to allow the politicians more time to whittle down their differences before they sat in parliament. The decision was a blunder, considering that the president had not consulted the Awami League before making his unilateral announcement. In a fraught condition, the new delay in calling the assembly to session was only to send up the political temperature a few notches higher. Yahya Khan's move inflamed passions in East Pakistan, where the reaction was swift. Spectators at a cricket match at the Dhaka stadium, furious at hearing of the presidential action, swooped on to the pitch, forcing the players to scatter for safety. Nearby in Motijheel, a crowd soon got ugly. Collecting bamboos piled nearby for a building under construction they marched through streets of the Gulistan business area. The Awami League hurriedly called a press conference at Hotel Purbani in Motijheel, where Mujib made it plain that the postponement was a frontal assault on democracy and a deliberate move to humiliate the people of Bangladesh. He called for an indefinite strike in the province which, in the circumstances then prevailing, was readily responded to by the population. The presidential move not only angered the Awami League but also made it even more resolute about adhering to its demands for a wholesale constitutional restructuring of the state.

The speed with which events unfolded in East Pakistan left both the military regime and Bhutto stunned. An immediate result of the move, one that left the army and the PPP at a loss to explain the slide in the situation, was the Awami League chief's de facto assumption of political authority in Dhaka. Crowds of supportive Bengalis marched to Mujib's residence where they expected the majority leader to hand down some significant decisions about the future of the movement. Mujib, who had publicly called for a non-violent, non-cooperation movement against the regime in the style of Mahatma Gandhi's struggles against the British colonial power in the 1930s and 1940s, relished his new-found authority. But he was also aware of the pressure that was building up on him, particularly from the students and the youth in his party, for a unilateral declaration of independence for Bangladesh. While he was well aware that politics had undergone a severe transformation with the 1 March announcement by the president, he was also conscious of the need to resist any form of militancy. As the days went by, Mujib issued political as well as administrative directives to the people on an everyday basis, thereby making it known to the central government authorities that their writ did not run in East Pakistan any more. Civil servants, teachers, the media, journalists, artists, and others, quickly embraced the position of the Awami League leader being the centre of authority in the province. Offices, shops and educational institutions in the province remained closed. Of greater import was a total ban on trade activities and postal communications between East and West Pakistan. Mujib had moved to stop any financial remittances from being sent to the west from Dhaka. In those early days of March 1971, it was the image of a militant Bengali nation which emerged to defy the state of Pakistan. The army was a subdued lot, though at a number of places it resorted to shooting into the crowds, which only worsened an already bad situation.

The students of Dhaka University symbolised the mood of the province when for the first time the flag of a projected independent Bangladesh was flown on the campus. With a red sun encompassing the map of East Pakistan displayed against a background of green, the flag was the earliest formal sign of a programme under way to steer the crisis towards a declaration of political sovereignty from Pakistan. As he faced mounting calls for independence, Mujib chose to tread a careful path, though he was not sure that his grip on the situation would not loosen. He was in principle reluctant to do anything that could undermine his credibility as the elected leader of not only the province but of the country as well. There was hardly any ambivalence in the situation: he needed to defy the regime and show who was in charge, while at the same time he was not willing to entertain the thought that this was the moment he had always craved for, the chance to make Bengalis a free people.

He chose a safe middle course. That of supervising the administrative and political functions of the province by way of having the Awami League issue directives on how matters ought to be conducted on a daily basis. With the complete erosion of Yahya Khan's authority in the province, the president was now effectively only in control of West Pakistan. Compounding the problems for the president was the refusal of Governor S.M. Ahsan to go along on the national assembly postponement issue. He resigned and flew off to Karachi. In Dhaka, his responsibilities as governor were taken over by the zonal martial-law administrator, Sahibzada Yaqub Khan. On 3 March, Mujib addressed a public rally where he reiterated his position that Bangladesh, as he called the province, was now in the control of his party. The time had arrived, he told the crowds, for the rights of the Bengalis to be reclaimed. He also cautioned everyone that any action in favour of Bengali self-expression needed to be carefully thought out in order for the nation to not lose its way.

The Awami League, sensing that it had put the regime and Bhutto on the defensive, now informed the country that Mujib would be announcing his next course of action at a rally at the Race Course on 7 March. Almost at once the air was rife with speculation of whether the Awami League leader would use the opportunity for a unilateral declaration of independence (UDI) for the province. There are reasons to believe that the Bengali leader did indeed weigh the pros and cons of a UDI. However, having been through the disturbing Agartala Conspiracy trial only a couple of years earlier, he was not ready to be branded a secessionist by his enemies. Moreover, he was drawn to the broader principle of arguing the case for his Bengalis within the parameters of Pakistan. The additional factor of his being the leader of the majority party in the national assembly, which placed him in the sure position of being the country's prime minister, possibly, held him back from leading the province out of the federation.

Mujib's arguments, as he placed them before his party colleagues and the radicals, were two-pronged. On the one hand, the Awami League as the majority party could not walk away from the thick of things. On the other, it was not for the Bengalis, being the majority of the national population they were, to secede from the rest of the country. But if the majority, even without seceding, found itself in a straitjacket, what happened then? To that question the answer was simple: the Bengalis would wait for the regime to stumble or commit a blunder. One that would give the Awami League the perfect reason to tell the world that a failure on the part of the regime to respect the democratic wishes of the people of Pakistan had finally compelled it to go its independent way. It was thus that Mujib kept the extremists around him at bay. He had yet not lost faith in negotiation.

At the other end, a sombre Bhutto, having precipitated the crisis, now came up with one formula after another to create a less harsh image of himself. Already a constant object of attack from nearly every political quarter in the West, for jeopardising the future of democracy, he now proposed that the national assembly bifurcate itself initially, with its Bengali bit to meet in Dhaka while the West Pakistani segment would convene in Rawalpindi or Islamabad to finalise separate drafts of a proposed constitution. Once that job was done, the overall assembly could meet as a single body to work out a compromise based on the two drafts which by then would have been made ready for deliberation. It was a proposal that left the Bengali politicians cheered, for they were now able to present the leader of the PPP as the man who was suggesting that East and West Pakistan effectively go their separate ways. The Urdu terminology that Bhutto had used while forwarding his formula for a settlement was '*Udhar tum idhar hum*'– you there, we here. The smaller parties in the west were appalled. For the radicals in the east, it was significant ammunition that they needed to argue their case for Mujib to opt for independence.

But Mujib still held on, resisting the growing pressure. A dilemma before him was a patent need to state a position at the rally scheduled for 7 March. Any declaration of independence on his part could swiftly push the army, increasingly jittery over the relative impotence it had been relegated to with the growing rise of Bengali militancy, into action. Mujib surely could not afford such a consequence to any decision coming from him. If there had been anything he had become convinced of in the weeks since the election, it was the feeling that the military regime, in tandem with the likes of Bhutto, would be quite happy to create the conditions that would portray him and his party as having provoked the crisis. As 7 March neared, he and his advisors huddled to adopt a strategy to tackle the issue. It was perfectly clear to him that even if he did not go for an outright declaration of independence for Bangladesh, he would still need to convince Bengalis that they were indeed headed for independence. He would thus achieve, as he hoped, two objectives. First, by skirting around the independence issue, he would leave the regime guessing about his future moves. Second, he would persuade his fellow Bengalis into believing that independence was what mattered in the end, but before that the state of Pakistan would need to be given enough rope to hang itself.

The absolute silence that the Awami League maintained in the days before the rally ratcheted up the suspense in West Pakistan. President Yahya Khan, Bhutto and everyone else who mattered in the western province feared that Mujib would actually take the plunge and bid farewell to Pakistan by declaring an independent Bangladesh. But if that eventuality came to pass, the army too was ready to deal with it. In the more than two weeks since the crisis erupted, noticeable contingents of the army had been moved, by air as well as sea, from the west to the east. While soldiers and officers descended on Dhaka, it was largely ammunition which was unloaded in Chittagong from ships arriving from Karachi.

A more ominous sign of what the regime might do, if things began to slip further out of its control, was reflected in the appointment of the ruthless Lieutenant General Tikka Khan as the new governor and zonal martial law administrator of East Pakistan. Already notorious for the harsh employed methods in quelling a rebellion by tribesmen in the province of Baluchistan in the 1960s, Tikka Khan was generally referred to as the butcher of Baluchistan. A man of inadequate intellect but formidable physical toughness, he was the right man for the regime. But even Tikka Khan found, to his dismay and bitterness, just how far the Bengalis had gone in their disillusionment with Pakistan.

The chief justice of the East Pakistan High Court, Justice B.A. Siddiky, in deference to the authority exercised by Mujib, refused to swear him in as the new governor. Tikka Khan was thus forced to fall back on using his powers as martial law administrator but could not enter upon the office of governor because the province was actually being administered by Mujib and the Awami League. A rattled Yahya Khan, unable to predict Mujib's next move, but afraid the Bengali leader might resort to a declaration of independence, made what he thought would be taken by Bengalis as a conciliatory gesture. He invited Mujib and the leaders of the other parties represented in the national assembly to an RTC in Dhaka on 10 March. But what he sought to give with one hand, he clearly took away with the other.

Yahya Khan did not disguise his irritation with the Awami League for the conditions in East Pakistan since his previous broadcast of 1 March, when he set out an invitation for another RTC. The president, to his Bengali listeners, appeared to see nothing wrong with Bhutto's stance in the crisis. There was thus the possibility of his new gesture coming to nought. East Pakistan, he failed to realise, had moved a good many miles beyond the anodyne of an RTC. As the junta waited for Mujib's response, Bhutto accepted the invitation to the RTC with alacrity.

On 7 March, a sombre Mujib stepped up to the dais at the Race Course to announce his next course of action in the proliferating crisis. As the million strong crowd armed with bamboo staves, more as a sign of defiance of the army than as an effective way of resisting a military onslaught should it come, raised slogans in favour of independence, a military helicopter circled overhead, ostensibly to keep track of Mujib and the crowd. Within the province, fear that the army would strike prevailed despite the enthusiasm in favour of a declaration of independence. Defying the government, the Dhaka centre of state-run Radio Pakistan stood by to broadcast Mujib's speech live to the entire province. However, the army soon forced it to scuttle the plan.

As the Awami League leader made ready to address the crowd and through them the Pakistani authorities, not a soul save his close associates in the party had any inkling of what he would say to his people and to the regime in Islamabad. The speech turned out to be one of the finest instances in the history of Bengali political oratory. Mujib, for years regarded as a natural when it came to speeches, began his Race Course address by drawing an outline of the twenty-three years in which successive Pakistani administrations had deprived Bengalis of their fair share in government and the economy. He then proceeded to respond to Yahya Khan's invitation to the RTC. Indeed, the president had held the Bengali nation responsible for the crisis that had erupted following the postponement of the national assembly session six days earlier. The words only whipped up more of militancy in the crowd. Mujib rejected any idea of an RTC with the president and Bhutto. 'With whom do I sit down to talk?' He asked with his standard rhetorical flourish. 'With those who have killed my children, who have made mothers in this land lose sons to the killers unleashed by the state?'

The climax was soon reached when the Awami League leader directly addressed Yahya Khan. 'You have called an RTC, but you must accept my demands before that.' Pausing for dramatic effect, with the audience waiting with bated breath, Mujib slowly ticked off his demands. The first demand elicited a roar of approval from the crowd. Martial law, declared Mujib, had to be withdrawn. That led to the next demand, which was the withdrawal of soldiers to their barracks. The third demand called for a swift judicial inquiry into the army shootings that had taken the lives of a number of Bengalis throughout the province. At this point, the Bengali leader paused once more. Then, slowly and firmly, came the last bit. He demanded that the regime transfer power immediately to the elected representatives of the people.

Wild cheering followed the articulation of the last demand. The Awami League leader had made his programme clear in a way that left the whole of Pakistan facing an entirely new situation. Mujib had been emphatic in his determination to change the whole ball game. Before he would agree to any negotiations, he wanted power to be transferred to him, which in essence meant he rejected the authority of the junta and in any case, when power came to him he would have little need to talk to anyone. Only when the four demands were met, he told the crowds, would he consider whether or not he would take part at any RTC. Simply stated, the RTC idea had simply been shot down by the Awami League. The speech was a remarkable indication of the way Mujib had manoeuvred his way out of a situation where he could not only avoid an outright UDI but also deprive the regime of any excuse to launch an armed assault on the rebellious province by holding back from treading the independence road. But the thought of political sovereignty for Bangladesh was not something he was content to consign to the winds. His concluding remarks, which would later be taken as a directive to his people, were meaningful without being hazy. 'The struggle this time,' he declared, 'is a struggle for emancipation.' The grand finale came in the next statement. 'The struggle this time is the struggle for independence.' The crowd burst into sustained applause.

A palpable sense of relief was noticed in West Pakistan after Mujib's speech. The nightmare of a Bengali declaration of independence which many in the regime and outside it had feared would come from the rally in Dhaka had not come to pass, which for General Yahya Khan was sign enough that there was yet room for negotiation. Mujib's demand for a transfer of power and withdrawal of martial law surely placed the regime in a difficult position, but the soldiers were already telling themselves that a negotiated way out of the crisis was possible. Deep within the junta, however, the Awami League leader's reluctance to go for independence was already being looked upon as an opportunity for the military to use the time to augment its presence in Dhaka. It was the height of naiveté in Mujib and other politicians in the Awami League that they did not, until the very end, suspect that the army would utilise the time Yahya Khan would spend in talks with them to make their own preparations to crush the Bengali nationalist movement. The very military assault that Mujib thought he could offset by avoiding extreme action on 7 March would ironically be unleashed with terrible ferocity at the end of the month. But before that happened, the army needed to keep up a pretence of good intentions.

President Yahya Khan and his advisors got down to serious business immediately after Mujib's declaration trying to schedule a new spate of talks with the Awami League. Many in the junta, among whom was the powerful Lieutenant General S.G.M.M. Peerzada, hoped the Awami League would formally approach the regime for talks. Their despair was telling, when no such overture materialised. It was then that the government began to send out feelers for a Mujib-Yahya meeting in Dhaka. Mujib, who had clearly turned into the sole focus of political authority in East Pakistan, made little effort to downplay his role.

When a Western journalist asked Mujib if he was not defying the authority of the government by controlling East Pakistan, his response was withering. 'What do you mean by government? I am the government,' he told the startled newsman. A couple of days later, when asked if he contemplated independence for the province, he was coy in his answer. 'Independence? No, not yet,' was the way he had left the possibility of freedom for Bengalis dangling in the air. At about the same time, he was telling *Newsweek*'s Loren Jenkins that there was no hope of salvaging the situation. 'The country as we know it,' said the Bengali leader, 'is finished.'

As reports began making the rounds about an impending trip to Dhaka by Yahya Khan, Mujib told the media the president 'is our guest' and so was welcome to visit Dhaka. It did not take an observer of Mujib's politics much to understand that he was, despite the absence of a formal declaration of sovereignty, giving out the message to the president and through him the rest of Pakistan that Bangladesh or East Pakistan was as good as foreign territory for them. Many in West Pakistan bristled at the suggestion. And yet there were men like Asghar Khan and Wali Khan who called for power to be transferred immediately to the Awami League leader. In East Pakistan, Nurul Amin, who had survived the Awami League juggernaut at the elections to win a seat in the national assembly, joined the rising chorus for the army to hand over power to Mujib.

An intriguing aspect of Mujib's demand relating to a transfer of power was the deliberate ambiguity of it. The Bengali leader did not, at any point in his speech, convey any hint that power would have to come to him as prime minister of Pakistan. Indeed, his focus throughout the speech was on East Pakistan, which was vague and by no means a sign that he might have been echoing what Bhutto had only recently suggested—that the national assembly meet in a bifurcated manner in the two wings of the country before coming together for a final thrashing out of the issues. But Mujib was shrewd enough to understand that he could not afford to go for a public endorsement of Bhutto's suggestion lest he be accused of being in cahoots with the PPP leader about breaking up the country. Besides, Bhutto's thoughts were by and large regarded as unabashed adventurism, prompted more by his need to save face than any serious attempt at getting the country to move on. In the days after 7 March, Mujib felt relatively relaxed as, in his view, he had thrown the ball back in the court of the regime. He was in little mood to invite Yahya Khan to talks with him in Dhaka, but he did expect the president to make the journey from Rawalpindi to the East Pakistani capital to discuss the issues he had raised. At this point, the Awami League leadership felt confident about its ability to ride out the storm and actually leave both the army and the PPP ruing the manoeuvres they had lately engaged in. Bengali intellectuals were happy that Mujib had forced the junta into a situation it could neither reject nor easily emerge free of. Dismissing Mujib's demands would only accentuate the Bengali struggle for freedom. Being caught in them meant that Yahya Khan was compelled to look for a way out of them that would not leave him looking sheepish before Pakistani and international opinion.

President Yahya Khan, accompanied by a powerful team of generals, economists and lawyers, arrived in Dhaka on 15 March. On their way to the president's house from the airport, they were first made aware of how long and deep Mujib's writ ran in the province. The streets were deserted of vehicles and all offices and other establishments stayed closed as part of the non-cooperation movement launched by the Awami League leader. No crowds stood on the pavements to applaud the president. Sullen, angry Bengali faces were everywhere. The next day, Mujib, accompanied by his own team comprising Syed Nazrul Islam, Tajuddin Ahmed, Khondokar Moshtaq Ahmed, A.H.M Quamruzzaman and Dr Kamal Hossain, met the president and his delegation at the president's house, in circumstances that were vastly different from what they had been in December when Yahya Khan had spoken of Mujib as Pakistan's future prime minister. At this meeting, the Awami League leadership went on the offensive, making it clear that the decision to postpone the session of the national assembly had been a mistake and aimed at depriving the Bengalis of their due place in the national scheme of things. For its part, the presidential team informed the Awami League that unless the Six Points were watered down, it would be difficult for the national assembly to arrive at a constitutional agreement. Mujib's response was to let the president know that there could be no compromise on the Six Points. However, there would be no obligation on the part of the four provinces constituting West Pakistan to accept the programme as the basis for their political future. The president's feeling on the question was understandable. The Six Points, he noted, would leave the central authority at the mercy of the provinces with nearly every subject so far handled by the centre, devolving to the provinces.

The talks between Mujib and the president went on for the next few days. Bhutto, meanwhile, waited anxiously in Karachi to be invited to participate in the parleys. It had been made obvious by the Awami League, even before Yahya arrived in Dhaka, that Bhutto was not welcome. Mujib, against the backdrop of his 7 March declaration, now considered that only he and the president could talk out the details of a political settlement. But he had quite underestimated the support the chairman of the PPP commanded in the military. Bhutto had down the years been seen as an establishment figure, a West Pakistani with enough experience in the Ayub Khan government to know that the interests of the Punjabi civil-military bureaucracy had to be preserved if Pakistan was to endure as a state. General Yahya Khan went into the job of persuading Mujib in Dhaka that any discussions on the future of the state would remain incomplete and therefore invalid without the participation of the leading political party in West Pakistan. On 17 March, Mujib's forty-ninth birthday, West Pakistani newspapers that had for years ignored or denigrated his politics in their reportage and editorial comments suddenly came forth with paeans to his political sagacity. Greetings went out to him from some unexpected quarters, which demonstrated the desperation that the elite had fallen into as a result of the crisis. The birthday tributes to the Bengali leader could not have come without a nod from the regime and therefore served as a potent reminder of how the fate of Pakistan hung in the balance and how only Mujib held the keys to a solution.

On 21 March, the Awami League finally gave the go-ahead to Yahya Khan for Bhutto to join. A visibly nervous Bhutto, who probably had had little idea earlier of the indignation he had caused in East Pakistan by his politicking over the national assembly session, was now witness to the sea change that had come over the Bengalis since his last visit to the province in late January. Before arriving in Dhaka this time, he had reassured his West Pakistani, more precisely Punjabi-Sindhi constituency, that no deal struck between the regime and the Awami League would hold validity without his party's imprimatur on it. It was a sentiment he was to reiterate to the media in the East Pakistani capital, which now seethed with Bengali nationalism.

The new Bangladesh flags, earlier seen fluttering on the campus of Dhaka University, were now ubiquitous in the city. It was a province up in revolt against Pakistan and it appeared that the population merely waited for a formalisation of Bangladesh's independence rather than saving a united Pakistan through negotiations. Bhutto's version of the first meeting with Mujib and Yahya remains interesting, though it has never been corroborated by other sources. During a break in the talks at the president's house, he was to note how Mujib took him by the elbow and led him out on to the lush green lawns of the residence, telling him on the way that their conversation inside could be tapped by government agents. Once outside, Mujib made a desperate appeal to the PPP leader. Pakistan, he told him, needed to be saved and it was a job that could be accomplished only by the two of them. Mujib, according to Bhutto, then suggested that the Awami League and the PPP form their separate governments in East and West Pakistan respectively as a solution to the crisis. Bhutto thus implied that the idea of a formal separation of the eastern province from the rest of the country came from the Bengali leader. Conveniently, in his narration of the tale, Bhutto made no mention of his own earlier prognosis of the same kind when he had come forth with his 'you there, we here' approach to the issue. Besides, Bhutto's claims of what he wished to be regarded as perfidy on Mujib's part were made later in the year when the Bengali leader was already in prison again, and a guerrilla war had begun testing the resolve of the Pakistani forces in East Pakistan. Between 21 and 23 March in Dhaka, however, the negotiations went nowhere, with all the three participants producing their own plans which were repeatedly amended over the language and other nuances in legal arguments.

As the talks remained deadlocked, much thought in the public arena was given to whether the national assembly would meet on 25 March, the new date that the president had set earlier after consultations with both Mujib and Bhutto. But by 22 March it was easy to see that the differences between the Awami League and the PPP were still too wide to allow for a meeting of the national assembly. Yahya Khan was forced to renege on his earlier announcement expected on 25 March. That move, however, created the brief illusion that the talks were taking a somewhat positive turn and Pakistan could eventually manage to walk purposefully away from the imbroglio.

On 23 March, the anniversary of the adoption of the 1940 Lahore Resolution by the All India Muslim League that was to pave the way to Pakistan and observed officially as Pakistan Day, Bengalis publicly repudiated the country they were part of. In the morning, the young student leaders of Dhaka University handed over a Bangladesh flag to a tired looking Mujib, to raise it over his residence as a demonstration of the course the Bengali nation was taking under his leadership. Till that moment, Mujib had resisted all attempts to make his preferences over the independence issue known publicly. This morning, however, it was the fatalist in the Bengali leader that seemed to have taken over. He raised the Bangladesh flag before the wildly cheering crowds. He knew well that the talks with the junta and Bhutto were going nowhere. Worse, reports of large-scale troop movements all over the province filtered in, a hint of the imminent crackdown he had so long tried to stave off. He had not trusted Yahya Khan or Bhutto right from the beginning and had little reason to start doing so now. The negotiations were being used by the junta to reinforce its strength in the cantonments, which could only mean that a major operation was in the offing. Neither Mujib nor his party could anticipate the scale of the assault that was to come.

On that day, however, Mujib drove down to the president's house once again for a fresh session of talks. This time, though, he was clearly in a new mode. His vehicle displayed the Bangladesh flag, enough to make it appear that he had already taken over as the leader of a free Bengali state. The day was spent with all the three sides in the negotiations dealing with a number of points relating to a possible transfer of power. And yet there were precious few signs of such a transition actually about to take place. On the morning of 24 March, the tension was visible in the Awami League leadership. In sharp contrast, the junta as well as the PPP demonstrated a surreal calm that could only be interpreted to mean the worst fears coming true. The talks held that day remained focused on the nitty-gritty of the positions put forth by the Awami League and the PPP. At the end of the talks on that day, General Peerzada, principal staff officer of the president, assured the Awami League that he would get back to it the next day.

25 March 1971 dawned in unease, both among the Bengali political leadership and the population. From early in the day, rumours began to make the rounds of an imminent army operation against the Bengali nationalist movement, which was now vociferously demanding that Mujib declare the independence of the province. The leaders of the Awami League waited to hear from the junta, but when nothing came from that side and the day slowly progressed to afternoon, Mujib and his colleagues knew that the end had drawn nigh. By early evening, the Awami League had given a call for a general strike all over the province on the following day even though it did not quite know the turn of events that would be between the evening of 25 March and the beginning of 26 March.

As dusk fell on 25 March, news began to circulate that President Yahya Khan and his team had flown off to West Pakistan. It did not take long for the Awami League to confirm that the leader of the military regime had indeed left Dhaka. His departure was the earliest hint that a major crackdown by the army could be only hours away. Angry Bengalis, in their determination to resist the soldiers erected makeshift barricades at important points in the city. In the Dhaka University campus, in Motijheel, the business district of the city and on the road leading out of the cantonment into the city, young Bengalis cut down trees and bamboos and picked up stones and bricks to litter the roads with obstacles that would make it difficult for the soldiers to break through. It was naiveté at work, with few citizens really aware of the terrible force the army might use in its attack. But it was, at the same time, a desperate move on the part of a population which was now confronted with circumstances that threatened the political movement which had gone on for nearly the past one month. From various parts of the city, slogans of Joi Bangla, victory to Bengal, made popular by the Awami League over the previous couple of years through its emphasis on the Six Points, were heard. But, at the same time, the streets cleared quickly as citizens went through deep foreboding at how the night would turn out.

At his residence in the Dhanmondi residential area, Mujib was being difficult with his party colleagues and workers, all of whom wanted him to make his exit from the city, and lead what they saw as a coming struggle for independence from Pakistan. The Awami League leader, uncharacteristically pensive and not wasting many words in his defence, refused to entertain any thought of going into hiding. He was, he told his party men, the elected leader of the majority party in the national assembly and therefore could not be expected to escape. Besides, if he left Dhaka, a maddened army would burn down every home, looking for him. He preferred to wait and let the army take him, as it had in earlier times, into custody. But he told the assembled leaders and workers that they should fan out into the country and prepare for the coming struggle for liberation. As the evening deepened, Awami League leaders, journalists, friends and others left Mujib's residence. He was now in the company of his family— wife Fazilatunnesa, daughters Hasina and Rehana and sons Kamal, Jamal and Russell. As the first sounds of gunfire were heard from the approach leading out of the cantonment, his elder daughter Hasina remembers, Mujib sent out a message through wireless proclaiming Bangladesh's independence. It was brief and to the point. With the army on its way, as Mujib knew, the elected leader of the majority party in Pakistan National Assembly and spokesman of the seventy-five million Bengalis inhabiting the province of East Pakistan, had the following directive transmitted to the outside world: 'This may be my last message. From today Bangladesh is independent. I call upon the people of Bangladesh, wherever they might be and with whatever you have, to resist the army of occupation to the last. Your fight must go on until the last soldier of the Pakistan occupation army is expelled from Bangladesh. Final victory is ours.'

Mujib's declaration of independence was swiftly borne out by a report distributed on 26 March by the US Defence Intelligence Agency to the White House Situation Room, Department of State and other government agencies in Washington. Titled 'DIA Spot Report', the agency noted thus:

Pakistan was thrust into civil war today when Sheikh Mujibur Rahman proclaimed the east wing of the two-part country to be 'the sovereign independent People's Republic of Bangladesh'. Fighting is reported heavy in Dhaka and other eastern cities where the 10,000-man paramilitary East Pakistan Rifles has joined police and private citizens in conflict with an estimated 23,000 West Pakistani regular army troops. Continuing reinforcements by sea and air combined with the government's stringent martial-law regulations illustrate Islamabad's commitment to preserve the union by force. Because of logistical difficulties, the attempt will probably fail, but not before heavy loss of life results.

Indian officials have indicated that they would not be drawn into a Pakistani civil war, even if the east should ask for help. Their intentions might be overruled, however, if the fever of Bengali nationalism spills across the border.

Sheikh Mujibur Rahman is little interested in foreign affairs and would cooperate with the United States if he could. The west's violent suppression, however, threatens to radicalize the east to the detriment of U.S. interests. The crisis has exhibited anti-American facets from the beginning and both sides will find the United States a convenient scapegoat.

Mujib, having sent out the declaration of independence, climbed the stairs leading from his library, from where he had sent out his message, and joined his sombre family on the first floor. He was poised, almost at peace with himself. But he knew, as well as anyone else in his family and among his colleagues, that his future was uncertain. The state of Pakistan was determined to get him and possibly finish him off.

—◦◦◦—

Genocide and Mujibnagar

The Pakistan Army launched Operation Searchlight between 11:30 pm and midnight on 25 March. Armoured vehicles, tanks and trucks carrying soldiers rolled out of the cantonment and made their way to targets designated earlier. A large group of soldiers moved towards the campus of Dhaka University and mounted an assault on the residential Jagannath Hall as well as the teachers' quarters. Squads of soldiers swiftly blasted the Kali Mandir, the Hindu temple in the centre of the Race Course, and the Central Shaheed Minar, the monument to the martyrs of the Language Movement of February 1952, into rubble. Two other groups moved fast to take hold of Radio Pakistan and Pakistan Television. Another group swooped upon the offices of *The People* newspaper in Shahbagh directly opposite the Intercontinental Hotel. The soldiers reserved particular wrath for the newspaper as it had, since the elections, played a rather vocal role in castigating the West Pakistani establishment over its failure to live up to democratic principles. The army marched into the Intercontinental looking for foreign journalists, a substantial number of whom had come from the Europe and the United States. All except the young British reporter Simon Dring, who concealed himself in the pantry of the hotel with the cooperation of the employees there, were rounded up, bundled on to army trucks, taken to the airport and put on a plane. The soldiers were in no mood for the overseas media to be witness to their murderous operations. A couple of days later, Dring would finally be spotted and packed off to Bangkok, from where he would file the first detailed report of the pogrom launched by the Pakistan Army in Dhaka.

A truckload of soldiers went to the buildings housing the Bengali language newspapers *Ittefaq* and *Sangbad*, both of which had worked as mouthpieces for the Awami League in the recent past. The army simply set fire to the buildings. An especially large contingent of the army travelled at lightning speed to the Peelkhana headquarters of the East Pakistan Rifles, whose members were all Bengalis, and mowed down anyone and anything that moved. More terrible was the carnage let loose at Rajarbagh police lines, where sleeping members of the provincial police force were murdered in cold blood. Back at the university, the soldiers broke open the gates of Jagannath Hall, where Hindu students of the university resided, and went on a rampage. Students were collected in separate groups in the open space before the hall building and shot. The killings went on till dawn, with the soldiers forcing the students they had so far spared to dig a mass grave on the open ground and dump the bodies of their comrades in it. Once the macabre job was done, the army killed those very students and kicked their bodies into the grave. By early morning, army bulldozers would flatten the grave, leaving little sign of the bodies squashed beneath the earth.

At the teachers' quarters, the soldiers moved around with lists of the names of particular academicians to be killed. In one of their first operations, they broke down the gate of the residence of the respected elderly professor of philosophy, Govinda Chandra Dev, and shouting obscenities went up to find him lying on a couch. They murdered him and then turned on the husband of his adopted daughter, shooting him in the head. In a nearby building, another band of soldiers, looking for Professor Maniruzzaman of the Bengali department of the university, mistakenly attacked the residence of his namesake who taught mathematics. He was killed, along with two relatives, and their bodies were dragged down the stairs and left on the open space before Jagannath Hall, where innumerable bodies of dead students had already been collected. The soldiers then attacked the quarters of Professor Jyotirmoy Guha Thakurta of the Department of English and shot him in the neck. Believing him to be dead, they left him and went looking for other teachers to kill. As dawn broke, Thakurta's wife managed to take him to the Dhaka Medical College, where bullet-riddled Bengalis from other parts of the city were being brought in as well. Thakurta struggled for his life for six days before breathing his last on 31 March. His body was then stolen by the army, never to be recovered by his family.

In the older part of the city, soldiers in armoured cars came upon a group of rickshaw pullers asleep in their three-wheeled bicycle carriages and pumped bullets into them. At Iqbal Hall of Dhaka University, residents were called out from their rooms and dormitories, lined up in the downstairs auditorium and shot. On Elephant Road, the soldiers stormed into the residence of Lieutenant Commander Moazzam Hossain, a former accused in the Agartala case, dragged him out on the road before the building and shot him in cold blood. On the university campus, Nurul Ula, an academic, watched from behind the curtains as the soldiers lined up students on the grounds of Jagannath Hall before shooting them. With his movie camera, Ula recorded the images, which were later shown around the world.

A little after 1:00 am on 26 March an elite force of the army rumbled down Dhanmondi Road 32, where Mujib waited. Once they approached the gates of his residence, the soldiers began firing indiscriminately at the building, shooting holes in the gate and the walls and killing the Awami League leader's security men on the spot. At one point, during what was obviously a lull in the shooting, an officer using a loudspeaker demanded that the Awami League leader come down and surrender to the army. It was then that Mujib went out on the balcony, to tell the soldiers to stop shooting. 'What do you want?' he demanded. The officer, already in the compound of the residence, told him that he was under arrest and would need to go with him. A few minutes later, having briefly consoled his petrified family, Mujib walked downstairs where the soldiers, some pushing him with the butts of their rifles, escorted him to a jeep and drove away.

About half a mile away, as Mujib heard gunfire pounding the city and saw flares thrown up by the army lighting the skies, the jeep stopped near the steps of the under-construction national assembly building. The building dated back to the years of Ayub Khan, who in his decision to declare Dhaka as Pakistan's second capital had actually meant for it to be the legislative capital of the country. The edifice of the parliament building was an offshoot of that decision. Tonight, as the military spread terror all across the city, Mujib was escorted out of the jeep and made to sit on the steps. Clearly, further instructions were needed by the soldiers who had arrested him. The officer who had taken the Bengali leader under arrest sent out a terse message on his walkie talkie, 'Big bird in cage. Small birds have flown.' The big bird was of course Mujib. The little ones that had flown were a reference to his colleagues in the Awami League. Apparently the officer was at that point in conversation with General Tikka Khan, the martial-law administrator now leading the operation against the Bengalis. Would he like Mujib to be brought before him? The general snapped, 'I don't want to see his face.' A few minutes later, Mujib boarded the jeep again, this time to be taken to Adamjee College in the cantonment, where he would be lodged under foolproof security for the next few days until he could be flown to West Pakistan. The army was not ready to make the mistake of keeping him in Dhaka, where he could turn into a focal point of Bengali resistance to the government's suppression of the nationalist movement.

As the offices of *The People* burned in Shahbagh, Bhutto watched from his suite in the Intercontinental. Although he would subsequently try to convince people that he had not been aware of the departure of Yahya Khan from Dhaka and the subsequent army action, the suspicion lingered that he had been kept posted about the entire sequence of events beginning on the night of 25 March. Early the next morning, Bhutto was collected by the army from the hotel, taken to the airport and put on a flight to Karachi. Arriving in Karachi in the evening, Bhutto was upbeat about the army operation against the Awami League. 'Thank God, Pakistan has been saved,' he told waiting newsmen. It was to be the understatement of the year. Even as he expressed his sense of relief at what he thought was an end to the crisis, the people of West Pakistan remained unaware of the orgy of killing that had been unleashed in East Pakistan.

When the state-controlled Radio Pakistan made an announcement in the early hours of 26 March that Yahya Khan would be addressing the nation in the evening, the expectation was that a solution to the political crisis was finally forthcoming and that he would announce a formula for a transfer of power to the elected leaders of the country. Such expectations were belied when a grave sounding president went on the networks to tell the country that Mujib and the Awami League had acted against Pakistan and thereby committed treason. 'This crime shall not go unpunished,' said the president, and he went on to impose a complete ban on the Awami League. It was the duty of the army, he said, to restore order in East Pakistan. As a sop to those who might doubt his overall intentions regarding a restoration of civilian rule, he reiterated his position that he would hand over power to the representatives of the people as soon as normal conditions were restored in Dhaka and elsewhere in the country's eastern province.

But a restoration of normal conditions would remain illusory. By the afternoon of 26 March, as Dhaka remained under a curfew and the army continued its mission of killing civilians and looking for senior leaders of the Awami League to arrest, resistance was taking its first tentative shape in the port city of Chittagong. With reports of the genocide in Dhaka seeping into the city, a small group of Bengalis at the Chittagong centre of Radio Pakistan took it upon themselves to rename the station as *Biplobi Shwadhin Bangla Betar Kendro*— Revolutionary Free Bengal Radio Station. Late in the afternoon, a prominent leader of the city branch of the Awami League, M.A. Hannan, arrived at the station and proceeded to read out what was purportedly a message of freedom from Mujib. It was the earliest public announcement of a declaration of freedom, though in later years, Siddik Salik, a major who served as public relations officer in the Pakistan Army in Dhaka when the crackdown commenced, would claim that as the soldiers went into action, the voice of Mujib was heard on a clandestine network telling Bengalis that Bangladesh was now a free state. The trouble with Salik's report as well as Hannan's announcement on behalf of Mujib was that in the fraught circumstances at the time, few people heard them. The Chittagong radio transmitter was not powerful enough to be received in the whole province. Despite such shortcomings, however, by late evening of 26 March, a good number of people in Chittagong as well as the Pakistan Army, in addition to a few elements in the Indian Border Security Forces only miles away from Chittagong, knew that a declaration of independence had been made and that East Pakistan was finally and truly on its way to becoming the independent republic of Bangladesh. The British journalist David Loshak, writing in *Pakistan Crisis*, his book on the unfolding events of the times, would note the clear move Mujib had made towards declaring Bangladesh a free state: 'Soon after darkness fell on March 25, the voice of Sheikh Mujibur Rahman came faintly through on a wavelength close to the official Pakistan radio. In what must have been and sounded like a pre-recorded message, the Sheikh proclaimed East Pakistan to be the People's Republic of Bangladesh. He called on Bengalis to go underground, to reorganise and to attack the invaders.'

A significant step on the road to independence was taken the next day, 27 March, when the men behind the Free Bengal Radio roped in Major Ziaur Rahman, a Bengali officer in the Pakistan Army who had before the crackdown been involved in unloading of ammunition for the army from the sea vessel MV Swat arriving from Karachi but had then turned against his superior West Pakistani officer, and invited him to visit their studio. It was there that Zia made another announcement of the independence of Bangladesh and for good measure appointed himself president of a provisional government for the new state. The radio officials, however, had to remind him that such a declaration would hold little water as it would be construed as a mutiny by a Pakistan Army officer rather than as a serious move towards a necessary struggle for armed liberation. Zia comprehended the situation and was soon on the air again. This time he announced the emergence of Bangladesh as an independent state on behalf of 'our great leader and supreme commander Sheikh Mujibur Rahman,' and appealed to the international community to recognise the new state. Zia's brief address was heard by a larger number of people than those who had earlier heard M.A. Hannan's declaration on behalf of Mujib, and had an electrifying effect on Bengalis. But for all the fervour associated with the declaration, Bengalis as a nation felt lost with an effective absence of news about Mujib and the other leaders of the Awami League. A substantial number of Bengalis believed that Mujib could not have remained alive, given the brutality of the army assault. And if he was dead, it could well be that his political associates too had met the same fate.

Over the next few days, as the army moved to retake the cities and towns of the province in a manner akin to a foreign military force capturing enemy territory, the government began to inform people that Mujib was under arrest. Its claims were dismissed because there was hardly any evidence in the nature of photographs or other documentary matter to show that the Bengali leader was in captivity. Besides, the Shwadhin Bangla Betar, which was soon forced to move out of Chittagong as the military moved in, continued to broadcast regular bulletins claiming that Mujib was organising the armed struggle on the war front. Such announcements were clearly aimed at keeping up the morale of the people. The scattered groups of Awami League political leaders and workers as well as common citizens really had no way of knowing whether their elected spokesman was alive. But it was necessary to keep up the myth that Mujib was around and directing the struggle.

Meanwhile, his senior colleagues in the party had, with a few exceptions, escaped from Dhaka into the villages, from where the only destination could be the frontier with India. Tajuddin Ahmed, left Dhaka as the army assault on the city began. Syed Nazrul Islam and Colonel Ataul Gani Osmany made their way out of the city. Dr Kamal Hossain, who would have joined Tajuddin and Amirul Islam, got caught up in the confusion and so missed the chance of leaving the capital. He was arrested by the army on 3 April and flown to West Pakistan with his family. Moshtaq, initially unable to escape, found refuge at the home of his friend Dr T. Hossain, where he spent some days until he could be safely spirited out of the place and across the frontier.

When the curfew was lifted for a few hours on 27 March, hundreds of families made their way to the suburbs around Dhaka and from there to the outlying villages. It would soon become a pattern. As the army reclaimed increasingly wider swathes of territory, Bengalis were left with little choice but to push on to the frontier with India. Politicians, academics and students all made a dash for the border. In the weeks and months after the crackdown, the numbers would swell alarmingly, enough to convince the outside world of the genocide being perpetrated by the army. By the time Bangladesh emerged as a free country nine months later, ten million Bengalis out of a population of seventy-five million would cross over into India, causing a logistical nightmare for the Indian authorities.

The Pakistan Army demonstrated a ferocity that left even the most cynical of observers stunned. It appeared to be particularly drawn to thoughts of killing any Bengali who looked like a nationalist (and all Bengalis were nationalists at that point) as well as Hindus. The military regime had convinced itself that the influence of Hindu culture on the Bengalis had become particularly pronounced and needed to be crushed. Within days of the crackdown, signs over shops and business establishments in Dhaka and elsewhere began to be written in Urdu, a clear affront to the population. The army had clearly expected that the ruthlessness of its action would bring the province to heel. It did not seem to have thought through the long-term consequences of its tactics, particularly aspects like the movement of large numbers of Bengalis towards the border with India. Most of those leaving the province in subsequent days were young men who would soon become part of the *Mukti Bahini*, or Liberation Force, that would steadily exhaust the army and push it into a situation where it would find itself trapped in the marshes and swamps of a country noted for the ubiquity of its rivers, lakes and ponds. Ill-equipped to deal with guerrilla warfare and, more importantly, having never taken into account the desperate measures the beleaguered Bengalis would adopt to defend themselves, the army was in a confused frenzy. By the time the war came to an end, the number of women kidnapped and raped by the soldiers of the Pakistan Army would go up to a figure of 200,000. Overall, the killings would reach the 3,000,000 mark by the time the war drew to its terrible conclusion. In the first few weeks after the crackdown, it became clear to Tajuddin Ahmed that quick action was necessary in order for the resistance to develop along a clear pattern. As general secretary of the Awami League he had developed a reputation over the years as one of the most incisive of Bengali politicians and had increasingly been looked upon as the theoretician of the party. Having played a principal role in the party, it fell upon him to take necessary action on the future of the Bengali movement.

Tajuddin Ahmed had to take charge of the independence movement by gathering the scattered party leadership at the earliest and devising a strategy to confront the Pakistanis militarily. His dilemma was compounded by the fact that, for the first time in recorded history, the Bengalis were being called upon to form a government for themselves. Never had the people of Bengal, on either side of the 1947 divide, been in a position to establish an independent government for themselves. The task for Tajuddin Ahmed, as he made his way to India at the end of March 1971, was therefore to send out a statement that the repression by the Pakistan Army in East Pakistan had not been able to douse the Bengali nationalist movement but in fact had only stoked it towards the bigger goal of independence. After 25 March, there could be no reason for Bengalis to remain part of the Pakistani federation. And that was the message Tajuddin Ahmed carried to Indian Prime Minister Indira Gandhi when he finally met her in Delhi in early April. It had been a tortuous flight from Dhaka to West Bengal and then, with the assistance of Indian border security, all the way to the Indian capital. Accompanied by Amirul Islam, the general secretary of the Awami League, he provided a detailed, first-hand account of the failed negotiations with the Yahya Khan junta and the subsequent military assault on an unarmed population to the Indian prime minister. Tajuddin's motive in meeting Mrs Gandhi was, first, to seek her government's recognition of Bangladesh as an independent state and, second, to ask for military assistance for the evolving guerrilla struggle against Pakistan. The Indian government, faced with a growing influx of Bengali refugees on its own soil in that early phase of the Bangladesh struggle, was perfectly willing to assist the Bengalis in their war against Pakistan. But the Indian leader also thought it prudent to impress upon her visitors that a necessary first step towards internationalising the issue was the establishment of a government for Bangladesh, naturally in exile. The myth that Mujib was indeed fighting the struggle for liberation was maintained, perhaps in the hope of compelling the Pakistani regime to reveal what they had done with him after taking him from his home.

The Indian and Bengali strategy on forcing the Pakistanis to acknowledge Mujib's whereabouts worked. In the second week of April, pictures of the Bengali leader under arrest and in the custody of police at Karachi Airport were splashed across the front pages of Pakistani newspapers. Apparently he had just been brought in from Dhaka and was in transit to wherever the regime planned to take him. Seated on a sofa and looking pensive, Mujib gave no hint of fear. It was an image that surely left Bengalis everywhere depressed. Contrary to what the Awami League might say, the Pakistanis appeared to suggest that the leader of the Bengali liberation struggle was actually a prisoner with absolutely little control over or knowledge of what was happening in his country. While that might have been true, now that it was confirmed that Mujib was in custody in Pakistan, it would be a valuable bargaining chip in the weeks and months ahead for his colleagues as also for the Indian administration. Mujib could not be physically eliminated without causing an outcry across the world. Already voices were being heard, apart from those of the Indians, about the escalating nature of the Bangladesh crisis. Soviet President Nikolai Podgorny was one among many world leaders to press for a return to negotiations in East Pakistan. His letter to President Yahya Khan in early April made it clear as to where Moscow stood on the crisis and that it would probably be playing a bigger role as the situation exacerbated. The Pakistanis were angry, but the anger subsided somewhat in their realisation that China had made no comment on the issue. The Pakistani authorities were, however, cheered by the disinclination on the part of the Nixon administration in Washington to support the Awami League. Its ambassador in Islamabad did not appear worried about all the reports of army killings that came to him from the US Consul, Archer Blood, in Dhaka.

Tajuddin Ahmed returned to Calcutta after his meeting with Mrs Gandhi and quickly set about shaping a strategy towards the formation of a government in exile. His efforts in getting the liberation struggle underway were hampered by the absence of news about other senior figures in the Awami League. By early April, it had become known that the respected member of the national assembly from Jessore, Masihur Rahman, had been arrested by the army and tortured to death in the local cantonment. In Comilla, the elderly Dhirendranath Dutta, in retirement from politics, and his son were picked up by the soldiers and shot on the street in a heavy downpour. Scattered reports made their way to the refugee camps which were being set up by the Indian authorities on their borders about the horrifying nature of the army's killing spree. The army had now begun to penetrate the villages where, with assistance from its local collaborators now organised under so-called peace committees (the members of these committees belonged to the right-wing parties which had been badly mauled at the December 1970 elections), they picked off Awami League supporters as well as members of the Hindu community. By April, the rape of Bengali women was turning into a systematic and organised affair.

In such circumstances, the only section of the Bengali political class that Tajuddin had around him were the members of the national and provincial assemblies who had made good their escape from

Dhaka. Tajuddin had already sent out feelers to many of these men about his thoughts on the issue of government formation in exile. But as he prepared to act on those thoughts, he found himself up against opposition from unexpected quarters. The younger elements in the Awami League and its affiliated bodies began to drop broad hints that Tajuddin Ahmed's bid to form a government would not go down well with large sections of the party. Articulated by such diehard loyalists of Mujib as his ambitious nephew Sheikh Fazlul Haq Moni, it was clear that the younger elements were in the mood to take over the leadership of the movement in the name of Mujib and push him aside. Tajuddin had long been expecting this opposition. Over the years, some of his long-time colleagues too had started to resent his growing importance in the party. In the manoeuvrings of Moni and his young followers, Tajuddin saw a well-laid plan of undermining his position and taking over the movement in a dynastic fashion. For all his devotion to Mujib, Tajuddin was not willing to let Moni or his more youthful radical supporters hijack the struggle.

Urged by his own followers to assume the role of Bangladesh's leader in the absence of Mujib, he took charge as the country's first prime minister. His next task was to record a message on tape and have it broadcast over Shwadhin Bangla Betar. The contents of the message were patently unmistakable: Bangladesh was engaged in war against Pakistan, a struggle that was now being spearheaded by a government set up by its elected representatives. The tape containing Tajuddin's speech was transported, over the reservations of Moni and his group, to the clandestine radio station then fitfully broadcasting from the north-eastern Indian border with East Pakistan. On the evening of 12 April, Tajuddin Ahmed's voice was heard in significant areas of what had by then become a country under Pakistani occupation. He clearly had a good understanding of the issues Bengalis would need to confront as they waged war against the state of Pakistan. The first few days after Tajuddin Ahmed's broadcast proved to be exciting, with news of the sightings of other senior figures of the Awami League in various parts of India contiguous to the border with Bangladesh. Captain Mansoor

Ali and Abu Hena Mohammad Quamruzzaman were picked up by the Indian security forces and brought to Calcutta, where Tajuddin had set up headquarters of the Bangladesh government in exile on Theatre Road in a building made available to him by the Indian authorities. Initially reserved on being told by the prime minister that he had taken charge and had in fact addressed the beleaguered nation over radio, the two men soon came round to endorsing the measures adopted so far.

Tajuddin was then flown to north-eastern India, where he welcomed Syed Nazrul Islam and a clean-shaven Colonel Osmany (the small, wiry, retired military officer, famed for his gigantic moustache, had apparently got rid of it to avoid detection by the army) and immediately acquainted them with the steps he had so far taken. Islam, a suave and decent man, was happy to know that in the absence of Mujib, he would serve as acting president and hold overall supervision of the war for independence. Once all the senior colleagues of Mujib had come together in Calcutta, it was felt that a formal inauguration of the Bangladesh provisional government would need to be organised on Bangladesh territory. With the Pakistan Army dominating most of the borders, Meherpur, a rural backwater in the Chuadanga region in the south-east of Bangladesh was chosen for the occasion. Tajuddin Ahmed and his colleagues quickly renamed the place Mujibnagar in honour of the jailed leader. The lawyer Amirul Islam, who had all along played a pivotal role in helping the prime minister to organise the government and at the same time act as his troubleshooter in his dealings with recalcitrant members of the Awami League, guided a posse of Indian and Western journalists from the Calcutta Press Club to the inauguration.

As acting president of the People's Republic of Bangladesh, the formal term now applied to the fledgling country, Syed Nazrul Islam swore in Tajuddin Ahmed as prime minister along with Khondokar Moshtaq Ahmed, A.H.M. Quamruzzaman and M. Mansoor Ali as ministers in the first Bengali government in history. Colonel M.A.G. Osmany was given charge, as commander-in-chief of the liberation army now known as the Mukti Bahini, to forge battlefield strategy for the armed struggle. The formal proclamation of independence, detailing the backdrop to the war, was read out by Professor Yusuf Ali, an academic turned politician who had been elected a member of the national assembly in the December 1970 elections.

The acting president and the prime minister delivered brief speeches explaining the background to the formation of the government. They told the assembled Bengali villagers as well as the newsmen come from Calcutta that no political solution other than the acceptance of an independent Bangladesh as a historical reality would be acceptable. The brief ceremony came to an end to the cries of *Joi Bangla* from the crowd gathered there. The die having been cast, it would now be for the politicians to flesh out the struggle in ways that would give the movement greater credibility in the coming days. But given the sheer might of the Pakistan Army in Bangladesh since 25 March, it would take a sustained, prolonged struggle to free the country of rule by distant Islamabad. The Mujibnagar leaders were quite aware of the need for a guerrilla response to the conventional tactics employed by the army.

It was such a need that led Colonel Osmany to confer with the Bengali army officers who had switched allegiance to Bangladesh moments after Operation Searchlight commenced. The outcome was a battle plan that segmented Bangladesh into eleven war zones, each of them under the supervision of a sector commander. Beginning in April, the Mukti Bahini would swell with Bengali deserters from the Pakistan Army, the police and East Pakistan Rifles. But the bulk of Mukti Bahini strength throughout the weeks and months to liberation would come from Bengali youths in the villages and district towns of the occupied country. Among the officers who would take charge of the eleven sectors of war were Major K.M. Safiullah, Major Ziaur Rahman, Major Khaled Musharraf, Major M.A. Manzoor, Lt Col Abu Taher, Major Nuruzzaman, and Major Rafiqul Islam. Of this group, Manzoor and Taher would escape from the cantonments in West Pakistan they were posted in and make their way to Mujibnagar.

From the air force, there were A.K. Khondokar and Khademul Bashar. Over a period of time, other military officers would turn up and join the war effort. There were many others who, while trying to cross over to India from West Pakistan, were detected by Pakistan's border forces and placed under arrest.

Apart from the operations launched by the Mukti Bahini against the Pakistani forces in various parts of Bangladesh, other guerrilla groups such as Abdul Kader Siddiqui's *Kaderia Bahini* operated inside Bangladesh and never crossed the border into India. The ferocity of the Kaderia Bahini in time became the stuff of legend and even had Pakistan's soldiers encamped in Kader Siddiqui's native Tangail district, fearing for their safety. Sheikh Fazlul Haq Moni and the younger elements opposed to Tajuddin Ahmed formed a new group of freedom fighters they called the *Mujib Bahini*, which was seen as a distinct move towards taking the initiative from Tajuddin's hands. Mercifully, it did not succeed, though the force continued to operate separately during the course of the war. Neither did a meeting of Awami League lawmakers, convened to deliberate upon the prime minister's actions in respect of the war, succeed in adopting a no-confidence motion against Tajuddin Ahmed. Broadly speaking, it was the Mukti Bahini that provided the thrust of the movement against the Pakistani forces. Trained under the supervision of Indian military officers in military camps around the frontiers of Bangladesh, the guerrillas, coming from middle-class Bengali families in the country's rural regions, quickly gained a reputation for swiftness of movement and precision attacks on the soldiers. They became adept in engaging the army in the villages and blowing up bridges that could otherwise help facilitate the movement of the soldiers. The Pakistani soldiers, of course, adopted their own methods of revenge. Once the guerrillas had moved off to safety after having harassed and killed or injured the Pakistanis, units descended on the villages where the guerrillas had camped before their attacks and simply set them afire. Shooting old men and women and abducting young women and girls had by then turned into a routine for the army.

The Bangladesh War of Liberation, contrary to the expectations of the Pakistan military authorities, turned out to be an inclusive affair that united Bengalis across the spectrum and beyond the confines of the occupied country. Justice Abu Sayeed Chowdhury, the vice chancellor of Dhaka University representing Pakistan at a human rights conference in Geneva at the time of the crackdown, denounced the military action and switched his allegiance to the Bangladesh cause. He was later deputed to take charge of the Bangladesh mission in London, where he played an instrumental role in organising overseas Bengalis towards disseminating information about the national cause in Europe. Bengali diplomats in Pakistani embassies abroad began to defect to the cause of independence within days of the crackdown and the declaration of independence. K.M. Shehabuddin and Amjad Hossain, stationed in the Pakistani consulate in Bombay, in a public statement condemned the atrocities committed by the army and switched loyalty to the Bengali cause. In Calcutta, the Bengali deputy high commissioner for Pakistan, Hossain Ali, hoisted the Bangladesh flag atop the building housing the mission and claimed it for his occupied country. When the Pakistan government, despite its efforts, was unable to reclaim the building, it simply closed down the mission. The office then became one of the focal points of the Bengali struggle. In the West, A.F.M. Abul Fateh, the senior-most Bengali, in an ambassadorial position, declared his rejection of Pakistan. Infuriated, the Islamabad authorities tried to have him recalled to Islamabad but failed. Shah A.M.S. Kibria, Humayun Rashid Chowdhury, Abul Maal Abdul Muhith, A.H. Mahmood Ali, M.M. Rezaul Karim, Waliur Rahman and Mohiuddin Ahmed, among a number of others, swiftly opted to serve the government in exile through public condemnation of Pakistan's actions in Bangladesh. The sinister nature of the war was not lost on a senior West Pakistani diplomat, Iqbal Athar. In a move that amazed not only his own country but also the Bengalis, he defected to the Bangladesh cause. In independent Bangladesh, he was to serve as an ambassador in a number of important countries until his death. In China, Khwaja Mohammad Kaiser, who belonged to the family of the erstwhile Nawab of Dhaka, faced a particular dilemma. He was Pakistan's trusted envoy in Beijing, highly regarded by the Chinese authorities. Clearly inclined to identify with the Bengali cause, he was unable to find the means to do it, given the vocal support China was giving Pakistan over the Bangladesh crisis. It was for Premier Zhou En-lai to advise him to carry on as best he could, a job he fulfilled till the end. In later years, Kaiser was to go back to Beijing, this time to serve as Bangladesh's ambassador in a country where he had for a long time upheld the interests of Pakistan.

Within West Pakistan, a large number of Bengali military as well as civilian officers were stranded as a result of the war. In the case of the military personnel, the authorities exercised particular measures to prevent them from escaping. The most senior officer in the army was again a man with roots in East Pakistan. Khwaja Wasiuddin, son of Ayub Khan's minister for information, Khwaja Shehabuddin, served as a lieutenant general in the Pakistan Army. Respected by his Pakistani colleagues, during the entire duration of the war, he nevertheless remained deprived of any specific responsibility. He was repatriated to Bangladesh after the war, and honourably retired from the army. The government would then send him off to Kuwait as the new country's ambassador.

Trial in Mianwali, Triumph in Dhaka

Sheikh Mujibur Rahman was lodged in Mianwali prison in the Punjab. The military authorities were quite clear about how they meant to treat him. General Yahya Khan, in his radio address on 26 March, had already accused him and his party of treason which in turn demonstrated an absolute unwillingness on the part of the regime to deal leniently with him. For Mujib, this latest spell of imprisonment was the worst he had faced in his entire political career.

In Mianwali, Mujib was placed in solitary confinement in a high security prison. He was given no access to radio and television. Newspapers which used to be regularly provided to him in his earlier spells in jail were now denied to him. The intention on the part of the regime was to subject him to psychological pressure through a denial of news and visitors. For the entire nine months he spent as Pakistan's prisoner, during which time his Bengalis waged war against Pakistan and eventually won, Mujib had nothing to do but pace around his narrow cell and sometimes, when the guards allowed it, take brief walks in the small compound before the cell. In the first few months of his imprisonment, no charges were brought against him officially and yet he was given reason to understand that sooner or later he would be put on trial. For Mujib, then, there was little hope that he would ever again walk out free and it was one of those rare occasions when a political leader who had initiated a mass upsurge against a military dictatorship and had rallied his people to the call to freedom, remained completely in the dark about the new realities taking shape.

While it is certain that Mujib had a fair idea of the ongoing repression in Bangladesh, he could hardly have calculated the enormity of the atrocities. The extent of the damage Pakistan's military regime was causing in Bangladesh was brought home to a team of West Pakistani journalists flown to Dhaka in April by the authorities. All the journalists save one were to help the regime in covering up its atrocities by informing their readers that everything was going well in the country's eastern province. Only Anthony Mascarenhas, a Christian, was sufficiently disturbed to return to Karachi and pack his bags for London. Mascarenhas was particularly troubled when a young army officer told him in Comilla that the military should be keeping the Bengalis in a state of slavery for as many as thirty years. It was not merely the murderous attitude but also the patent racism that appalled Mascarenhas. He arrived in London and made contact with the *Sunday Times*. In June, his description of what he called the rape of Bangladesh was splashed on its pages and fuelled opinion in Britain and in the West as a whole against the genocidal actions of the Pakistan government. Following Mascarenhas' report, the Western media began to take greater interest in the Bangladesh struggle and over the weeks and months focused on the crisis.

Meanwhile, Mujib's captivity was becoming a major concern for the Bangladesh government in exile as well as for the Indian authorities. With the number of refugees growing, India was finding it difficult, given its own economic constraints, to handle the problem. But even as Mrs Gandhi called for Yahya Khan to negotiate with Mujib, she realised that it was an option the Pakistanis would not exercise and that sooner or later Delhi might have to go to war as a means of bringing Pakistan to heel. The training facilities India provided to the Mukti Bahini, apart from everything else Tajuddin Ahmed and his government needed in order to function in a credible manner, was a big pointer to where Delhi wanted the Bengali liberation struggle to go.

The biggest factor in that struggle, of course, remained the Mujib persona. Even in his absence, the Bengali leader was an all-pervading influence on the course of the war. The Free Bengal Radio made it a part of its programme to begin its bulletins with the signature tune of Joi Bangla and follow it up by a broadcast of the final two lines from Mujib's 7 March exhortation for freedom. A large number of the patriotic songs broadcast by the station were thematically composed around the personality of the Awami League chief. He was obviously the very basis and the international face of the struggle for liberation. Only, he did not know that an entire movement for freedom was being waged in his name and that indeed he had already been honoured as the father of the Bengali nation. Two of his sons, Kamal and Jamal, had meanwhile made good their escape from Dhaka and joined the war. The rest of the family was shifted from Mujib's Dhanmondi residence and lodged in a house nearby. With Pakistani soldiers guarding access to the house, his wife, two daughters, of whom the elder was pregnant with her first child, and youngest son, were prisoners in Dhaka.

It was not before 9 August that the Pakistani authorities released any official news about Mujib. A terse announcement from the government informed the country that the Bengali leader would be placed on trial before a special military tribunal on charges of waging war against Pakistan and that the trial would commence two days later, on 11 August. It was given out that A.K. Brohi, a prominent Pakistani lawyer, would defend Mujib at the trial. After that, there was no more news on the trial, which was being conducted in camera, and people in West Pakistan as well as occupied Bangladesh had little idea of how the proceedings were being conducted. It would not be until Mujib was finally freed in January of 1972 that some idea of what had happened at the trial would emerge. There is as yet no record of the defence Mujib put up before the tribunal, though there are good reasons to think he did not recognise the legitimacy of the court. Having called for Bangladesh's independence only moments before his arrest on 25 March, he certainly could not have defended himself as a loyal Pakistani, unlike the position he had adopted at the Agartala trial three years earlier.

Mujib also refused to accept Brohi as his defence counsel on the ground that he had been given little choice in the matter of choosing his lawyer. But he did ask that Kamal Hossain, his constitutional advisor at the March talks with the regime and Bhutto, be allowed to defend him. The court demurred and told him that it was not possible for Kamal Hossain to speak for him. The shrewd Mujib gathered, from that nugget of information that the young lawyer must have been taken into custody as well. As Mujib would later narrate the story, the regime went to every possible length to convince Kamal Hossain to turn accuser by providing evidence against his leader, a suggestion he spurned. But if Kamal Hossain, who on the suspicion that he had become a turncoat at Mujib's secret trial was being regularly berated on the Shwadhin Bangla Betar, other Bengalis (among whom were two journalists for whom Mujib had particular affection) turned up to damn him before the tribunal. Despite his move to grant amnesty to members of the national and provincial assemblies and thereby secure their cooperation in restoring normal conditions in East Pakistan, Yahya made it clear that Mujib was not on the list of those being considered for pardon. At one point, speaking to a Western television channel, the president made the egregious remark that were he to free Mujib, his own Bengalis would kill him for all the misery he had caused them.

On 1 September, General Tikka Khan, who had since 25 March been serving as both governor of East Pakistan (Justice B.A. Siddiky had finally sworn him in under duress in the changed circumstances) and zonal martial-law administrator, relinquished both offices and left for West Pakistan to join as a corps commander in Rawalpindi. Into the office of governor stepped the Bengali Dr Abdul Motalib Malik. He had earlier served as minister for health in Yahya Khan's government and prior to that, in the Ayub Khan years, had been ambassador to countries such as Indonesia. His appointment as governor was an attempt by the regime to demonstrate a return of normality in the province. No one was fooled. Instead, Malik only tarnished his own reputation by accepting the job and quickly began to be reviled as a collaborator of the regime. Tikka Khan was replaced as martial-law administrator by Lieutenant General Amir Abdullah Khan Niazi, a Punjabi noted for his womanising habits and lewd jokes. It was under Niazi that the killing of Bengalis and the kidnap and rape of Bengali women would assume greater dimensions throughout the province.

As the crisis intensified in Bangladesh, with India now massively involved in arming and training the freedom fighters, there appeared to be a particular rush among the authorities to bring Mujib's trial to a speedy conclusion. There was little doubt about the government's intention. It needed a conviction and, in essence, a legally sanctioned opportunity to hang him. In October, Mukti Bahini guerrillas entered the home of former governor Abdul Monem Khan in the exclusive Banani residential area of Dhaka and sprayed him with bullets. Khan was buried hastily in the evening. The next morning, however, his family and friends were shocked to see his body sprawled outside the grave where it had been interred. The freedom fighters had made it plain that he had no place in the soil of Bangladesh. By the third week of November, the Pakistan Army did not only have to combat the Mukti Bahini but also the Indian Army which had begun to shell Pakistani positions across the border in the eastern region of Akhaura and Comilla. The systematic manner in which the Pakistan Army appeared to be pushing Bengali refugees towards India only compounded the situation. Prime Minister Indira Gandhi travelled to Europe and the United States, asking governments there to exercise their influence on Pakistan to stop the killings in Bangladesh. Mrs Gandhi had certainly been fortified by the treaty of friendship and cooperation her country had reached with the Soviet Union earlier in August, a deal which worried both Washington and Islamabad. Yahya Khan knew he had friends he could depend on in Washington. However, the growing belligerence of the Indians caused a multiplicity of fears in the Yahya regime. Fully aware that Mrs Gandhi had refused to be browbeaten in

Washington, the regime now turned to the Chinese. Towards the end of November, a high-powered delegation comprising such individuals as the chief of the air force and the foreign secretary travelled to Beijing under the leadership of Bhutto. For a regime that had so long tried to convey the impression of its being on top of the situation, the choice of Bhutto as leader of the delegation betrayed its nervousness. The PPP leader and former foreign minister was expected, because of his friendship with the Chinese leaders, to come back to Pakistan with Chinese reassurances about standing by Islamabad in any eventuality of military conflict in South Asia. It was a cheerful Bhutto who came back to Islamabad and reported to Yahya Khan, misleading as it turned out, that if India attacked Pakistan, China would mount its own assault on India from the north. Just how precarious a position Pakistan occupied in November 1971 was thus made patent. In order to protect its territory, it needed the Chinese army to divert the attention of the Indian government through a military attack in a manner similar to the assault it had launched on Indian positions in 1962.

Pakistan had been making matters worse for itself. In East Pakistan, its active encouragement to such political parties as the Jamaat-e-Islami in the task of Bengali killings had further alienated the population. The Jamaat, through its murder squads *al-Badr* and *al-Shams*, had actively been helping the military authorities in selecting Bengali nationalist targets from among political workers, civil servants, academics and students to kidnap and kill in the mission of upholding the 'solidarity and integrity' of Pakistan. Other political parties, the various factions of the Muslim League, the Pakistan Democratic Party and Nizam-e-Islam, had become active collaborators of the army and as a consequence, had seen a good number of their workers killed by the Mukti Bahini. A number of right-wing Bengali politicians—Nurul Amin, Moulvi Farid Ahmed, Fazlul Quader Chowdhury, Mahmud Ali, Shah Azizur Rahman, Professor Golam Azam, Hamidul Haq Chowdhury, Moulana Mannan, together with Chakma ruler Raja Tridiv Roy, eagerly linked up with the army and systematically went into the job of undermining the

Bengali nationalist cause. Mahmud Ali was chosen by the regime to lead Pakistan's delegation to the session of the UN General Assembly beginning in September. With him were Shah Azizur Rahman and Syeda Razia Faiz, a former member of the national assembly from the Convention Muslim League. The regime also went exploring the possibility of securing support among Bengali academics and was happy to come across quite a few collaborators, ready and willing to identify with its programme to de-secularise Bengalis. Among such collaborators was Syed Sajjad Hussain, a scholar in English literature whom Tikka Khan had appointed vice chancellor of Dhaka University. Hussain would be sent by the government to argue its case abroad. He would add newer dimensions to the meaning of collaboration with the enemy by his absolute refusal to agree that the Pakistan Army had engaged in any killing. Dr M.O. Ghani, vice chancellor of Dhaka University in the time of Ayub Khan, happily accepted Yahya Khan's offer to be Pakistan's ambassador to Tanzania. Collaborationist elements were found elsewhere as well. Begum Akhtar Suleiman, daughter of Suhrawardy, then residing in Karachi, issued statements, obviously at the behest of the regime, condemning the Awami League for having undermined the state of Pakistan. A member of the provincial assembly from the Awami League, S.B. Zaman, regularly denounced his party, to the delight of the rulers. On the Dhaka station of Radio Pakistan, two Bengali journalists happily scripted and presented an anti-India and anti-Awami League programme they called Plain Truth. For its part, the Pakistani government made public, what it called a White Paper, detailing the many perfidies Mujib and his party had allegedly resorted to at the March negotiations and earlier.

With the Mukti Bahini making steady gains in Bangladesh and India providing overt assistance to it, Pakistan was in a difficult spot. In the west, General Yahya Khan began to believe that a semblance of civilian rule, albeit with the military in charge, would help Pakistanis rally the cause of beating back the Bengali resistance as well as what was given out as Indian aggression. Almost overnight, 'Crush India' posters began to appear in West Pakistan. In East Pakistan, there was not much time for such elaborate propaganda as General Niazi and his forces were forced into a defensive posture against gains of the Mukti Bahini. The man who was known to his men as Tiger Niazi found it hard to live up to the old reputation.

In Mianwali, sometime in early December, Mujib's trial before the special military tribunal drew to a close, with the verdict still to be announced. On 3 December, the Pakistan Air Force strafed Indian cities in the western sector, thereby signalling the formal beginning of a war that would hasten the end for Pakistan. The Indians had obviously been prepared for such an eventuality, as their vigorous response to the attack was soon to demonstrate. Prime Minister Indira Gandhi, then on a visit to the Bengali refugee camps in West Bengal, rushed back to Delhi to inform her country that for the third time since the Partition, India and Pakistan were at war. The difference between the two earlier wars and the new one was that in 1971, the bone of contention was not Kashmir but the freedom struggle of the people of Bangladesh. Within days of the declaration of war, Pakistan reeled from the Indian attacks. Its air force in East Pakistan was systematically destroyed in the air as well as on the ground. In the west, Indian forces penetrated deep into Pakistani territory and its jet fighters pounded Karachi. The beginning of hostilities was also the point at which President Yahya Khan sought to provide a civilian facade to his regime. Rather too late in the day, and with the wrong people, he appointed Nurul Amin, the Bengali politician who had supported the military action in East Pakistan, as prime minister. For good measure, the president also placed Bhutto in the government as deputy prime minister and foreign minister. The gimmick was not destined to work and almost everyone in Pakistan and outside comprehended the absolute absence of credibility involved in the new arrangements. But Yahya Khan did send off Bhutto to the UN Security Council, which had begun debating the conflict, in the hope that the politician could save through diplomacy what the army was losing through war in both wings of the country.

As the war progressed, the Indian government officially announced its recognition of Bangladesh as a sovereign nation on 6 December. The Indian move was followed by a similar act by the tiny Himalayan kingdom of Bhutan. Sometime between 6 December and the end of the war, Mujib was sentenced to death by the military tribunal. In Dhaka, as it became increasingly apparent that the Pakistan Army was collapsing in its eastern province, Governor Malik and his ministers took shelter in a bunker in the compound of the governor's official residence. Frightened and shaking all over, Malik drafted his resignation on the inside of a cigarette packet and handed it to the chief of the UN mission in Dhaka for onward transmission to President Yahya Khan in Rawalpindi. Even as Malik and his ministers were conducted to the safety of Hotel Intercontinental, declared a neutral zone by the International Committee of the Red Cross, General Niazi appeared before the media to dispel rumours that he had escaped to West Pakistan. The Indian forces, he declared with typical bravado, would have to take Dhaka over his dead body.

The most scandalous act perpetrated by the army and its local Bengali collaborators in the final hours of Pakistan in Bangladesh was the careful, systematic picking up of leading Bengali intellectuals from in and around the city, between 13 and 15 December, by the murder squads of the Jamaat-e-Islami and the brutal manner of their killing. Their bodies, blindfolded and with hands and feet tied, were dumped at the brick kilns of Rayerbazar and were only discovered a day after Bangladesh emerged as a free state. At the UN, as Pakistan tried desperately to have India agree to a ceasefire, one resolution after another was introduced to bring about an end to the conflict. The Bangladesh government in exile, now sensing the arrival of independence a lot earlier than it had anticipated, certainly did not want a ceasefire that would allow the Pakistanis to hold on to chunks of Bangladesh territory as leverage for future negotiations aimed at undermining Bengali independence. The Indians clearly obliged, with considerable help from the Soviet Union. As one of the five permanent members of the Security Council, Moscow vetoed every resolution in favour of a ceasefire and clearly had little desire to put a stop to the Mukti Bahini-Indian Army advance towards Dhaka. The strategy worked.

On the afternoon of 16 December, General Niazi along with 93,000 soldiers of the Pakistan Armed Forces surrendered to the joint command of Indian and Bangladesh forces, led by General Jagjit Singh Aurora, at the Race Course in Dhaka. Tens of thousands of Bengalis poured out on the streets to welcome the arrival of freedom. Nine months after the launch of a genocide that had left three million Bengalis dead and its villages, towns and infrastructure destroyed, Bangladesh was finally a free republic. All over the country, young men emerged with posters of Mujib, a clear assertion of the pre-eminent role he had played in the liberation of the country. As the Father of the Nation, he was held in deep veneration. And yet, in that moment of historic triumph, no one in Bangladesh had the foggiest idea whether he was alive or had been put to death in Pakistan.

The Indian Army did not stop its advance into West Pakistan even as Bangladesh was formed on 16 December. There were all the reasons to assume that the Indians were in a position to move deeper and bring about the total collapse of Pakistan. It was a flurry of messages from the Nixon administration to the Soviet leadership in Moscow that ultimately influenced Prime Minister Indira Gandhi into announcing a unilateral ceasefire on the western front on 17 December. Meanwhile, moments after Pakistan Television had telecast images of General Niazi's surrender in Dhaka, Pakistanis in Rawalpindi, Peshawar and other cities went on a rampage demanding the ouster of the junta and its punishment. For a nation which had over the past nine months been led to believe in the superior quality of its army as well as in the fact that the government was in absolute control of East Pakistan, the surrender of the military and the emergence of Bangladesh was a rude awakening.

Left with little choice, Yahya Khan summoned Bhutto, who had dramatically stormed out of the UN Security Council in New York as Dhaka appeared close to falling to the Bengali guerrillas and the

Indian Army, back to Rawalpindi. Bhutto returned on 20 December and was escorted straight from the airport to the president's house. He was in discussion with Yahya Khan and the rest of the junta for several hours. By the time he emerged from the meeting, he was the new president of Pakistan. Ironically for a man who had won a majority of seats in the national assembly from West Pakistan at the December 1970 elections, Bhutto also took over Yahya Khan's other responsibility, that of chief martial-law administrator. In the course of his negotiations over the transfer of power, he rejected Yahya Khan's suggestion that he be allowed to execute, as a final act, the death sentence earlier handed down to the imprisoned Mujib. Such a move, Bhutto told the disgraced military ruler, would finish off any chances the country might have of getting back its defeated soldiers, who were now prisoners of war (POW), from Bangladesh. Thwarted, the president handed over charge of what remained of Pakistan to the chairman of the PPP. Minutes later, as the country's new chief, Bhutto placed Yahya Khan and his fellow generals in the junta under house arrest.

Late in the evening of 20 December, President Zulfikar Ali Bhutto spoke to Pakistanis over radio and television. The speech lacked substance, with the new leader trying to impress upon his audience the idea that 'East Pakistan' was under enemy occupation and would be recovered soon in the interest of 'our brothers', by which he clearly referred to the Bengalis. He promised to build a new Pakistan out of the ashes of the old and also announced a certain amount of restructuring in the armed forces. The title of commander-in-chief, he told Pakistanis, would henceforth not exist and instead the chiefs of the army, air force and navy would be known by the more humble sounding title of chief of staff. By the time Bhutto finished, he felt a mixture of triumph and gloom within him. The triumph was in the reality of his having finally made it to the leadership of Pakistan. The gloom came in the knowledge that a long, arduous struggle lay ahead of him in a fulfilment of the task he had set for himself. In every sense of the meaning, East Pakistan was gone, though he still entertained the faint hope that he could work out something with Mujib, who was now his and not Yahya Khan's prisoner. There probably was not much likelihood of that happening, as he well knew. Mujib had certainly not been ready to concede anything in Dhaka nine months earlier and he would surely, once the facts were presented to him, not agree to any compromises now. Bhutto knew that in the next few days, a major priority for him would be to reconnect with the Bengali leader.

Flight to Freedom

On 22 December 1971, the Bangladesh government in exile came home to a liberated country. As the sun went down, Acting President Syed Nazrul Islam and Prime Minister Tajuddin Ahmed, along with the rest of the cabinet and other Awami League political figures, arrived at Dhaka's Tejgaon Airport from Calcutta. The arrival of the government signalled the second significant step in the new nation's history, the first having been the defeat and surrender of the Pakistani Army six days earlier. But the return home from exile was a subdued affair owing largely to the absence of the founding figure of the new country. The acting president told the assembled crowd that Bangladesh's victory would remain incomplete until Mujib was free to return to the country he had led to freedom. He called upon the Pakistani authorities to release Mujib, warning that keeping the leader of the Bengali nation in continued detention would only worsen conditions in the subcontinent.

Unknown to the Mujibnagar leaders, however, on the very day they arrived in Dhaka, Bhutto had ordered Mujib's removal from his cell in Mianwali and transfer to a guest house near Rawalpindi. As Mujib would relate the story to the well-known Indian journalist Kuldip Nayar subsequently, a few days after he had been shifted to the guest house, Bhutto turned up there. It was a thoroughly surprised Mujib who saw Bhutto stride towards him. He yet had no clear conception of what had happened in the country or outside it in all the nine months he had spent in solitary imprisonment in Mianwali. But when for a few days the jailer, a friendly Pakistani who sensed some danger befalling his prisoner in the dying days of the war, had moved him to his own quarters, Mujib guessed that some major developments had taken place. There was little place, however, for the belief that Bangladesh had actually become a free country. Therefore, on that morning when Bhutto called on, Mujib wondered at what might have happened, or gone wrong. As Nayar relives the drama of the moment in *Distant Neighbours: A Tale of the Subcontinent*, on seeing Bhutto arrive at the guest house, Mujib asked him, 'Bhutto, how are you here?' The new leader of Pakistan replied, 'I am the president of Pakistan.' The incredulity in the Bengali leader at Bhutto's revelation was unmistakable. There was a bigger surprise in the answer to his next question, 'How can that be? You know that position belongs to me.' Mujib's claim on the presidency was a legitimate one, only he did not know of the circumstances that had placed Bhutto in power. 'As if to frighten me,' Mujib later told Nayar, 'Bhutto said, "I am also chief martial-law administrator."' That was the beginning of a new phase in the lives of the two men whose political differences had thrown up an entirely new equation in South Asia.

Over the next few days, Mujib and Bhutto met over several rounds of talks at the guest house. The Bengali politician, still a prisoner of the Pakistan government, did not fail to understand the subtle pressure Bhutto was trying to exercise on him. Pakistan's new president did not appear to have acquainted him with the full details of the circumstances that had overtaken Pakistan after 25 March. He confined himself to explanations of how the Indian government had taken advantage of the breakdown in the Dhaka negotiations to send its forces marching into East Pakistan. But he did refer, without going into details, the presence of an administration in Dhaka now led by Mujib's close political associates. Bhutto's overriding purpose in talking to Mujib was clearly one of extracting certain undertakings from him about the future state of relations between East Pakistan and West Pakistan, as he still referred to the broken country. Mujib, who was once again assisted by Dr Kamal Hossain (the lawyer had been brought out of his own confinement and reunited with his leader), told Bhutto that he could not make any promises until he was free to return to Dhaka and judge conditions for himself. Deep in his heart, though, Mujib was well aware of the fact that a sweeping transformation had come over the political scenario. Whether it was a free Bangladesh waiting for him out there he did not know. Neither did he know of the millions of lives lost and the devastation wrought upon his country. The fact that the crisis had spawned an international uproar, that the Indians had thoroughly mauled Pakistan in war was unknown to him. Mujib wanted to know from Bhutto whether he was a free man. Bhutto's affirmative response came with the information, again with a view to creating a good impression for himself—of how he had prevailed upon General Yahya Khan to refrain from hanging the Bengali leader. But on the issue of Mujib's departure from Pakistan, its new leader was of the opinion that he needed to prepare his people, traumatised as they had been by the turn of events in the country's eastern province, for the Awami League leader's release. Mujib, of course, understood Bhutto's predicament and agreed to give the latter the leeway he needed.

On the afternoon of 3 January 1972, as a rising chorus of demands from Bangladesh and elsewhere rose for Mujib's freedom, Bhutto rose to address a public rally in Karachi. He meandered through his speech, the understandable goal being to rekindle faith in the crowd about the future. After the customary noises had been made and populist bugles sounded, Bhutto explained the situation relating to Mujib's captivity in Pakistan. Knowing as he did that Pakistanis were at that point ready to go along with whatever he decided about the future, Bhutto nevertheless resorted to drama once more. He worked up the assembled crowd by saying clearly that he would not go against their wishes, that indeed his government was a people's government that had brought an end to dictatorship. As the crowd cheered, Bhutto raised the question: 'Do you allow me to free Mujib?' Predictably, his audience roared its approval. Relieved at the response, though he had never doubted it would be thus anyway, the president thanked the crowd three times. The people of Pakistan, he was quick to remind everyone present, had taken a huge burden off his shoulders.

Four days later, late in the evening of 7 January, President Bhutto accompanied Mujib and Kamal Hossain to Chaklala Airport in Rawalpindi, from where the Bengali leader would fly out of Pakistan. It had been agreed that Mujib would fly to London, though Bhutto had earlier suggested that he travel to Tehran and from there make his way to Dhaka. Mujib's preference had, of course, been for a direct flight to the capital of Bangladesh but Bhutto did not appear too keen on it. One of the reasons could be that it was too early yet for an aircraft of the PIA to travel to Dhaka. Another and more probable reason was that it was Bhutto's intention that Mujib survey the situation from neutral territory before making up his mind about his future course of action. Having known the Bengali leader for years, it was certainly naïve on Bhutto's part to entertain the notion that Mujib would have second thoughts, if any, about the course his people had taken.

It was a silent farewell that Bhutto and Mujib bade each other. The two men who had dominated politics in Pakistan for the better part of the past decade or so had now found the means to go their separate ways, as leaders of their independent countries. Pakistan's new president knew that it was the president of an independent Bangladesh he was sending off to freedom that evening. Mujib walked briskly up the gangway. He must have wondered at yet another momentous turn in his life. Nine months ago, he had been brought to Pakistan as a prisoner, with little hope that he would ever return home. And now he was free to go home. Pakistan, as soon as the PIA aircraft took off, was finally behind him. With Mujib and the Kamal Hossain family on the plane were officers from the Pakistan Air Force and PIA, responsible for escorting the Bangladesh leader safely to London.

Early in the morning on 8 January 1972, Heathrow Airport security scrambled to receive the aircraft carrying Mujib. The news of his impending arrival had already been passed on to the Foreign and

Commonwealth Office. For M.M. Rezaul Karim, the Bengali diplomat who had only months earlier defected from the Pakistani Foreign Service to be part of his country's independence struggle, it was sheer disbelief. He took out his own small car and drove furiously towards Heathrow. Arriving there and quite out of breath, he entered the VIP lounge to find Mujib standing with his trademark pipe between his lips. Also present were Dr Kamal Hossain and his family as well as the Pakistani officers who had accompanied Bangladesh's leader on the long flight from Rawalpindi. Once the officers knew that a Bangladesh diplomat had arrived to take charge of Mujib, they stood up, saluted and left without a word. As for Mujib, his excitement appeared to be greater than Karim's. The founding father of Bangladesh was relieved and happy to see the diplomat and without much ado began pelting him with questions. 'Rezai Karim'—he would always say 'Rezai' rather than 'Rezaul'—'is it true that Bangladesh is really a free country?' In later years, Karim was to look back at the sheer nervousness he felt as he kept answering Mujib while keeping an eye on the road, as Mujib had opted to travel with the diplomat in his car instead of the assigned government vehicle.

News of Mujib's arrival in London spread quickly. Journalists, the general public, British officials and politicians and Bengali residents in the city made their way to Claridges. After a quick huddle with Rezaul Karim and other Bengali diplomats, among whom was the young Mohiuddin Ahmed, he welcomed people who had come to see him. Everyone cheered the political figure who had paved the road to Bangladesh's freedom. News bulletins on the BBC and other media organisations made note of the Bengali leader's arrival in their headlines. By early afternoon, Mujib had met Prime Minister Edward Heath and opposition Labour leader Harold Wilson. He called Dhaka and for the first time since his arrest by the Pakistan Army in March, spoke to his family. A long conversation then followed with Prime Minister Tajuddin Ahmed. The conversations with his family and with Tajuddin were emotional affairs, but they nevertheless left Mujib thrilled. He now had a clear picture of all that had happened in his absence in Bangladesh. It gave him immense satisfaction knowing that he had truly liberated his people.

Mujib's opening words at a crowded news conference that evening at Claridges was a touch poetic. He was happy to share, he said, the unbounded joy of freedom achieved by his people in an epic liberation struggle. Bangladesh, he told the assembled crowd, was a reality and would fulfil its obligations as part of the international community. Asked why he had decided to come to London instead of going home directly from Pakistan, he retorted, 'The decision was made by Mr Bhutto. I was his prisoner.' But Mujib also made use of the opportunity to convey his gratitude to Pakistan's leader for saving his life. He then related the story of how Bhutto had prevented Yahya Khan from ordering his execution before handing over Pakistan's presidency to the PPP leader. For all his gratefulness to Bhutto, however, Mujib was not at all ambivalent about his own plans. He made the emphatic statement that Bangladesh would have nothing to do with Pakistan anymore. He wished Pakistan well and hoped that it in turn would wish Bangladesh the same. The Bangladesh leader made special mention of India, to whose prime minister and people he was thankful for the moral and material support they had provided to the people of Bangladesh. On the question of the genocide, he made it clear that the officers of the Pakistan Army would be tried for war crimes by his government.

Mujib left London for Dhaka in the evening of 9 January 1972. On the way he would stop over in Delhi to convey his personal thanks to Prime Minister Indira Gandhi and other Indian leaders for their assistance to Bangladesh. He was welcomed at Delhi's Palam Airport in the morning of 10 January by President Verahagiri Venkata Giri, Prime Minister Indira Gandhi, West Bengal Chief Minister Siddhartha Shankar Ray and the chiefs of the Indian Armed Forces. Also on hand was Abdus Samad Azad, the new Bangladesh foreign minister sent to the Indian capital to escort him home. Mujib stayed in Delhi for about two hours, in the course of which he addressed a public rally where he was profuse in his thanks to Mrs Gandhi and the people of India for the tremendous help they had provided to the Bangladesh struggle, especially the sanctuary given to the ten million Bengalis who had fled their homes when the genocide began in March.

Then it was on to Dhaka, where millions had begun to crowd before the airport and line the road leading from it to the Race Course, where Mujib was expected to speak before joining his family at home. On the tarmac at the Tejgaon Airport, badly damaged by Indian bombing during the war but sufficiently restored to welcome Bangladesh's founder home, soldiers of the Indian Army and the Mukti Bahini were on standby to present Mujib with his first ever guard of honour as Bangladesh's president. Members of the wartime cabinet waited in the winter sun, as did a horde of newsmen. Sometime after 1:30 pm the Comet aircraft made available to Mujib by the British government in London landed in Dhaka.

As soon as the doors of the aircraft opened, the discipline that had so long been maintained on the tarmac swiftly came apart. The young student leaders who had in March 1971 played a pivotal role in pushing the message of independence forward went inside the plane and moments later emerged with a tired looking Mujib. It was clear he had lost weight in prison and had aged unmistakably in the nine months away from home. A grin played on his face as he swept back his hair with his right hand. Prime Minister Tajuddin Ahmed then moved forward and buried his head in his leader's chest. Both men broke down. Their tears soon led to moist eyes in nearly everyone else present around them. Colonel Osmany had his men clear the area somewhat for Mujib to inspect a guard of honour. Once the formalities at the airport were completed, Mujib climbed aboard an open truck, with the Mujibnagar government figures and the firebrand student leaders crowding around him, and headed for the Race Course. The two mile stretch of road would take the procession almost three hours to cover. At the Race Course, Mujib wept at remembrance of the sacrifices Bengalis had made in the war against Pakistan. He told the million strong crowd how the military junta had tried to intimidate him during his trial. 'I told them I was a Bengali and a Muslim, who only dies once.' He had defied the men who had put him on trial and had been ready to walk to the gallows with his head held high. He then referred to Bhutto, to let him know that Bengalis had earned their freedom and would have nothing more to do with Pakistan. The people of Bangladesh, declared the nation's founding father, had acquitted themselves well. They had become the golden children of a Golden Bengal. Quoting the poet Rabindranath Tagore, who once had complained that the people of Bengal had remained mere Bengalis but were yet to become true human beings, Mujib told the jubilant crowd that the poet had been proved wrong. 'Come back, O poet,' he intoned dramatically, 'and see how your Bengalis are today transformed into worthy men.'

Moments later, as dusk and the winter haze settled over Dhaka, Mujib made his way back to his family, who waited for him at the house in Dhanmondi where they had been kept under house arrest by the Pakistan Army throughout the course of the war of liberation.

PART
6

In Power

Two days after Mujib returned to Dhaka, he decided that the country would adopt a Westminster-style government for itself and that he would be its prime minister. Those who had secretly hoped that Mujib would take upon himself the role of founding father, in the mould of Mahatma Gandhi in India, were disappointed. Having been in the forefront of the Bengali struggle for self-expression for nearly a quarter of a century, Mujib was not willing to have anyone else in the driver's seat. He was thus, in a way, emulating Pakistan's Mohammad Ali Jinnah who, despite being governor general, went on to demonstrate the inordinate authority he gave himself over his prime minister. Moreover, Jinnah also saw to it that he was president of the Muslim League as well as president of the constituent assembly. In the case of Mujib, it was quite clear that he would not be content to remain president of Bangladesh, a position to which he had been placed at the time of the establishment of the provisional government in April of the preceding year. His lifelong political activism precluded any notion of his being a figurehead, either as president or as one following in the footsteps of Gandhi. Thus, on 12 January 1972, when Mujib stepped down from the ceremonial office of the presidency and took charge as prime minister, he could not but remain chief of the Awami League as well. In the Westminster system that would be the norm and he was not willing to move away from it.

triumphed over the erratic National Awami Party leader Moulana Bhashani. He had proved to be a far better strategist than all of them. A common thread of thought making the rounds in the early days of Bangladesh revolved around the possibility of how things might have gone wrong had he not returned from imprisonment in Pakistan, and had in fact been executed by the Yahya Khan regime. To a large extent, it was true that after liberation, the Mujibnagar government was worried about the law and order situation. None of the freedom fighters agreed to give up the weapons and only when guerrillas like Kader Siddiqui publicly killed some Urdu speaking Biharis, who had allegedly collaborated with the Pakistan Army, did the precarious condition under which Tajuddin Ahmed and his colleagues tried to work come to light. Worsening the situation was the absolute defiance coming from the young radicals who had opposed Tajuddin all the way in Mujibnagar. Moni, Tofail Ahmed and others still harboured the notion that the wartime prime minister had come by his position through usurpation. It was with a huge sense of relief, therefore, that Mujib's arrival in Dhaka was greeted. Tajuddin certainly hoped that the presence of the nation's supreme leader would make it far easier for him to tackle such areas as the economy, which had gone haywire.

It was reasonable on Tajuddin's part to expect to be allowed to carry on as prime minister given the record he had already established as a wartime leader. Bengali civil society as a whole thought that with Tajuddin remaining prime minister, Mujib would confine himself to the role of a figurehead, a meaningful one at that. That was, of course, not the way things turned out to be. Once Mujib had taken over as prime minister, Tajuddin Ahmed was handed responsibility of finance, a job he was well qualified to do owing not only to his background as a student of economics but also to his thorough understanding of politics as a whole. Syed Nazrul Islam moved from being acting president to being minister for industries. Abdus Samad Azad remained foreign minister. Moshtaq, over the next few years, would serve as water resources as well as commerce minister. In that early phase of Bangladesh's independent existence, Dr Kamal

Hossain was appointed law minister, his specific task at that point being the framing of a constitution for the country. Mujib was not willing to repeat the Pakistani mistake of spending years over framing the constitution and then seeing the initiative slipping from the hands of the Awami League government. Mizanur Rahman Chowdhury came in as minister for relief and rehabilitation, with Abdul Mannan and Professor Yusuf Ali stepping in as minister for home affairs and education, in that order. Mujib decided to keep quite a few porfolios, such as the establishment division and defence, in his own hands. As he set out to stamp his authority on the country, the prime minister told Bengalis that he would need three years to get things back in order. Over the next three years he repeated at the rallies he addressed throughout Bangladesh, there should be no expectation of a miracle on the part of the population. Having gone through the trauma of war, Bengalis were only too willing to give their leader the time he needed to set conditions right for them.

One of the earliest tasks facing the government was the matter of handling the Pakistani POW, who had meanwhile been shifted to POW camps in India through a deal with Bangladesh, as well as dealing with the local right-wing elements who, in their role as quislings for the Pakistan Army, had engaged in systematic kidnapping, killing and raping of the local population. At the same time, Mujib was worried that unless the Indian Army left Bangladesh, the country's independent status would come under a cloud abroad. The Pakistani government of President Bhutto had already embarked on its mission of portraying the emergence of Bangladesh as a result of Indian machinations. He was finding some rather good listeners in China, Saudi Arabia and Libya, countries that had remained hostile to Bangladesh throughout the war.

In February 1972, Mujib travelled to Calcutta, where he met Mrs Gandhi. Those who recall the meeting have often related the tale of how the Bangladesh leader bluntly but politely asked the Indian prime minister when she would be taking her soldiers home. Gandhi's reply was that she would do it whenever Mujib wanted it. And then, on her own she suggested 17 March as a possible date. Mujib would be fifty-two on 17 March. If the soldiers did go back days before the scheduled date, making it possible for Mrs Gandhi to be in Dhaka on 17 March, there remained the question of how Bangladesh and India would handle the Pakistani POWs issue. The Indian authorities, for reasons of security, had transported all the POWs, military as well as civilians, to India but clearly were not in a position to free them or strike a deal with the Pakistan government without a clearance from Mujib and his administration. Mujib had already declared his objective of putting the soldiers on trial in Bangladesh on charges of genocide. At nearly every rally he addressed following his return home, he reiterated his intention, thereby convincing Bengalis that the army which had run riot in 1971 in their country would soon be facing the consequences of their actions.

But Mujib's plans would soon run into serious difficulties. President Bhutto, himself under immense pressure in Pakistan to have the prisoners freed and brought back home, made it clear that Bangladesh would be making matters hard for itself if it went ahead with the trial. There were, after all, as many as 100,000 Bengalis, all working for the central government as well as the armed forces, stranded in Pakistan at the time. Any move by the Bangladesh authorities to place Pakistan's soldiers on trial would, therefore, lead to a risk of the Bengalis in Pakistan facing danger. But for Mujib, matters were simpler than what Bhutto made them out to be. In Bangladesh, 250,000 Urdu speaking Biharis, Muslim refugees from Bihar who had settled in East Pakistan in the aftermath of the Partition and who had identified with the Pakistan administration in the war of 1971, had been given the option of adopting Bangladesh citizenship or going over to Pakistan. Almost all of them, with stray exceptions, chose the latter course. In terms of Mujib's arithmetic, these Biharis, euphemistically referred to as stranded Pakistanis, would be exchanged for the Bengalis in Pakistan.

As far as his government was concerned, the soldiers were an entirely different issue. Predictably he refused to cave in to the threat that Bhutto held out. As he went about repeating his arguments for a trial, his government enacted the Collaborators' Act that would serve as the legal mechanism for a criminal prosecution of those Bengalis who had cooperated with the Pakistan Army in the killings of 1971. Most of the collaborators belonged to the Jamaat-e-Islami, which had played an instrumental role in the creation of such squads as al-Badr and al-Shams, collectively known as *Razakars*. In addition to the Jamaat, right-wing political parties such as the various factions of the Muslim League, Nurul Amin's Pakistan Democratic Party and the Nizam-e-Islam had also been active associates of the army, which could only mean that a large number of their leaders and workers would face legal action under the Collaborators' Act. Some prominent right-wing politicians, among whom were Khan Abdus Sabur Khan and Fazlul Quader Chowdhury, had already been jailed. Both men, who had been part of Ayub Khan's government, had been vociferous supporters of the army. The last governor of East Pakistan, A.M. Malik, and his ministers had already been moved from the neutral zone of the Intercontinental Hotel to Dhaka Central Jail. But some others the government would have liked to place on trial had gone missing, either dead or absconding. Moulvi Farid Ahmed, a scholarly Islamist politician and chief of the Nizam-e-Islam party, was never traced after 16 December. The general assumption was that he had been killed by the victorious Mukti Bahini soon after the Pakistani surrender.

Nurul Amin, appointed Pakistan's prime minister as a last-ditch attempt by Yahya Khan in early December to save East Pakistan, was stranded in Pakistan. Like him, Professor Ghulam Azam of the Jamaat-e-Islami and Mahmud Ali, who had led Pakistan's delegation to the UN in September 1971, found themselves away from home in Islamabad. In subsequent weeks, the Bangladesh government, having already proscribed all right-wing religion-oriented political parties in the country, would deprive these men, along with a few others, of citizenship rights in the new country. Nurul Amin, appointed by Bhutto to the largely ceremonial post of vice president, would eventually die in Pakistan and be buried beside Mohammad Ali Jinnah. Mahmud Ali, who would never waver in his belief that 'East Pakistan' would return to the fold of Pakistan, would serve a number of years as a minister in the Bhutto government. Raja Tridiv Roy, after a stint as a minister in Bhutto's administration, would serve Islamabad as ambassador to quite a few countries. In the Chittagong Hill Tracts of Bangladesh, where he had been chief of the Chakma tribe until 1971, he would be replaced by his young son Debashish Roy.

The most immediate problem for the government concerned the restoration of infrastructure in the country. During the war, hundreds of bridges and culverts had been destroyed, mostly by the Mukti Bahini to prevent troop movements by the Pakistan Army. For its part, the military had razed a number of towns and villages which in early 1972 presented a picture of desolation. Railway tracks had been uprooted in a number of areas; Dhaka Airport was yet in need of repairs and Chittagong Port was riddled with mines that eventually would force the government to appeal to the Soviet Union for help in bringing conditions back to normal. In the course of the nine months of the war, education had also taken a mauling with students either staying away from classes or moving off to join the resistance. A good number of teachers at all levels of education had been killed or had gone missing in the war.

An extremely serious problem for the new country was the chaos that marked its civil administration in those early days. With not much of a trained civil service, except for the erstwhile East Pakistan provincial civil service and a few members of the Pakistan central civil service, Bangladesh was in acute need of experienced personnel to run its administrative structure. Years after liberation, an Awami League politician who would serve as a minister of state in the Mujib government would reflect on the fact that the circumstances thrown up by the war created a situation where not many people knew how the country should be going about conducting diplomatic relations with the outside world. Bengalis had never been a strong presence in the Pakistani diplomatic structure; the handful of diplomats who had thrown in their lot with the government in exile, were largely officers at the junior levels.

A similar condition prevailed in the military. With the exception of Colonel Osmany, who despite his seniority in the Pakistan Army had repeatedly been superseded in the matter of promotions, while all other army officers remained at the level of majors during the war. With the arrival of independence, the Mujib government sent off Osmany into retirement before co-opting him as minister for shipping and inland waterways in January. In his place as chief of the army came Colonel Safiullah, who like his deputy Colonel Ziaur Rahman, had been a major in the freedom struggle. A similar condition defined the hierarchy in the air force and the navy. The police force, battered in the war, was in urgent need of rebuilding. The paramilitary East Pakistan Rifles, largely assigned to border duties in the old days, went on doing the same job, though under a new name as the Bangladesh Rifles.

In the early stages of freedom, the government went in for populism as a policy. The Awami League, never having been a revolutionary party, realised after the war that it had ended up causing a revolution in the country and so would need to demonstrate its belief that it was aligned with popular expectations. The fact that it was still a middle-class organisation, that its members and followers were bourgeoisie, did not seem to matter, though its critics pointed out, even at that stage, that there was a huge gap between what the Awami League was, and what it pretended to be. Some of the student leaders who had been vociferous fans of Mujib before and during the war now demanded that he form a government of national unity given that the War of Liberation had been an inclusive affair with Bengalis from all sides of the spectrum, and not just the Awami League, taking part in it. Indeed, the participation of non-Awami League politicians in the war—and prominent among them were Moulana Bhashani, Professor Muzaffar Ahmed of the pro-Soviet NAP, and the elderly Moni Singh of the CPB—had been a pointer to the broad nature of the struggle. All these three politicians had been part of an all-party advisory group during the war, but it was evident their role was more a formality than a direct involvement with the course of the war.

The Awami League made sure that the initiative never slipped from its hands, though Tajuddin Ahmed, socialist as he was, may have welcomed a larger role for people coming from outside the Awami League. He was himself in a state of siege, which clearly precluded any forceful role he might have been able to play in ensuring a bigger piece of action for non-Awami Leaguers. The trouble with the demand for a national government in early 1972 was, therefore, not that it was being raised, but that the Awami League was not willing at all to entertain the notion. There were the many instances when the arrogance of Awami League ministers and parliamentarians was not missed. The attitude on the part of the party towards appropriating credit for the successful conduct of the war was understandable, but in the developing economic crisis in the country it did not go down well with many people. Such growing disillusionment was compounded by the patent incompetence that was beginning to undermine political and administrative work throughout the country. At industries like the gigantic Adamjee jute mills in Narayanganj, nationalisation was running into problems. Absence of good management was glaring.

Yet the Mujib government's move towards nationalising all banks and large-scale industries in Bangladesh in the early stages of independence had been made with considerable justification as a way of substantiating the nature of the state being a people's republic. In the excitement of liberation, the chasm that separated such radical nationalisation from the constitutionalism the Awami League had all along applied as its political belief, was not really given adequate thought. The public impression was that with Mujib ordaining such a fundamental restructuring of the system, everything would turn out well in the end. Mujib's popularity was what kept the government going, though the same could not be said of many of his colleagues. It was a time when Mujib's word was clearly law. His status as the father of the nation gave him a unique advantage over everyone else. When he decreed that the four fundamental principles of policy, democracy, secularism, socialism and nationalism would determine the political course for the country, the public response was enthusiastic.

Mujib was determined that Bangladesh would be a complete turning away from the Pakistani legacy of communal politics through its emphasis on secular democracy. It was thus that for the first time since the division of India in 1947, religious minorities in Bangladesh found themselves being treated at par with the majority Muslim segment of the population. The overriding objective of the government was the promotion of a nationalistic Bengali spirit. As an early measure, the government decreed that English-medium education would give way to Bengali, across the country. Considered in seriousness, the move made good sense in that it envisaged the promotion of a common education programme all over Bangladesh. Obviously, the urban elitism that was often the result of education at English-medium missionary schools and colleges was a legacy the government wished to roll back. Much would be made in later years in what would be seen as the damage done to education by the banishment of English. It was not so. The Mujib government never banned a study of English in schools and colleges. It merely sought to remove the disparities that expensive English-medium academic institutions created between the various classes of citizens. Like any other nation, Bengalis were expected in 1972 to reinforce their cultural legacy through educating themselves in their own language, with English remaining a necessary part of the curricula at the appropriate stages in education. But by far the biggest threat to the government was beginning to come from some rather unexpected quarters.

In the months after January 1972, with no real opposition to the Awami League in parliament or outside, it fell to Bhashani to voice the earliest of grievances against the government. But that stance quickly took the shape of communalism in what appeared to be new garb. Having propagated secular politics since he first became associated with the Awami League in 1949, and later in the gathering movement for Bengali autonomy and eventual independence, Bhashani now raised the issue of what he called Muslim Bangla. To the government and the country as a whole, it was a frontal assault on the secular principles which had only recently led to the emergence of Bangladesh. For

Bhashani now to argue for a Bangladesh with emphasis on its Muslim majority population sounded like a reversal of gears for him. It was a particularly risky proposition at a time when the state was engaged in strengthening the foundations of the Westminster-style democracy upon which it would work. Bhashani's gimmick, as the government and its well wishers saw it, was in the circumstances about to serve as fresh ammunition for those quarters in Bangladesh who had never reconciled themselves to the break-up of Pakistan. But for observers of Bhashani's brand of politics, the Muslim Bangla idea was vintage moulana. His reputation for unpredictability, indeed melodrama had always been part of his political character. The mercurial nature in Bhashani certainly did not help matters. It was in such a context that his demand for a Muslim Bangla in 1972 was assessed, though his unpredictable nature this time could not but increase the dangers for Mujib. The prime minister was of the emphatic view that Bhashani was playing into the hands of Bangladesh's enemies, internal as well as external. The harsh language that went into the weekly newspaper, *Haq Kotha* that Bhashani edited in criticism of the government went into a fuelling of disaffection towards the government. Not all of the allegations hurled at the government were untrue. With his hands already tied with the cumulative problems confronting the government, Mujib would have liked to have Bhashani on his side. The moulana was clearly not willing to oblige.

Apart from the opposition from Bhashani, the Mujib government faced new forms of threats from sections of the media. Early in 1972, Abdus Salam, the respected editor of the *Bangladesh Observer* (the newspaper, the oldest English language daily in the country, had till liberation been known as the *Pakistan Observer* and was owned by the right-wing politician Hamidul Haq Chowdhury) was forced to resign after he suggested in an editorial that the Awami League government was not *de jure* in terms of its authority since it had been elected to frame a constitution for Pakistan. The editorial was seen as an affront to the state, considering that it did not appear to take account of all the developments that had taken place since the elections. What increased

Shaping Foreign Policy

In the strictly political sense, 1972 was a mixed bag for Mujib. Diplomatically, he was ecstatic about the quick pace of recognition being accorded to Bangladesh by nations around the world. The British government was one of the earliest to recognise the country, an act that promptly resulted in Bhutto's decision to take Pakistan out of the Commonwealth. For reasons that had little practical basis, the Pakistani president and his administration did not accept the emergence of the new state, contributing to the continuation of hostilities between the two countries. The Pakistani media went on referring, in a somewhat egregious manner, to the Bangladesh government as the Dhaka authorities, which did not help matters. Moreover, the Bhutto government dispatched anti-Awami League Bengali politicians as emissaries to various countries with the specific objective of influencing them into staying away from recognising the new state. The Saudis would remain hostile to Bangladesh for as long as Mujib lived. The Libyans under Colonel Gaddafi, effusive in its support for Bhutto, effectively meant non-recognition of the Bengali state. And, of course, there was the relentless opposition to Bangladesh by China, which would not only refuse to accord diplomatic recognition to Bangladesh but would veto its efforts to gain membership of the UN for three years in a row.

Having made it known that his country would as a foreign policy practice friendship for all, Mujib did not express his displeasure at

Mujib did not fail to present as a sign of his government's successful pursuit of diplomacy. Where regional alliances or international organisations were concerned, Bangladesh swiftly made its entry into the Commonwealth, the NAM, World Health Organisation, and others. Relations with the Middle East were by and large excellent, with most countries in the region establishing diplomatic ties with the new country. But the Saudis and the Libyans continued to be a problem. Mujib's meeting with Saudi King Faisal at the summit of non-aligned nations in Algiers in 1973 came close to being a shouting match and Mujib was clearly angry at what he saw as an attempt on King Faisal's part to be patronising.

With the Chinese, Mujib adopted a more discreet position. The Bangladesh struggle had been similar to the long battles waged by the Chinese communists against Chiang Kai-shek's nationalists. Given such a similarity in the background of the Bengali War of Liberation and the Chinese movement for revolution, Bangladesh's politicians had been pretty much perturbed at the clear pro-Pakistan position Mao and Zhou En-lai had adopted in 1971. Not even the appeals made in letters sent to the Chinese leadership by Bhashani, considered a good friend of Beijing's, during the war for support to the Bengali cause, elicited any response. In the post-war situation, however, the Bengali leadership remained acutely aware of the need for China and Bangladesh to establish diplomatic links at the earliest.

Tempers flew in Dhaka every time Beijing vetoed its attempt to enter the UN as a member, but Mujib took good care that such displeasure did not emerge in the open. He would need China in future, just as he would need India and the Soviet Union and the United States. Never having expended much time or effort on questions of foreign policy, Mujib discovered, somewhat to his consternation that apart from the domestic crises he was facing, diplomacy was one particular area that needed his direct attention. He was clear in his belief that for Bangladesh to make any impact in the world there was a necessity of adopting policies that underlined its independence in conducting foreign relations.

As part of such a policy, the country had applied for entry into the Commonwealth and been accepted as a member, despite the fact that as a state which had come into being not through gaining independence from the British but through waging war against a Commonwealth country, it was under no obligation to join the club of former colonies. But Mujib needed all the friends he could collect in that critical phase in Bangladesh's history. Much the same outlook defined his view of the Non Aligned Movement (NAM). To the prime minister of Bangladesh, the movement was a formidable group for Third World nations but in need of a larger involvement in global politics. By taking Bangladesh into the organisation, Mujib demonstrated the definitive, all-encompassing nature of the country's foreign policy objectives.

Where Pakistan had never been a part of the NAM but had since its birth pursued a foreign policy unabashedly inclined to friendship with the West, particularly the United States, Bangladesh was opting to be different. The goodwill and support that the Bengalis had come by during the war, to say nothing of the political stature of near mythic proportions that Mujib had achieved, were the perfect grounds on which to disseminate Bangladesh's idealism and goals before the international community. Mujib clearly saw himself as part of a group of statesmen who were heirs to the original founders of the NAM. It was Tito, the president of Yugoslavia, along with India's Indira Gandhi, Egypt's Anwar Sadat and Bangladesh's Mujib who would shape the new perspectives of the NAM. Having come through an ordeal of fire in the years of his struggle in Pakistan, Mujib was now prepared to play his full role on the international stage.

It was such an ambition that manifested itself at the 1973 Algiers summit. Bangladesh's prime minister, having largely confined himself to politics of the rebellious sort in Pakistan, now found himself happily, in the spotlight of the wider world. In the Algerian capital, his interaction with statesmen who had been around for quite a while created a new image for him, one that was not lost on the crowds back home. Fidel Castro, one of the first global leaders to meet him, marvelled at the manner in which the Bangladesh liberation struggle had been shaped before it reached fruition around the personality of a captive Mujib. Anwar Sadat and Mujib clicked instantly, as did Tito and the Bengali leader. The host and chairman of the conference, President Houari Boumeddiene of Algeria, found it easy dealing with Bangladesh's prime minister as did many others. Mujib came back home happy in his new-found international role. He had even gone out of his way to meet the young Muammar Gaddafi, whose backing for Pakistan over the Bangladesh issue had already come in the way of his country's links with the new country. Their meeting was a polite affair, unlike the acrimonious nature of the earlier meeting between the prime minister and the king of Saudi Arabia.

But if 1973 was a time for Bengalis to feel happy about the impression their leader was making in the councils of the world, it was also proving to be a difficult phase in dealing with matters in the immediate vicinity. An impasse seemed to have settled into the atmosphere regarding relations with Pakistan, with particular reference to the POWs. In public, Mujib kept repeating his determination to try Pakistani soldiers for genocide in Bangladesh. Privately, he was under pressure, not only from Bhutto but also, rather unexpectedly, from Mrs Gandhi. Islamabad was stubborn in its view that the POWs could not be tried by Dhaka and unless they were freed, no Bengalis stranded in Pakistan would return to their homeland. Eventually, it was Mujib who blinked first. Instead of keeping up the argument for a wholesale trial of Pakistani military officers for genocide, his government now decided that only 195 officers in the POW camps in India would face prosecution. But even that failed to settle the issue. The Indians now tried gently arm-twisting Bangladesh, the argument being that a quid pro quo was necessary in Dhaka's dealings with Islamabad. With Pakistan refusing to recognise Bangladesh officially, Mujib did not quite see why he should be compelled to go for a rethink on the POW issue. At the same time, he was not prepared to have the issue of the repatriation of the Bengalis from Pakistan linked with the question of the POWs trial. But, as the weeks and months went by, the Bangladesh position progressively weakened, to a point where as a consequence of a tripartite deal involving Pakistan, India and Bangladesh, Dhaka saw all Pakistani POWs going free. Not even the 195 officers slated to be put on trial in Dhaka could be held back. Mujib had little choice in the matter. By the third quarter of 1973, Pakistan's imprisoned soldiers had begun their long journey back home from their camps in India. Simultaneously, the Bhutto administration put into operation its own plan of repatriating the stranded Bengalis to their new country. But in all this exchange of people, the two issues that mattered crucially, the repatriation of the Biharis to Pakistan and a settlement of the question of assets and liabilities of pre-1971 Pakistan, remained untouched. Down the years, Bangladesh would find it increasingly painful to engage successive Pakistani governments in deliberations on them.

The release of the POW was one overt indication of failure of the government. For its enemies who were increasing by the day, that absolute failure to try even a single POW on charges of genocide exposed the administration to charges of pusillanimity. Not even diehard supporters of the prime minister could find it easy to digest what was now a rather unpalatable truth—that the country's foreign policy in so far as it involved South Asia had received a mauling at the hands of Bhutto and his men. The general refrain was that the Pakistani prime minister had, in his drive for a new Pakistan, seized victory from the jaws of defeat, while the Bangladesh leader, with all his compelling moral and political reasons for ensuring justice for his people by trying their tormentors, had slipped. And if the POWs could go free, it would only be a matter of time before their local Bengali collaborators, detained under the Collaborators' Act of 1972 would go free as well. And they did go free in September 1973 when the government announced an amnesty for a significant number of Bengalis detained as quislings of the Pakistani army. Mujib took care to let the country know that no one who had engaged in killing and rape would be released from jail. And yet there were the many instances when collaborators had walked out of prison because there was insufficient evidence to convict them. The problem was not that the men were proved innocent. It was that the cases against them were badly framed and shoddily pursued. As for the release of such prominent Muslim League politicians as Khan Abdus Sabur Khan from prison (Fazlul Quader Chowdhury had died of a cardiac arrest in prison months after his arrest in 1972), the government's explanation lacked substance. The amnesty granted to the collaborators was distinctly damaging. Although the pardon did not lead to a lifting of the ban imposed on right-wing political parties in early 1972 (and the Collaborators' Act stayed in place too), it did open a window to the revival of communal politics in the country.

As long as Mujib lived his brief life these communal elements would stay quiet. But they were biding their time, and would strike at an opportune moment. Their ranks would swell, to the consternation of the country, by the entry into the administration of a section of Bengali officials, now beginning to make their way back to Dhaka from Islamabad. Not all of these officers were swayed by patriotism towards their new country. Many had happily been part of the Pakistani civil service even as many others were moved off to the detention camps in the aftermath of December 1971. The government's failure to put all these officers, as well as a number of returning soldiers through a screening effectively stymied administrative work and proved detrimental.

Mujib's faith in his people, both common citizens and returning officials, was unflinching. It was not for him to contemplate a situation where his own people would need to go through scrutiny before the government could decide whether or not they could be part of Bangladesh. Syed Najmuddin Hashim, a senior Bengali bureaucrat repatriated to Dhaka in 1973, would later relate the stories of the many Bengali officials serving in the Pakistan government unable to contain their criticism of the break-up of Pakistan and yet would subsequently rise to high positions in Bangladesh. Some Bengali diplomats would go on serving in Islamabad until as late as 1974, when the Pakistan government's move to ease them out of their jobs would force them to relocate to Bangladesh. Once in Dhaka, they were swiftly absorbed in the foreign office of the new country. The arrival of officers from the central service of Pakistan was, in that particular perspective, a boon for the government. Much the same argument could be made in respect of the military officers and soldiers who came back, to be absorbed in the armed forces of the new country.

Emerging Cracks

Bangladesh's Constituent Assembly adopted a constitution based on the parliamentary system of government on the first anniversary of liberation in December 1972. In terms of political import, the constitution was a milestone in the history of the country, for it not only reflected a clean break with the past but also demonstrated the universally accepted principles of pluralism and rule of law that the government now presented before the nation as its testament to history. An additional reason why the enactment of the constitution was seen as a triumph for the government was the speed with which it had been formulated, debated and adopted. The contrast with Pakistan was remarkable. Where the Bengalis finally had a constitution by December 1972, the Bhutto government in Pakistan was yet muddling through in its own search for a constitution acceptable to all four provinces of the country. As a result, Pakistan's new constitution, the third in its history, would not be adopted until August 1973.

However, in the year when the Bengalis gave themselves a constitution, politics was beginning to go through a certain measure of permutation and combination. With the Awami League operating unchallenged after the war, largely because there was not much of a parliamentary opposition to speak of, politics initially presented a lacklustre image for itself. Outside parliament, the two factions of the NAP, one led by Moulana Bhashani and the other by Professor Muzaffar Ahmed as well as the Communist Party of Bangladesh (CPB) with Comrade Moni Singh in the forefront, were the only significant political parties that mattered. Worrying though, was the presence of underground extreme leftist parties which as time went by made matters harder for the government. The *Purba Bangla Sarbahara* Party led by Siraj Sikdar, an engineer who had switched to underground politics as a way of preparing for what he believed would be a revolution of the masses, quickly gained strength in the north-western region of the country. Analogous to the Sarbaharas was the presence of the East Pakistan Communist Party (EPCP) of Abdul Haq, which stubbornly refused to acknowledge the emergence of Bangladesh as an independent state, as its very name suggested, and propagated the notion that only armed revolution could dislodge the government of Mujib. The EPCP would turn increasingly bitter in its attitude to the Mujib government. It was telling that its leader Abdul Haq wrote to Pakistan's Bhutto government in 1974 soliciting assistance in removing Sheikh Mujib from power. In its infancy, therefore, the new state found itself compelled to deploy a considerable portion of its strength in steps to suppress these two outfits. The government's worries were not made any easier by the activities of Ziauddin, a major in the army, whose article in the weekly *Holiday* detailing the excesses and corruption of the government caused a major scandal for Mujib. As a serving army officer, Ziauddin had clearly violated service rules by publicly commenting on the state of politics. But when he was asked to retract his views, he refused and promptly went underground from where he would continue to harass the government.

Not all of the problems the government faced were the result of the machinations of its enemies. Within the first year of freedom, the decision to set up a paramilitary force called the Jatiyo Rakkhi Bahini or National Security Force had been made. The move was certainly not looked upon favourably by the fledgling Bangladesh Army, whose officers grumbled that the JRB had been established to keep an eye on the armed forces. Outside the military, opinion was harsher. The force, it was suggested, had come into existence to provide security to the prime minister and his political party. The JRB only increased such suspicions through the particular brutality it deployed in handling dissent in the interior of the country.

In the midst of all such developments, in July 1972 Prime Minister Mujib was invited to the annual conferences of the two factions of the Bangladesh *Chhatra* League, the student front of the Awami League. The Chhatra League, a united body of secular students and a major force behind the mass upsurge of 1969 as well as the build-up to a movement for an independent Bangladesh in March 1971, had within months of liberation split into two factions. With one faction led by Nur-e-Alam Siddiqui and Abdul Kuddus Makhan, the other went into the hands of A.S.M. Abdur Rab and Shahjahan Siraj. Mujib's initial response to the invitations was politically astute. He asked both factions to bridge their differences and go back to being a single entity. When the suggestion did not work or, more specifically, was spurned by the Rab-Siraj group, the prime minister turned up at the rally of the Siddiqui-Makhan faction and thereby effectively put the seal of his preferences.

In hindsight, it is tempting to think that Mujib's patronisation of a faction of the student organisation at the expense of the other may have exacerbated conditions for him. The reaction of the Rab-Siraj group was predictable fury. The two young men, till that point of time fanatical supporters of the prime minister, now perceived a need to go on an offensive against the government. They were fortified in adopting such a position by the strong hold they exercised on the young people, who for better or worse, were drawn to what they saw as the necessary radicalism of the faction. By October, A.S.M. Abdur Rab and Shahjahan Siraj had roped in M.A. Jalil, a former major and freedom fighter who had meanwhile gained a measure of popularity by his opposition to Indian soldiers taking away military hardware from the border areas after liberation, in the job of exploring the prospects of a new political opposition to the government. In this task, all three men were clearly assisted by the brilliant Sirajul Alam Khan, himself a young former student leader and freedom fighter, then in the process of developing his own theories of socialism as a means of defining Bangladesh's perspectives in the future.

A direct fallout of the schism in the Chhatra League in July 1972 was the formation of the *Jatiyo Samajtantrik Dal* (JSD), or National Socialist Party. It quite escaped the notice of the organisers of the party that its English nomenclature was a strong reminder of Adolf Hitler's National Socialists or Nazis in Germany. One reason why the new party faced little embarrassment about how it called itself surely had to do with the fact that it was generally referred to by its Bengali name, JSD or *Jashod*. In their enthusiasm to provide a credible opposition to Mujib, the young leaders of the new party seized upon the catchy but rather misleading theme of 'scientific socialism' as the underlying principle of the JSD. Over the next few months and years, Major Jalil, A.S.M. Abdur Rab and Shahjahan Siraj would wage a relentless, if often misguided, war of attrition against the Awami League. Young people, drawn to the equally youthful leadership of the JSD, would join the party in droves and would eventually come to grief as its leaders lost the way through a series of miscalculations and risky adventures. But in the two years between 1972 and 1974, the growing appeal of the JSD was a matter of worry for the government. Not even Mujib was immune to the phenomenon. At public rallies organised by the Awami League, the prime minister disdainfully described the JSD leaders as callow young men on whose lips their mothers' milk was yet to dry. Such expressions of prime ministerial umbrage did little to help the government, but with an array of problems ranged around it, Mujib and his administration saw conspiracies against them building up everywhere.

The only people with whom the prime minister felt comfortable were the politicians in Professor Muzaffar Ahmed's NAP and Moni Singh's CPB. He would have liked to come by a little more understanding from Bhashani, but the elderly and increasingly cantankerous politician was hardly in the mood to oblige him. In fact, Bhashani now began to berate the prime minister at every rally he addressed and did not forget to remind his audiences that when he was president of the Awami League in the 1950s, Mujib had been only one of the many joint secretaries of the party. It was his way of trying to demonstrate the prime minister's lack of ability to be where he was in politics at that point of time. Other critics of Mujib, notably Oli Ahad, his one-time contemporary in the 1950s, and Amena Begum, the assertive woman who had once been one of his key lieutenants in the Awami League, lost little chance to flail away at the administration's failure to prevent the economy from collapsing. With the prices of essential commodities going up in the market, effectively pushing citizens into a state of desperation, it was of little wonder that politicians like the lawyer Alim al-Razee would point a finger at the prime minister for the gathering confusion in national life.

In public, Mujib gave little hint of the doubts that were beginning to gnaw away at him. Once the constitution had come into force, he decided to go for a fresh mandate from the electorate. The first general elections in independent Bangladesh were set for 7 March 1973. There was symbolism attached to the date. Two years earlier, on 7 March, Mujib had given the call for freedom in what was yet Pakistan. It was now his way of demonstrating the distance he and his people had travelled since those tumultuous times. There was little question that for all the discontent building up around its administration, the Awami League would obtain a massive majority in the Parliament, or *Jatiyo Sangsad* as it came to be known in the Bengali language. The personality of Mujib was yet the biggest asset of the Awami League and was therefore a natural symbolism for the country. When the results came in, the predictions made of a near total sweep by the Awami League turned out to be correct. The party garnered 293 of the 300 seats in parliament. A handful of non-Awami Leaguers, including the JSD's Abdullah Sarkar, won seats in the Jatiyo Sangsad, whose benches promised to be occupied almost fully by the supporters of the prime minister. For all the triumph though, there were a few election related incidents that definitely did not enhance the credibility of the ruling party. Moshtaq, the minister for water resources and a highly unpopular figure, clearly was in danger of losing his seat to his rival in his constituency in Comilla. Soon, however, the entire administrative machinery went into action trying to manipulate the results in his favour. He was duly declared elected to parliament in Dhamrai near

Dhaka. Zealous supporters of the government did not appear ready to accept the victory of the veteran politician and former Awami Leaguer Ataur Rahman Khan. It took Mujib's personal intervention to ensure that Khan's election was not tampered with. After all, with Ataur Rahman Khan, in whose provincial cabinet Mujib had once served as a minister in the 1950s, in parliament, a semblance of an opposition, however minuscule, would be noticeable.

The government which Mujib formed after the 1973 elections remained essentially the same cabinet he had formed in January 1972. The major exceptions were in the shifting of Moshtaq from water resources to commerce and Kamal Hossain from law to foreign affairs. Abdus Samad Azad was moved to agriculture from foreign affairs, with Manoranjan Dhar becoming the new law minister. Food was the responsibility of the elderly Phani Bhushan Majumdar. As the year wore on, however, political violence targeting Awami Leaguers in the rural regions began to take an increasingly ominous shape. Quite a few members of parliament were gunned down. In general, rising crime was proving difficult for the government to control. Mujib's exhortation to businessmen to desist from increasing the prices of food went unheard. His constant warning to hoarders made little impact as rice disappeared from the shops and the government found it necessary to issue food coupons, known as ration cards, to increasing numbers of families in the urban centres of the country. But it was in the villages where the pain of hunger was beginning to be felt stronger than ever.

Already analogies were being drawn to the unprecedented Bengal famine of 1943, though the comparison was unfair as the number of people affected by food shortages in 1973-74 was considerably lower than the three decades previously. But such facts were poor consolation for the government as it came under heavier pressure to check smuggling and the hoarding of food and ensure that enough rice reached the market to keep prices down. Mujib's expectations of help from the United States were to be dashed when Washington chose to have a shipload of foodgrains headed for Chittagong turn back as a punitive measure for Bangladesh's export of jute and jute goods to Cuba. But if Mujib was disappointed with the Americans, he was clearly shocked at the reluctance of his friends in Moscow to come to his country's aid. Apart from a minimal supply of food aid, the Soviet Union did not appear overly keen on bailing Bangladesh out of its difficulties. And, of course, the door to China was yet shut. There was little sign of the Beijing leadership preparing for a diplomatic recognition of the new South Asian nation or lifting its objections to Dhaka's membership of the UN.

In December 1973, politics in Bangladesh took a surprisingly unexpected turn when President Abu Sayeed Chowdhury resigned from office. No explanation was offered, either by Justice Chowdhury or the government, for the resignation. But there had been clear hints in the preceding months of the president and the prime minister being unable to agree over certain broad areas of policy. The nature of their differences was never made public. Chowdhury was officially reassigned as the country's roving ambassador abroad, which in point of fact was a way of sweetening the break between head of state and head of government. His replacement as the country's new president was the lacklustre Mujib loyalist Mohammadullah, at that point the speaker of parliament. A staunch Awami Leaguer, Mohammadullah thus became the first in a line of presidents owing fealty to a political party.

—◦⊛◦—

In Lahore, Once More

The government of Mujib spent nearly three years trying to master the art of international diplomacy as it sought to construct a structure of friendship with other nations. The arrival of Dr Kamal Hossain, a lawyer educated in the United Kingdom and trusted by the prime minister, as foreign minister was surely the point at which Bangladesh's foreign policy picked up speed. Hossain was an articulate spokesman for the country in the tripartite negotiations involving India, Pakistan and Bangladesh in New Delhi. Moroever, he had already burnished his credentials through his pivotal role in the framing of the country's constitution in 1972. When, therefore, Kamal Hossain assumed charge of the foreign office after the March 1973 elections, his fundamental responsibility became one of adding fresh doses of energy to Bangladesh's case for entry into the UN. Pakistan was still putting up objections to Dhaka's entry into the global body and it was clear that the Chinese, courtesy their veto, were willing to help Islamabad in meeting its objectives. Hossain, with a reputation for friendship with the West, was in a position to use his influence to bear on the United States and other countries in the development of a positive image of Bangladesh in the outside world. He must have realised though, how strenuous a job it was considering the goodwill the new country had received during its liberation war and in the times immediately afterwards, was being frittered away through mismanagement and administrative incompetence.

By early 1974, it became pretty much obvious that problems relating to Pakistan required to be dealt with without further delay. The impediment, however, was still the Bhutto government in Islamabad. Despite the deal on the return of his country's POWs to Islamabad, Pakistan's leader did not appear to be ready to accept the reality of Bangladesh's being an independent state, even if the rest of the world had already welcomed the Bengalis into their councils. But an inevitable crisis lurked for Pakistan as it prepared to host a summit of the leaders of Islamic countries in Lahore in February 1974. The Organisation of Islamic Countries (OIC) could not afford to ignore Bangladesh as more than 80 per cent of its population comprised Muslims. Moreover, there was the problem of the OIC needing the presence of Bangladesh in its councils if it did not wish to be accused of hypocrisy.

Perhaps the organisation would have had a simpler way of dealing with the Bangladesh question if the summit had been set in a country other than Pakistan, whose prime minister was intent on demonstrating before the world that his country had come to terms with its past and was indeed in a position to provide leadership to the global Islamic community. It was once more time for Bhutto to engage in a bit of self-publicity. And why not? He had successfully steered Pakistan to a position of respectability after the disastrous military defeat in 1971. Furthermore, he had adroitly managed to bring all Pakistani POWs back home and had thereby prevented Bangladesh from putting a single soldier of the Pakistan Army on trial. Bhutto's popularity in his country was scaling newer heights. He understood full well that an OIC summit in Lahore would finally anoint him as a statesman and thus enhance his standing in the international community.

All said and done, it was once more Bangladesh that plagued Bhutto. He was, for all his evident pride in being able to host the summit, in a quandary about the ways and means of bringing Mujib to the gathering. The Bangladesh leader had already dismissed any thought of travelling to Pakistan unless Islamabad accorded full diplomatic recognition to his country. Additionally, by way of demonstrating his own position towards Pakistan, Mujib had begun to speak of mutual recognition, by which he meant Dhaka and Islamabad recognising each other as distinct political entities. The upshot of this stand-off was that by the time the leaders of the Islamic nations began arriving in Lahore, a greater sense of urgency took over the Bangladesh issue. Eventually, it was through the efforts of countries like Kuwait that a deal was struck. Pakistan would declare its recognition of Bangladesh, which in turn would be persuaded to drop its objections to dealing with the former mother country. The announcement of the deal was made in the run-up to the inauguration of the summit. What followed was again a mini drama. The Kuwaiti foreign minister flew from Lahore to Dhaka, met Mujib and eventually accompanied him and his delegation to the summit.

In terms of history, it was a breakthrough in that Mujib was finally able to claim that the Pakistanis had bowed to the inevitable by acknowledging the emergence of Bangladesh as a free country. The Bangladesh prime minister, accompanied by a team that included Foreign Minister Kamal Hossain and his political secretary Tofail Ahmed, the former student leader, arrived in Lahore to a reception pregnant with irony. He was greeted at the airport by President Chaudhri Fazle Elahi and Prime Minister Bhutto. The latter dispensed with the more formal handshake and instead gathered his old political rival in an embrace. After that, Mujib and his team, in a pretty emotional state, heard the Pakistan Army play the Bangladesh national anthem, *Amar Shonar Bangla* (My Golden Bengal), in honour of the Bangladesh prime minister. Mujib, in the company of President Fazle Elahi and Bhutto, inspected a guard of honour, after which he was conducted to the reception line where senior Pakistani civil and military officials were introduced to him by Bhutto. When Mujib approached General Tikka Khan, now Pakistan's army chief of staff, the man who had initiated the genocide in March 1971 in Bangladesh and refused to see Mujib after he had been taken under arrest, saluted the Bangladesh leader. A smile wreathed in subtlety played on Mujib's lips as he held out his hand to the soldier. 'Hello, Tikka,' he said, before moving on.

For Mujib and his government, the recognition of Bangladesh by Pakistan was an unqualified triumph and so too was Bangladesh's participation at the Islamic summit in Lahore. The prime minister was clearly elated that his country had finally claimed its rightful place in the global community. The OIC summit had been a necessary opening for Dhaka in the Islamic world given that a number of Muslim nations had felt rather queasy about supporting the Bengali struggle for liberation because of their conviction that Pakistan represented a fortress for the defence of Muslim interests. Mujib's attendance at the Lahore summit certainly broke the ice, but it still left countries like Saudi Arabia sullen in their attitude to Bangladesh. On a slightly larger scale, the prime minister's acceptance of the invitation to the OIC summit helped dispel the notion among large numbers of Bengalis that the country's close ties with India came in the way of its efforts to develop an independent foreign policy for itself. Mujib's decision to take the country into the OIC had left the Indian government of Mrs Gandhi surprised. The Bangladesh prime minister had felt little need to consult the Indian leader on the question and indeed there were certain stories given out at the time that when some individuals in his administration ventured the mild suggestion that Mujib let the Indians into the plan, the prime minister brushed the whole idea aside. But there was a second aspect of the OIC-related move as well, one that left quite a large body of Bengalis pretty wary about the way things would turn out now that Bangladesh had formally identified itself with the Islamic world. For these people, the country's secular basis had been compromised by membership of the OIC and could eventually mean a turning away from the nationalistic principles on which the state had been founded.

—◦◦◦—

PART
7

Gaining UN, Losing Tajuddin

Towards the end of June 1974, Zulfikar Ali Bhutto arrived in Dhaka as the head of an eighty-member delegation that included nearly everybody who was anybody in Pakistan. The ostensible goal was to hold discussions with Mujib and the issues of the stranded Biharis and the liabilities and assets of pre-1971 Pakistan.

Bangladesh's stand on the future of the Biharis had already been weakened as a result of the tripartite agreement of the previous year allowing Pakistani POWs to return home and at the same time facilitate the departure of Bengali civilians and military personnel and their families from Pakistan for Bangladesh. Of greater importance was the assets and liabilities question. The Pakistanis clearly resisted any demand made by Bangladesh on the issue. Mujib as well as the wider Bengali civil society had argued, for good reason, in the pre-December 1971 years that the prosperity which marked conditions in West Pakistan was a direct offshoot of an exploitation of East Pakistani resources. Jute and tea happened to be the country's principal foreign exchange earners and yet the profits derived from them had not been spent on the east as much as they had been expended in the west. As the Bengalis saw it, the separation from Pakistan in 1971 had as much to do with the rejection of the 1970 election results by the west and the consequent military crackdown as with the twenty-four year neglect of East Pakistan's economic imperatives by the rulers in Islamabad. It was these matters that Mujib now intended to place before Bhutto. But the Pakistani prime minister was not prepared to listen, as the results of the visit would show.

Bhutto's visit was a disaster from the beginning. If the Bengalis were prepared to let him know that his being in Dhaka was hardly a big deal given the bad reputation he had already acquired among them, he only justified that impression. Grumbling and angry, he went to the *Jatiyo Smriti Shoudho* (JSS), the National Memorial erected in memory of the Bengali martyrs of 1971 outside Dhaka, to pay his respects to Bangladesh's freedom fighters. As he stepped out of his car, a large group of Bengalis carrying placards demanding that he go home raised slogans excoriating him over his role in the 1971 killings. A sullen Bhutto was conducted to the memorial, where he showed not the slightest intention of demonstrating any respect to the dead. He refused to doff the Mao cap and as Tofail Ahmed, the Bangladesh prime minister's political secretary, offered him the visitors' book, Bhutto huffed. 'Enough of this nonsense,' he said angrily as he pushed the book away. Back in Dhaka, his negotiations with Bangladeshi government was a repeat of the abortive talks he and Mujib had held in January 1971. Only this time, the two men were dealing with each other in a new capacity, as leaders of two independent states. Bhutto's intransigence kept coming in the way. When the two-day visit came to an end, a grim-looking Mujib accompanied Bhutto to the airport in the fading light of day. Little of the warmth that had earlier marked the restoration of contacts between the two leaders back in Lahore in February of the year was on display. It was the last time Mujib and Bhutto would meet. Their visceral dislike for each other would only increase in the coming months. After Bhutto's departure, the Bangladesh prime minister informed waiting newsmen that the stubbornness of the Pakistani leader had caused a collapse in the talks.

The People's Republic of Bangladesh was admitted to the UN as a member in September 1974, with the Chinese government finally not raising any more objections against its entry. What upset sensibilities in Dhaka over the Chinese attitude was the sheer indifference Mao

Zedong and Zhou En-lai had demonstrated towards the Bengali cause in 1971. The Chinese attitude of hostility also embarrassed those leftists in Bangladesh who had traditionally considered themselves closer to Mao than to the Soviets. The CPB of Moni Singh, a staunch ally of the Soviet communists, and the Muzaffar faction of the NAP could now gleefully point to the failings of the pro-Beijing communists and indeed paint them as agents of the power circles in the Chinese capital. Men like Siraj Sikdar and Abdul Haq, it was pointed out, were only echoing the sentiments of the leadership in Beijing.

Once the membership of the UN came through, Mujib was elated despite the fact that China was yet to accord diplomatic recognition to his country. What cheered him was something that came wrapped in his essential nationalism. He was now in a position, to present the world's Bengali speaking people before the global community. For him, it was rather immaterial that a good chunk of Bengalis remained part of the Indian union. At a press conference soon after his return to Bangladesh in January 1972, a reporter evidently tried to put him in a spot when he wanted to know if in future the Bengalis of West Bengal could be incorporated in a wider Bangladesh state. Mujib could not afford to trip up. His calm response impressed those who heard him that day. 'I am happy,' said he, 'with *my* Bangladesh.' That was all he said. It was a clever way of giving his perspective on the times he was part of. At the same time, it was a calculated way of leaving any question about the future in a state of ambiguity.

Days after the grant of membership, Mujib flew to New York, in the latter part of September 1974. It was an enviable distinction, in terms of diplomacy, that he had reached. He would address the UN General Assembly and would then make a visit to Washington to see President Gerald Ford. The trip to Washington would not be an official one, but the Bangladesh leader clearly wished to add a new feather to his cap by meeting the leader of one of the world's most powerful states. One wonders if Mujib would have wished to meet Richard Nixon, who had resigned only a month earlier, given the mutual antipathy the two men shared. In addition, the Bangladesh government was in an upbeat mood about presenting its leaders before the international community in as many ways as possible. His trips to Britain and Europe, to the Soviet Union and India and his presence at the summits of Islamic nations and the NAM had all been a remarkable recognition of him as a strong, charismatic leader for his country. It was charisma that would be put to good use in New York and Washington.

For Mujib, no moment could have been more poignant than the time he spent delivering his speech before the General Assembly. He had achieved yet another first for himself and in his country. He had spoken in his native Bengali, for which a number of young men had sacrificed their lives on the streets of Dhaka in 1952, and twenty-two years later was being heard all over the world. It was one of Mujib's finest hours. For his nation, many of whom were glued to the radio sets back home, pride was the unmistakable sentiment that defined the moment. It had been a bad year in terms of the economy. The number of people who had died from hunger was high, but there was the drought and international conspiracy to explain it away. With the government having opened thousands of gruel kitchens all over the country, the famine was in recession and the prime minister looked forward to a happy year ahead.

At the UN, he was visited by Henry Kissinger, the man who had more than anyone else positioned America in a tilt towards Pakistan in 1971. Nixon and Kissinger had gone overboard in their move to prevent a complete collapse of Pakistan. The dispatch of the US Seventh Fleet to the Bay of Bengal during the war had been considered a hostile act by the Bengalis. That the Soviet Union and India had put paid to the Nixon-Kissinger plans and that Bangladesh was now a close ally of both Delhi and Moscow rankled the secretary of state. He was determined, therefore, that Bangladesh should be spliced away from its socialist moorings. Mujib, however, ever the hospitable Bengali invited the US secretary to Bangladesh to dispel the notion that his country was the basket case Kissinger had once disparagingly said it would be.

Between Mujib's appearance at the UN in September and Kissinger's visit to Dhaka, an event of far-reaching implications was to occur. A few weeks after Mujib's return from New York, in October 1974, Finance Minister Tajuddin Ahmed arrived from Washington after talks with the World Bank and the International Monetary Fund. For a man who had been an ardent socialist all his life and who had, since 1971, seen absolutely little cause to seek aid from the West and its lending institutions, the visit to Washington certainly hurt his pride. It hurt the socialist in him to no end to be eventually dealing with the very people he had generally regarded as emblematic of capitalism and economic exploitation. The government he was part of had turned to the West, which he saw as a self-defeating move that could only land Bangladesh in a position where its political sovereignty would stand compromised by the economic demands made on it by the Bretton Woods institutions. As he stepped off his plane in Dhaka, Tajuddin was asked by newsmen if the prime minister had approved of his negotiations in Washington. Already under pressure from Mujib loyalists who had never quite ended their campaign against him, the finance minister snapped that he knew what needed to be done in the national interest. After all, the War of Liberation had been waged and won without Bangabandhu, he said in what was taken as a clear reference to Mujib's absence from the war in 1971. That comment more than any other would seal Tajuddin's fate in the government.

A couple of days after Tajuddin's return from Washington, a terse official announcement made its way into the news bulletins. The finance minister, it noted, had asked to be relieved of his responsibilities and the prime minister had accepted the resignation. As Tajuddin Ahmed lapsed into silence and seemed to withdraw from politics, refusing to divulge what had happened between him and Mujib, a series of speculations began to make the rounds in Dhaka. Neither Mujib nor Tajuddin sought to reveal it before the country. The anti-Tajuddin elements in the Awami League greeted the news of the finance minister's departure with great relief. Tajuddin's successful prosecution of the war as also his formidable intellectual prowess had been a threat to Mujib loyalists like Moni, who clearly felt that the wartime prime minister could someday manoeuvre into a position where he just might supplant Mujib as the nation's leader. Large sections of Bengalis, however, believed that if Tajuddin had not been at the helm in 1971, matters would have turned out a lot worse for the country. Interestingly, even as Tajuddin Ahmed came under pressure in 1974, in that same year Moni became the owner and publisher of a new English language newspaper in the country. The *Bangladesh Times* quickly became a popular newspaper. Almost threatening to eclipse the *Bangladesh Observer*, the new newspaper was a weapon Moni would wield to demonstrate his influence in the country.

A few of Tajuddin's friends have over the years sought to add their own views to the issue, suggesting that in the few times the wartime leader attempted to draw Mujib's attention to the subject of the Mujibnagar government, the country's founding father was quick to let him know that there would be time for all that later. That time never came. What added to Tajuddin's miseries was the animosity of Moshtaq. The latter had never forgiven Tajuddin for the unceremonious manner in which he had been prevented from travelling to the UN in September 1971 to argue Bangladesh's case before the world body. Insult was then added to injury when, soon after the government in exile returned to Dhaka in December, Moshtaq was quickly replaced as foreign minister by Abdus Samad Azad. For Tajuddin, it had become imperative to stop Moshtaq from going to New York in 1971 to plead Bangladesh's case when reports surfaced, largely through Indian intelligence reports, of his secret meetings with American diplomats in Calcutta about a probable compromise between the Awami League leadership and the Pakistan government. The Americans had clearly aimed at putting Moshtaq's right-wing politics to good use by encouraging him to agree to a confederal arrangement with Pakistan and thereby undercut the guerrilla struggle for full independence for Bangladesh.

It is interesting that even as the guerrilla struggle continued, Moshtaq was the only member of the government to argue for a policy that would have it choose between Mujib's release from prison and the struggle for liberation. Tajuddin's response was emphatic:

Bengalis would wage war for freedom and at the same time work towards securing their leader's freedom. He saw no dichotomy between the two issues. Fortunately for Tajuddin and the other members of the government, the intelligence reports on Moshtaq's links with Washington came to light just as the foreign minister was preparing to leave for New York. The prime minister was justified in assuming that once in the United States, Moshtaq would publicly repudiate the Mujibnagar government and so drive a clear wedge in the armed struggle. With Moshtaq grounded, the job of presenting the Bangladesh cause before global opinion fell to Justice Abu Sayeed Chowdhury, already in London managing the country's unofficial mission there.

By October 1974, Tajuddin Ahmed was thus under siege from a number of quarters. On the one hand, Sheikh Moni and his band of young supporters made it clear to Mujib that Tajuddin's presence in the government was an invitation to potential trouble, an argument that the prime minister inexplicably did not or could not brush aside. On the other hand, Moshtaq was taking full advantage of the anti-Tajuddin moves by the young Awami Leaguers to add fuel to the gathering sparks. There was a third group of people who went around peddling rumours and innuendoes about the pro-India bias in Tajuddin Ahmed's politics, to a point where the intention was patently one of projecting the finance minister as Delhi's puppet in Dhaka. Finally, there was the coincidence of Tajuddin's ouster from the government coming only days before the arrival of Henry Kissinger in Dhaka.

The US secretary of state was received warmly by the leaders of the Bangladesh government. The prime minister himself was present at the news conference Kissinger addressed at the *Ganobhavan*, the official residence of the head of government. The Kissinger trip was to serve as a defining moment in relations between Dhaka and Washington, in that, it formalised a restructuring of diplomacy between the two countries. Mujib was now in a position to claim that his foreign policy of friendship for all and malice towards none had been vindicated. Except for China,

Bangladesh was now on good terms with nearly every country that mattered in the particular Cold War climate which prevailed.

The Kissinger visit marked a reorientation in Bangladesh's diplomatic priorities, a clear shift away from its leanings towards Moscow and Delhi and towards Washington. Mujib's visit to the Lahore meeting of the OIC as well as his participation at the NAM meeting in Algiers and the Commonwealth summit in Ottawa were moot indications. For Mujib, though, the priority was not so much of a shift as it was a need for the country to balance its ties with the world's powerful nations. He remembered only too well the charges of pro-Americanism that had been levelled at Suhrawardy when the latter served as prime minister of Pakistan in the 1950s. Mujib was not willing to be the target of similar accusations in Bangladesh. Henry Kissinger, despite his notoriety, was a powerful figure, which is why his arrival in Dhaka was regarded as a milestone by his government.

As far as Kissinger was concerned, the visit was part of the geo-political strategy of the United States. Washington had since 1971 found itself in a straitjacket in South Asia, with a distinctly independent India ignoring all its pleas for accommodation with Pakistan, until at least the liberation of Bangladesh. Furthermore, the alliance between Moscow and Delhi, sealed by the treaty of friendship and cooperation signed in August 1971, had sent waves of fear through the administration in Washington. America's relation with China, despite the breakthrough made in July 1971 and the subsequent visit to Beijing by President Richard Nixon in February 1972, was yet in a state of wary experimentation. Pakistan was still weak, and any move towards a further strengthening of ties with it, as Kissinger figured, would prevent Washington from making a re-entry into the subcontinent. It was thus in the context of America's wider South Asia vision that Kissinger undertook his mission to Bangladesh. He found Mujib and Kamal Hossain, the foreign minister, receptive to thoughts of closer links with Washington. Mujib, through his long political career, had in terms of diplomacy been more inclined towards the West than to the socialist power structure symbolised by the Soviet

Union and to a lesser extent, China. It was the direct influence of his political mentor Suhrawardy, who had never made any secret of his preferences for the United States when it came to dealing with the world's powerful nations. Mujib's happiness, therefore, at the opportunity that came with the Kissinger visit for forging of links with America was understandable.

For all his consolidation of powers at home and successes abroad, however, Mujib was rendered immeasurably weak and indeed lonely by the departure of Tajuddin Ahmed from the government. The fallen finance minister was the one man who provided the necessary political balance and intellectual content to the government. Though Mujib was determined to demonstrate in public the image of a leader not shaken by his departure, in private he was a lonely man after October 1974. Tajuddin strenuously avoided journalists and made absolutely no reference to Mujib or to the causes that had led to his resignation. In the few months that would remain of his life, as also that of Mujib and the other principal leaders of the 1971 government in exile, he made no statement, appeared at no public gathering, and gave no newspaper interviews. There are reasons to believe that he and Mujib met after October 1974 and that the prime minister asked him to come back to government. For Tajuddin, it was not easy to forget the wound that had been inflicted by the very man he had served with unquestioned loyalty through the decades.

Towards the end of 1974, Mujib was forced to direct attention away from foreign policy to domestic affairs. The state of law and order had continued to decline. Runaway prices leading to hoarding of foodgrains continued unabated and underground leftist elements as well as the old, pardoned associates of the Pakistan Army were busily going about trying to undermine the government. An exasperated Mujib decided he was left with no choice than resort to drastic measures. Parliament swiftly passed the Special Powers Act (SPA), a sweeping measure that gave the government blanket authority to detain and prosecute individuals on grounds of national security.

The long-term ramifications of the SPA would be tragic. In the immediate term, it was a clear pointer to the failure of the Awami League government to roll back the slide that had already set in. For Mujib, the SPA was an admission that constitutional politics had hit a bad patch. Not even the SPA seemed to be enough to help the government deal with its enemies. In December of the year, a state of emergency was declared in the country. It was proof, if proof was at all needed, of the beleaguered state only three years after the arrival of independent statehood. As the year drew to a close, rumours were rife about drastic changes being contemplated around the political system that had been in vogue since January 1972. Mujib, it was whispered, was seriously mulling the question of a switchover from the parliamentary form of government to presidential rule. The air was thick with doubts and fears about the future.

From Pluralism to Second Revolution

Between December 1974 and January 1975, events moved at dizzying speed for Bangladesh. Mujib's government now clearly saw itself beset with enemies everywhere and obviously looked determined to adopt some pretty harsh methods to contain the situation. Talk of a drastic change in political patterns was not discouraged or dismissed by the government, which was again a hint of the regressive steps it was planning to take. The beginning of January was spent in convincing Awami League leaders and members that such a change was necessary in national interest. At the same time, Mujib was receiving some much needed support for his probable new venture from his natural allies among Moni Singh's communists and the NAP of Professor Muzaffar Ahmed. It was a harassed Mujib who governed in January 1975, a far cry from the decisive national leader who gave out the call for freedom in March 1971 and then returned to resume his leadership of the country in January 1972. There was a reason behind Mujib's discomfiture.

Early in January, the security forces had nabbed Siraj Sikdar, leader of the extremist left-wing Sarbahara Party responsible for murdering a number of Awami League workers in the country. He was taken before the prime minister as a prisoner, which in itself was a curious affair. Obviously the exchange between the two men did not go well. Removed from the prime ministerial presence by the police, ostensibly to be placed in jail, Sikdar was soon afterwards shot by security forces.

The country was informed that he had been shot while making an attempt to escape. The killing horrified Mujib, who clearly had reason to think that Sikdar had been eliminated as a way of embarrassing his government.

Overall, the troubles his government now faced had a string of reasons attached to them, not least of which were the wrong policies the prime minister had adopted in the preceding three years. Those policies reflected themselves in the failure of the government to keep the economy from collapsing. Politically, the decision to pardon the old collaborators of the Pakistan Army as well as a failure to reach out to other political parties had proved costly. The establishment of JRB had done little credit to the government as its operations merely served to fuel the suspicion that it was not only an organisation responsible for ensuring the security of the Awami League and the government it led but was also a countervailing force to the army. Besides, discontent in the army had begun to come to the fore in the earlier part of 1974, when the prime minister had first ordered the soldiers to act against smuggling and hoarding but then had them return to the barracks.

Reports that the army had been recalled because it had begun nabbing local Awami League politicians and supporters engaged in sordid economic activities surely did not enhance the image of the government. The more important fall-out of the move was the feeling among citizens that at the end of the day, with the civil administrative machinery rendered helpless in checking the slide, the government had been forced to fall back on the soldiers. For Mujib, whose entire political career had been based on a need to keep the military out of politics and under civilian control, the deployment of the soldiers was but a way of demonstrating his authority over the armed forces. To his fans and foes alike, however, it looked like an admission of failure. Worse, the quick withdrawal of the soldiers from the drive against smuggling and hoarding created a strong impression that when it came to defending its own interests, the Awami League would go to an extent where it would stubbornly uphold its own partisan interests.

Certain sections in the army, particularly those who had been co-opted into it after their return from service in the Pakistan Army in pre-1971 Pakistan, clearly were left sulking. In addition, the lack of screening of the repatriated officers and soldiers entering the Bangladesh Army would lead to grave results, with the Pakistan returnees eventually upstaging the freedom fighters and thereby adding to the political turmoil in the country. In 1974, however, there was clearly little sign that it might act against the civilian authority. Mujib was still the powerful symbol of popular government and no one in the military could contemplate a situation where a revolt or a *coup d'état* could be launched against his administration. For all the weaknesses and flaws of the government, no one in Bangladesh could contemplate the possibility that the officers and men of the Bangladesh military could someday act against not only their elected prime minister but also a man who was the Father of the Nation.

Reports of CIA activities were on. India's prime minister, it later transpired, had repeatedly conveyed to Bangladesh's leader her fears about his security. Mujib had never left the residence that had been his home in all the years he had shaped the Bengali nationalist movement and then led the struggle for freedom. While the Ganobhavan, or House of the People, was where he conducted official business, he and his family resided in Dhanmondi with security that was as lax as it had been since the late 1960s.

Crowds of people, ranging from politicians to visiting diplomats, newsmen to common citizens, had free access to the residence but none of that appeared to bother the prime minister. He still clearly relished being with the crowds, for the crowds had always supported him. His growing troubles in governance were not going to create a distance between him and his people. Even in his worst moments, he trusted his people. He knew that the earlier taboo on criticism of his political style, no more existed, with ever larger numbers of people speaking out on the mishandling of conditions they saw developing around them. He bristled at the criticism but in public made little mention of it. His earlier call for the nation to give him three years to remedy conditions in the war-ravaged country did not appear to have produced much of a result in economic terms. In January 1975, the three years he had asked for were over.

The apprehensions and predictions about Mujib's growing desire for a complete overhaul of politics came true on 25 January when parliament swiftly passed the fourth amendment to the constitution. For his supporters, the implications were not merely shocking but horrifying as well. The Westminster-style of government which the prime minister had promoted in all his years of struggle in Pakistan and which he finally found possible to adopt in independent Bangladesh was with alacrity supplanted by a presidential system of government. And that was not all. The more telling feature of the fourth amendment turned out to be a constitutional ban on political pluralism through the creation of a single political party known as the Bangladesh Krishak Sramik Awami League, or peasants-workers' Awami League. But, of course, Mujib and his political associates were not willing to present the case for a change to a single-party system in that way. According to them, the new party, BAKSAL as it came to be known by its acronym, was essentially a national platform of all secular parties, including the Awami League, which had taken part in the War of Liberation or were ready to uphold the principles on the basis of which the independence struggle had been waged.

In his new enterprise, Mujib found two willing partners, the CPB and the Muzaffar faction of the NAP. Obviously, none of the other political parties, for instance Bhashani's faction of the NAP and the JSD of A.S.M. Abdur Rab and Shahjahan Siraj, were willing to join the bandwagon. Those parties automatically, through the provisions of the new amendment to the constitution, stood dissolved. Within the Awami League, Mujib's policy of a changeover to a single party system had not been a unanimous affair. An incensed General Mohammad Ataul Gani Osmany, commander-in-chief of the Mukti Bahini during the war and in early 1975 a lawmaker and minister in Mujib's government, chose to resign from parliament rather than go along with the new measures. In a blistering speech on the floor of parliament before walking away, Osmany recalled the original principles upon which the people of Bangladesh had gone to war against Pakistan and pointed out to Mujib and all the other members of the legislative body that a one-party system was a negation of those principles. In what was surely his parting shot, the crusty old soldier told a silent, embarrassed house that having struggled long and hard against Ayub Khan, the old dictator in the Pakistani era, he was not willing to serve under Mujib Khan, that last bit a clear allusion to what he considered the growing authoritarian tendencies in the Bengali leader. Osmany's resignation from parliament was followed by that of Mainul Hosein, a young barrister and owner of the largest circulated Bengali daily newspaper *Ittefaq*. Hosein had been a particular object of Mujib's affection owing to the prime minister's close association with the young lawmaker's father, Tofazzal Hossein Manik Mia in the 1950s and 1960s. Both Mujib, as a rising politician, and Manik Mia, as editor of the *Ittefaq*, had been protégés of Suhrawardy. During the Six Points movement in 1966, Manik Mia had clearly come down on the side of Mujib and had paid a terrible price for it. His newspaper was proscribed and he was carted off to jail, remaining there for nearly three years. He died in June 1969. Mujib knew he could do little to persuade Osmany not to desert him, but the young Mainul Hosein's decision to emulate the general infuriated the prime minister. To him, it was a clear betrayal of a link that had been forged in the days of Hosein's father. But Hosein was not to be cowed. He stood by his decision to give up his seat in parliament.

Before the end of the day on 25 January, things moved quickly. Mujib addressed the parliament and in what was clearly an emotional speech expressed his sorrow that he would not be part of the legislative body any longer. He was, after all, about to take over as an all-powerful president in a new system that would make him not only head of government but head of state as well. In his speech, he went to great lengths to reassure the country that democracy was not dead. On the contrary, the new step he had taken aimed at creating an inclusive society for everyone in the country. In the new set-up, he explained, power would begin at the grassroots and flow all the way up to the national level. Hearing Mujib describe the new conditions, one would almost believe that a real decentralisation of authority had been put into place. The paradox is that the prime minister's arguments on decentralised, expanded local government and a thorough restructuring of the civil administration did indeed make sense to a nation which had for three years only muddled through one crisis after another. Under the new system, the prevailing nineteen administrative districts of the country, so long under the authority of bureaucratic district commissioners, would be restructured and expanded into sixty districts altogether. Each of these districts would be administered by a governor who could be a political figure or a civil servant. Indeed, as the following days and weeks would reveal, a pretty good number of men in the civil service would be appointed to gubernatorial positions. But what was troubling was that all the restructuring was coming at the expense of universally accepted standards of democracy. Mujib told the lawmakers, and by extension the country, that elections on the basis of adult franchise would continue to be the norm. In his assessment, the new national party, as he would call BAKSAL, would nominate a plurality of candidates for seats in local bodies as well as the national legislature in order for the electorate to choose their representatives on an assessment of the merits of the candidates before them. In his opinion, the new political steps were a necessary Second Revolution, or *Ditio Biplob*, for the country. Obviously, the first revolution had been the struggle for and attainment of political liberation from Pakistan in 1971.

Late in the evening on 25 January 1975, Sheikh Mujibur Rahman was sworn in as Bangladesh's president in the new scheme of things. As president, he now had overall authority over all aspects of administration as well as politics. He was supreme commander of the armed forces and chief of BAKSAL. The hand-picked man who had been president for the previous year, Mohammadullah, made his exit from office by submitting his resignation to the speaker of parliament. But that was not the end of the road for Mohammadullah. He was taken into the new cabinet that President Sheikh Mujibur Rahman formed immediately after the adoption of the fourth amendment to the constitution. In the new presidential system of government, the cabinet comprised a vice president, prime minister and a whole range of ministers. To a certain extent, that is, without the pluralistic aspects of it, Mujib's new system resembled the Fifth Republic in France, where the powers of the prime minister were fewer or less far-reaching than those of the president.

Mujib's choice for vice president was Syed Nazrul Islam, who had served in the same position during the war and had therefore been acting president with Mujib imprisoned in Pakistan. The new prime minister was Mansoor Ali. Moshtaq stayed on as commerce minister and Kamal Hossain, ambivalent about the new system, nevertheless remained foreign minister. In fact, all of Mujib's long-time political associates continued to hold ministerial positions. The one exception was Tajuddin Ahmed, who certainly was not willing to be part of the new dispensation. But Tajuddin, rather than creating any fresh scope for new disagreement with Mujib, went quietly along when he was nominated a member of the newly created central committee of the new national party.

A particular feature of the new set-up was the inclusion of individuals at all levels of politics and administration in BAKSAL. Ministers, members of parliament, civil servants and the chiefs and deputy chiefs of the army, navy, air force, police, Bangladesh Rifles and JRB were inducted as members of the central committee. Not much wisdom was needed for people to know that BAKSAL meant to be the new guiding philosophy in Bangladesh's politics. At its best, it was reminiscent of the communist system as it then prevailed in the Soviet Union and China. At its worst, it was a reminder of Baathist politics in Syria and Iraq. But, of course, Bangladesh's ruling circles did not see it that way at all. For Mujib, BAKSAL was a political necessity resting on indigenous national factors.

Over the days and weeks after the assumption of presidential powers by Mujib, the government went into a detailed presentation of the new system to the country. It was announced that the governors appointed to head the sixty political and administrative divisions of Bangladesh would undergo training courses before they took charge of their offices. Meanwhile, an immediate and positive fall-out of the BAKSAL move was the discipline and order that swiftly made its way into national life. The government was buoyed in its new ideas by the spectacle of people from the various professions making their way into BAKSAL. It must, in fairness, be said that outside the structure of the administration Mujib and his government did not exercise any authority to coerce people into joining BAKSAL. Even so, a wide range of individuals, especially in the media, made a beeline for the party. Some were clearly ardent believers in Mujib's new political philosophy. Others, despite their reservations about the president's policies, came into BAKSAL more as a way of keeping their future intact than in evincing a new interest in politics.

There was yet a third group of journalists keen to project themselves as loyal newsmen, fundamentally a set unwilling to miss out on opportunities that could arise from the new arrangements. On 26 March, the fourth anniversary of the declaration of Bangladesh's independence, Mujib, his vice president, prime minister and senior members of the cabinet made a journey back to the old Race Course, now known as Suhrawardy Udyan in honour of the founder of the Awami League. The crowds were thinner than the huge masses of Bengalis who had earlier turned up at the same place in earlier years to hear Mujib outline his plans for autonomy and, subsequently, national freedom. On 10 January 1972, the crowds that had turned up to hear him speak after his return from Pakistan had spilled over onto the roads around the vast grounds. On 26 March 1975, though, it was quite different. Mujib still demonstrated his ability to work up energy in his listeners, but there was also the clear perception that he and his government were running out of steam. For all the enthusiasm with which the government was then engaged in promoting the BAKSAL philosophy, there was the unmistakable feeling that Mujib's decision to bring an end to pluralist democracy had taken the wind out of the country's sails. With no political opposition, whatever the government did or spoke of amounted to little more than propaganda. Not even the president could have failed to notice the sullen calm that had descended over the country. His speech at Suhrawardy Udyan, the last he was to make there, clearly lacked focus despite the plans he outlined about the future. On that afternoon, as the rally drew to a close, there was no mistaking that Bangladesh's government and its people had grown equally exhausted through the tumult of the preceding four years.

On 16 June, the government, in light of its new policy of streamlining life and politics in the country, decreed all but four newspapers out of existence. It was a bad move and was justifiably considered a brazen assault on the press. The general feeling that command politics had come into operation, freedom of press was now a matter to be handled and dispensed by the state. The government, of course, tried to reason that the presence of two Bengali language and two English language newspapers would bring about a sense of discipline in the media sector. Radio and television, in government control since the Pakistani era, were not a problem at all. But with the decision over newspapers, the authorities made it obvious that they did not intend to leave any loopholes as the new political system went to work. This move, apparently decided upon through discussions between Mujib and a few senior journalists, including at least one who was later to develop and demonstrate a pathological dislike of the president, came as one of the rudest of shocks to have assailed the country since the January changeover to one-party government. But protest was limited to private grumblings. At that early stage of the new experiment and with the SPA in force, no one was willing to raise the hackles of the administration by voicing dissent.

The immediate impact of the shutdown on the newspaper industry was the sudden state of unemployment for the thousands of journalists and press workers at the proscribed newspaper establishments. But the government, it appeared, had been prepared for its next move, which came through making the official announcement that all retrenched newsmen would be absorbed in the various organisations and departments of the government. That would not be quite the same as the journalists making use of their pens to comment on the affairs of the state, but there was the dubious satisfaction, though, that in an atmosphere of redefined socialism, the affected members of the journalistic community would at least not be forced into the streets through a loss of their jobs.

Through the end of July and early August, plans for the training of governors went on apace, with senior members of the government taking it in turns to enlighten the men appointed to the jobs on the nature of the work they were expected to perform. One of the sessions was addressed by Moshtaq, the commerce minister. A shrewd political operator, Moshtaq had kept his ire around his earlier removal from the foreign office to himself. Indeed, he had scored something of a triumph when Tajuddin Ahmed, a colleague he detested heartily, was forced out of the government. The fact that Moshtaq had covertly engaged in negotiations with American diplomats in 1971 had not come in the way of his closeness to Mujib.

The truth was that before his resentment of Tajuddin Ahmed, he had been resentful of Mujib himself. In the nearly four years since the liberation of the country, Moshtaq had remained in private frustration over what he plainly considered Mujib's unwillingness to let him play a bigger role in the administration. But he never let the frustration and the anger show. When Mujib returned from Pakistan, Moshtaq, unlike the rest of the Bengali leadership, publicly kissed his leader on the cheeks as a demonstration of his affection. At cabinet meetings and public rallies, he remained sufficiently ingratiating towards Mujib to convince the Father of the Nation that his loyalty was above board.

Moshtaq's friendship with the American embassy had never been a secret. The links that he had established with Washington, through its diplomats in Calcutta in 1971, had simply been carried over to Dhaka, especially after the United States granted diplomatic recognition to Bangladesh in April 1972. He was on friendly terms with Davis Eugene Boster, the US ambassador, and in October 1974, when Henry

Kissinger visited Dhaka, had spent some good moments with the American secretary of state. A guest at the official dinner hosted for Kissinger remembered years later how he had noticed the American and Moshtaq get up from the table and leave the room, within seconds of each other. Moments later, as the guest himself went out to visit the washroom, he noticed Kissinger and Moshtaq ending what looked to him a quick conversation before they both made their way, separately, back to the banquet hall.

Unknown to Mujib or any other senior member of the government, discreet activity had already been initiated by junior elements in the army to mount a coup against the president. It appears that the momentum for a change had begun tentatively following Kissinger's visit in October 1974 and indeed gathered pace following the switchover to the one-party presidential system in January. Mujib had little way of knowing that one of the men he trusted completely and whose presence around him was ubiquitous, minister of state for information Taheruddin Thakur, was in league with Moshtaq and the military officers planning the overthrow of the government. And Moshtaq found other soulmates in such individuals as Mahbubul Alam Chashi, the bureaucrat who had been removed as foreign secretary in the wartime government in 1971 by Tajuddin Ahmed, at the same time that Moshtaq himself had been stopped from going to New York. Like Moshtaq, Chashi had never been able to swallow the insult and was naturally prepared to team up with his old boss again in any move against Mujib. Another member of the team was A.B.S. Safdar, the chief of national security intelligence who owed his job to Mujib.

By mid-1975, even as Moshtaq made pretences of going along with preparations for an official inauguration of the BAKSAL system, contacts appeared to have been well established between him and the majors and colonels, among whom was his nephew Abdur Rashid. In hindsight, it is amazing that no one in the administration, not a single Mujib loyalist holding any position of power and security, was aware of the plot. The army chief, Major General K.M. Safiullah, remained absolutely ignorant of the conspiracy, as did the chiefs of the air force, navy and Bangladesh Rifles. Though the role of the army deputy chief of staff, Ziaur Rahman, has remained unclear, there have been the periodic comments made by some of the coup leaders after the overthrow of the government had taken place, about his knowledge that a major move was afoot. Zia, if one were to go by the statements of these officers, was not willing to take direct part in a coup but would not discourage anyone else from taking such a step.

There is a clear feeling that American Ambassador Boster, despite his knowledge of something serious brewing, was not willing for his embassy to be involved. But the same was not the sentiment of the CIA station chief holding a diplomatic cover post in the embassy. The extent to which the plans for a coup were developed and improved upon were subsequently to be revealed in fair detail in Lawrence Lifschultz's incisive study of the Mujib assassination and the execution of Colonel Abu Taher, *Bangladesh: The Unfinished Revolution*. The intricate networking the leaders and planners of the coup went into leaves little doubt that it was well coordinated. Only days before the soldiers struck, Taheruddin Thakur, Mahbubul Alam Chashi and A.B.S. Safdar met at the Bangladesh Academy of Rural Development (BARD) in the rural environs of Comilla and would turn up in Dhaka on the morning of the coup. No one noticed that they had all gone missing. In the JRB, which had already established a pro-Mujib reputation, not even the faintest hint of anything about to go wrong was detected. As for military and civilian intelligence, everyone remained blissfully unaware of the plans that were now in place to finish off the president and his government. Mujib, of course, had never believed that any of his Bengalis could ever nurture any wish to assassinate him.

Yet in the two years proceeding August 1975, a streak of fatalism had made its way into the Mujib persona. For a man who had exuded confidence all his life and had consistently believed that democratic politics was a forceful way of sending all conspiracies scattering, it was rather uncharacteristic that brooding became part of the last few years of life. The precise moment when he was jolted into awareness about his vulnerability as Bangladesh's pre-eminent politician was when he was given the news of the death of Chile's Salvador Allende in September 1973. By the time news of the bloody coup by General Augusto Pinochet Ugarte and the killing of President Allende filtered through to Dhaka, it was already 12 September. Those who saw Mujib that day recalled the deep sense of foreboding that suddenly seemed to envelop his whole being. He had for months kept in touch with the growing darkness in Chile and in the gathering troubles around Allende saw a reflection of his own problems. It was clear to him that Allende's difficulties were his own. Both he and the Chilean president had been elected to office and enjoyed broad support across the spectrum. And yet both were now trapped in a web of conspiracy that was only becoming increasingly thicker with time. When Allende finally succumbed to the conspiracy against him, Mujib was convinced that he would be next. He was shrewd enough to know that the same foreign forces, in league with local elements, which had put an end to the Allende government, would come after him. In his Ganobhavan office on the day he received the news of the Chilean coup, Mujib was unable to concentrate on his work. He went home early and did not emerge again until the next day.

By July 1975, the sense of euphoria Mujib went through months earlier as he decreed a change in the political structure had largely been replaced by worry. He gained weight. A tall man, towering above six feet and therefore at a height above the average Bengali, Mujib now was a gigantic figure in the literal sense. But what made conditions even more pronounced at this stage in his life was the swift, almost brutal ageing he appeared to have gone though in the years in power. His years in Pakistan's prisons had certainly left their mark on him physically, but it had been the years in power as Bangladesh's supreme leader that had done the most damage to his physique. His hair, always ample, was now a lot greyer than it had been four years earlier and the furrows on his forehead had deepened. Having always been a gregarious man, he now seldom smiled. The old laughter that once symbolised the extrovert in him was missing. In July, he saw two of his sons marry, within days of each other. If in private he felt happiness as a parent, in public the images of him in the company of his family, including the two new daughters-in-law, only added to the perception that he was a worried, to a certain extent harassed, head of state. But he soldiered on, still resolute in his belief that at the end of the day the country was with him. He had, after all, made it possible for his Bengalis to win independent nationhood for themselves.

While he relished his role in the creation of Bangladesh, he was at the same time particular about his conviction that it was the love and support of his people that had made everything possible. He had never deviated from the principle that government rested on the consent of the governed. Even when he had made the move to BAKSAL, he honestly believed it was a decision acceptable to the nation. If three years of parliamentary government had been a disappointment, his new measure, he reasoned, could not but lead to a better deal for the country. He was right about the new deal, as statistics subsequently produced by the Bangladesh authorities would reveal. In the eight months after the introduction of the BAKSAL system, agricultural production would register a rise, food distribution throughout the country would improve greatly and, overall, lawlessness would be significantly curbed. In what amounted to uncomfortable irony, Mujib was beginning to do in 1975 what he had been unable to put in place in the years from 1972 to 1974. Where parliamentary democracy had gone haywire with him, the one-party system was beginning to prove that he could get things done after all.

But that was just part of the story. The more significant aspect of the tale was the vacuum that had descended on Bangladesh as a result of the ban on pluralistic democracy. With just four newspapers allowed to run, journalists chafed under the new system despite the assurances they had been given about employment outside their profession. Mujib knew that BAKSAL would only work around his personality. Throughout the period from May to July 1975, he hammered away at the need for the bureaucracy to embrace the changes he had put in place. He had become convinced that the system of elitist administration that had been introduced in the subcontinent by the British and had been emulated by India, Pakistan and Bangladesh was not working for his country. The Second Revolution, he told the country over and over again, was a way of reforming not just politics but the administrative system as well. The programme of segmenting the country into sixty administrative zones highlighted a system where civil servants would, through operating under political governors, push themselves closer to establishing links with the general masses. By any measure, the plan to have civil servants interact with the public was revolutionary and was a clear step towards stripping the bureaucracy of the aloofness, some would say hauteur. In language characteristic of his sometimes earthy style, Mujib demanded of civil officials that they discard their formal trousers in favour of shorts, meaning they emerge from their ivory tower and identify with the masses that were paying them their salaries. Not many civil servants appreciated the rebuke, but it was vintage Mujib. He had never been forgiving of arrogance and anything that bore the odour of elitism in his impoverished country, and he was not about to spread balm over any hurt bureaucratic sentiments.

When Mujib visited Bhashani in Santosh in March 1975, ostensibly as a measure to earn the old man's approbation for his new political schemes, he was happily surprised at the effusive nature of the welcome the elderly politician gave him. His severe criticisms of the government notwithstanding the storm he had been trying to raise over the Muslim Bangla question, Bhashani remained a typical avuncular figure for Mujib. People who saw the two together often remarked on the stern yet affectionate way in which Bhashani dealt with Mujib, who in turn knew that despite his position as Bangladesh's supreme leader there was hardly any point in trying to be patronising towards Bhashani. Mujib's respect for Bhashani had endured through the years. Besides, any amount of support he could extract from the elderly politician for his latest political moves would be a boon for him. When Mujib arrived in the village of Santosh, which had over the years become a spiritual destination for Bhashani's supporters and others, the man who had been the first president of the Awami League before the break came in Kagmari in 1957, walked up a good many yards to welcome the president. The old man gathered Mujib in a hug and Mujib, in the manner of a prodigal son returning home. Later the two men had lunch from the same bowl, which was quite in line with the Bengali tradition of individuals strengthening their bonds through a sharing of meals. Mujib bade Bhashani goodbye in an upbeat mood. The NAP leader had assured him of his support for his political programmes. Nothing could have cheered the president more.

On 8 August, there was a special reason for Mujib to think anew that his policies were on the right track after all. He had been able to convince former president Abu Sayeed Chowdhury, who had left the country and been travelling abroad as roving ambassador, to return and be part of his government. Justice Chowdhury was sworn in as a minister without portfolio. There was a bit of symbolism attached to Chowdhury's return to government, especially since his resignation from the presidency in late 1973 had given rise to all sorts of questions about the difficulties he was having with Mujib. Now that he was back, Mujib could demonstrate to his critics that there was after all a sense of purpose to his new politics. Abu Sayeed Chowdhury, who had repudiated the Pakistani junta in March 1971 over what he plainly considered to be its violation of human rights in East Pakistan, was now of the view that helping Mujib to implement the Second Revolution was a duty that went beyond personal or partisan interests. Mujib had already been hurt by General Osmany's decision not to stand by him when BAKSAL replaced the old political order. In Chowdhury's return, some of that hurt was assuaged.

At that particular stage in his political career, Mujib needed as many national figures as he could possibly gather to be with him in his mission of giving politics a much needed shake-up. He was not overly bothered that a single party system was essentially his repudiation of his own beliefs, given that he had been a votary of multi-party democracy all his life. As far as he knew, BAKSAL was a necessary step in the right direction, at least for some time, especially since it was never his intention to keep the country in a state of regimentation in the way the communist parties of eastern Europe or the ruling circles in the Middle

East often did. All his life he had believed in the righteousness of the many causes he initiated or undertook to defend at various points in his career. The system he had brought in in January 1975 was just the latest cause he thought would help his people find a way out of the gathering darkness around them.

In those last few days, Mujib looked forward to another event of significance for him. He would be addressing a convocation at Dhaka University, in his position as chancellor of the university, on 15 August. There was something triumphant in that. In 1948, Mujib had been rusticated from the university, for his role in organising a strike by menial workers of the university. Although the expulsion order had subsequently been rescinded, Mujib never went back to his classes. In any case, he was becoming sufficiently involved in politics at that early stage to think of resuming life as a student. It was to this same university, whose radical students had helped him over the years in promoting his political programmes, that he was now going back, this time not merely as president of the republic and chancellor but also as the Father of the Nation. Brisk preparations went on to have the campus ready for the convocation. Late in the evening on 14 August, the president's eldest son Sheikh Kamal made a round of the university to ensure that everything was in place for the convocation the following morning.

Earlier, on the afternoon of the same day, Mujib welcomed to his office a special representative of South Korean President Park Chung-Hee. One other responsibility he carried out was sending a message of felicitations to the president and the prime minister of India on the occasion of Indian Independence Day on 15 August. He also kept himself posted about news relating to Foreign Minister Kamal Hossain's ongoing visit to eastern Europe. It was rather late when he travelled back to his residence in nearby Dhanmondi. At dinner, three members of the family were absent. Mujib's elder daughter Hasina, her husband, the nuclear scientist Wajed Mia and younger daughter Rehana were in Europe on a visit.

⤙☙⤛

Murder of Caesar

Shortly after 3 am on 15 August, Colonel Farook Rahman gathered his fellow conspirators in the Dhaka cantonment to go over the final details of the operation against President Sheikh Mujibur Rahman and his government. He was clearly the man in charge. With him were his brother-in-law Colonel Abdur Rashid, who was also related to Commerce Minister Moshtaq, and a handful of other officers and a good number of soldiers from the Lancers Regiment. In an inexplicable manner, the plotters had asked for, and been given, permission to take their tanks, gifts to Mujib from Egyptian President Anwar Sadat, out in those quiet hours in what was given out as a routine exercise. What was curious about the request was that no one in the senior ranks bothered to know why the exercises needed to be done at that particular time. Once the permission had been given, Farook Rahman and his men simply led the tanks and accompanying armoured cars out of the cantonment and into the city.

It was a little after 4 am when the tanks rumbled down the empty roads, on their way to their destinations. One team would head for the Dhanmondi residence of the president. Another would move towards Minto Road, the area that housed government ministers and a third would go to another part of Dhanmondi where Mujib's powerful nephew Sheikh Moni lived with his family. The plotters had evidently decided to attack the three places simultaneously and with a maximum of shock and surprise. The tanks headed for Mujib's residence went past the headquarters of the JRB, situated behind the under-construction parliament building, where Mujib had been made to wait in March 1971 as Pakistan's soldiers awaited instructions on what to do with him. It is quite possible that some members of the force witnessed the tank movements, but no one appeared to be troubled. Mujib's political secretary Tofail Ahmed, responsible for liaising with the JRB, was at home in another area of the city, unaware of the approaching calamity. The coup leaders and their men swiftly covered the stretch of road before the JRB headquarters, rumbled past Ganobhavan, the president's office, and turned left. Straight ahead lay the short distance to Dhanmondi Road no. 32, where the president and his family, as were the rest of the Dhaka population, in slumber. Road no. 32 led off the main Mirpur Road, on which was situated the Kalachand sweets shop. A few soldiers quickly climbed to the roof of the shop and placed a few machine guns there. The guns targeted Mujib's residence, quite visible from the place. Meanwhile, a few tanks stopped at the head of Road no. 32 while a few others went in, coming to a stop at the gates of the presidential residence.

The first group of soldiers alighted and ordered the security personnel at the gates to let them in. The presidential guards, completely taken by surprise, refused and were swiftly mowed down. Meanwhile, other soldiers arriving before the house began firing into the residence, obviously to generate as much panic as possible. The sounds roused Mujib and his petrified family as well as the entire neighbourhood. Sheikh Kamal quickly rushed down the stairs and ran smack into some soldiers who had already entered the passage downstairs. He was shot at close range. A young boy who worked as a servant was killed as well. Meanwhile, Mujib was frantically trying to contact the army chief. Finally, when he got through to him, General Safiullah, in what was surely one of the darkest moments in his life, proved unable to help his president. He asked the pretty pointless question, 'Can you come out of the house, Sir?' The next call made was to his security chief Colonel Jamil. The colonel, who had only been repatriated from Pakistan the previous year, rushed out in his dressing gown and pyjamas, got behind the wheels of his car and drove towards the president's residence. Meanwhile, Mujib began receiving calls from Abdur Rab Serniabat, his brother-in-law and a minister in the cabinet, suggesting that his residence on Minto Road had also come under attack. At Sheikh Moni's residence, a similar situation prevailed. The soldiers were running amuck everywhere.

Mujib's helplessness was complete when the telephone lines at his residence soon went dead. The commotion downstairs prompted the president to emerge from his bedroom, in his white kurta and lungi. As he stood at the top of the stairs, a major was seen running up. He suddenly stopped when he saw Mujib standing there, a looming presence. Mujib demanded, 'Where is Kamal? What do you want?' The major, Bazlul Huda, stammered, 'You have to come with us, Sir.' It is not clear what response came from Mujib, but there have been the varying nature of reports that have been flying around for years. There can be no knowing what Mujib thought as he stood facing a shaky Major Huda there. Suddenly, another officer Major Noor rushed up the stairs. Shrewd enough to guess what was happening he shot Mujib in the chest and stomach. The impact led to the president rolling down the stairs and coming to rest on the landing that led to the ground floor. He was dead. One of the bullets had gone right through his stomach and emerged from his back. Blood streaked the walls and the staircase. The sound of the gunfire brought the president's wife Fazilatunnesa running out of the room. She was immediately shot. Her lifeless body lay sprawled in the corridor.

Once Mujib and his wife had been shot, the soldiers ran riot all over the residence. They stormed the rooms of the house looking for the other members of his family. Some of them had lined up a few individuals, one of them a personal employee of the president, by the wall near the gate and in due time Mujib's youngest son, Russell (who had been named by the president after the British philosopher Bertrand Russell) was brought there. The ten year-old boy, shivering in fright and wailing to be taken to his mother, was made to stand in the line. He asked the personal secretary, Mohitul Islam, if the soldiers were going to kill him. Islam, terror struck himself, nevertheless reassured the boy that he was safe. In the house, the remaining members of the president's family comprising his second son Jamal (a lieutenant in the army who had recently returned after completing a course at Sandhurst in the United Kingdom), Mujib's newly-wed daughters-in-law and his younger brother Sheikh Naser took shelter inside the bathroom attached to the main bedroom of the residence. It did not help, as the soldiers soon broke down the door and mowed them all down with machine gun fire. Their bodies fell in a heap. Outside, as Russell kept asking to be taken to his mother, one of the soldiers, in a moment replete with unmitigated cruelty, brought him upstairs, over the body of his father on the stairs and to the spot where his mother lay dead. Without further ado, the soldier pumped a round into the boy's head.

Across town the group of soldiers which had earlier made its way to Minto Road, finished off Minister Abdur Rab Serniabat and his family. In another part of Dhanmondi, soldiers rushed into the home of Sheikh Moni and shot him and his pregnant wife Arzoo, before their two young children. When they left, one of Moni's brothers rushed him and his wife, both of whom were still barely alive, to the hospital where they succumbed to their injuries. Meanwhile, Mujib's chief of security, Colonel Jamil, who had earlier left his home when he heard of the attack on the presidential residence, approached Road no. 32. He certainly did not know that by then the whole family had been wiped off. Soldiers stationed there by Farook Rahman stopped him at the entry to the road and asked him to turn back. He refused. The soldiers murdered him in his vehicle.

The killings were over before dawn broke. As the call to prayer was heard in the mosques of the city, the assassins went about ransacking Sheikh Mujibur Rahman's house and laying hands on everything of value they could find. As the sun rose, Farook Rahman and a band of the men who had taken part in the killings, made their way back to the cantonment, obviously to rally other men as also to inform them of what had been done. Colonel Rashid, in the company of another group of soldiers, rushed to the residence of Moshtaq in the old part of Dhaka to inform him that Mujib and his family had been killed and that it was time for him to take over. In later years, Moshtaq was to deny that he had anything to do with the assassinations and that indeed the first time he knew anything about the coup was when the majors and colonels visited him and asked him to be the country's new president. His protestations were laid bare by the killers themselves, who in various interviews with the media would all say emphatically that he had always had full knowledge of the conspiracy as his had been the leading personality behind the planning and implementation of the overthrow of the government of Sheikh Mujibur Rahman. Down the years, there have been unconfirmed reports that as Moshtaq would not take over as president unless he was sure that Mujib was actually dead; he had to be taken to Road no. 32 to show the body of the president.

At first light on Friday, 15 August 1975, no one in Dhaka and in the rest of Bangladesh, save Mujib's neighbours in Dhanmondi, knew of the calamity that had come over the country. For the late president's government, the vice chancellor, teachers and students of Dhaka University, it was going to be a momentous day because Mujib would address the convocation in the earlier part of the morning. Sarkar Kabiruddin, the well-known newsreader on Radio Bangladesh, made his way to his office in Shahbagh to read the first news bulletin of the day, around 6:30 am. He was surprised to see tanks and soldiers before the gates of the radio centre and quickly tried to turn back. The soldiers blocked his path and compelled him to enter the station, where he quickly realised the situation. A few of army officers, who had occupied the radio station once they had killed Mujib and the members of his family, ordered him to broadcast the announcement that the 'autocrat' Mujib had been overthrown. Prior to Kabiruddin's arrival, though, Major Shariful Haq Dalim had already gone on air to make the announcement, shrill and triumphant, that Mujib had been killed and that country had been placed under martial law. For good measure, Dalim added that Bangladesh was now an Islamic republic under the leadership of Moshtaq. For the better part of the morning, it was this message, now in Sarkar Kabiruddin's voice, that would be heard throughout a stunned country.

A stunned silence greeted the announcement of the coup and the murder of the president's family. In the cantonment, the leaders of the coup swiftly got in touch with the senior figures of the army. Breaking all rules of discipline, Farook Rahman and his fellow plotters marched into the office of the army chief of staff and ordered him to go with them to the radio station. Elsewhere, similar action was being taken in the case of the chiefs of the navy and air force. At the Bangladesh Rifles, whose chief was away on a trip abroad, his deputy was collected and taken to the radio office. Some of the plotters made their way to the offices of the chief of general staff, Brigadier Khaled Musharraf, and acquainted him with the details. Likewise, Colonel Shafaat Jamil was informed of the coup. When some officers with no link to the coup turned up at the home of the deputy chief of army staff, Major General Ziaur Rahman, to inform him of the violent change that had taken place, they found him shaving. He coolly responded that the vice president was around to take charge. But even as Zia said that, other soldiers, having finished off Mujib and his family, went looking for other senior leaders of the fallen government. They quickly placed Vice President Syed Nazrul Islam, Tajuddin Ahmed and A.H.M. Quamruzzaman under house arrest. The Prime Minister M. Mansoor Ali had gone into hiding and would not be found until a few days later.

As the morning progressed, all the three services chiefs as well as the heads of the police and Bangladesh Rifles were brought to the Radio Bangladesh office in Shahbagh, where each one of them read out a statement of loyalty to the new regime. They were then escorted back home by the army officers, who were now clearly in charge of the country. After the statements of loyalty had been made, Moshtaq addressed the country, telling them that he had taken over as president of Bangladesh in what he described as a moment of historical necessity. He made no mention of Mujib and his family, but he did not forget to salute the soldiers who had carried out the *coup d'état* as children of the sun who, in his view, had done the country proud.

As the day progressed to afternoon and then evening, the question that was being asked in whispers around the country was about the fate of Mujib's family. By now people were convinced that Mujib was dead. If he were yet alive, Moshtaq would not take over. But even as the bodies of the president and his family lay where they had fallen before dawn, no one in the country knew that an entire household had been massacred by the soldiers of an army that Bangladesh's founding father had assiduously built in the three and a half years since the country's liberation from Pakistan in 1971.

Early on the morning of 16 August, the soldiers collected the bodies and placed them in rough, makeshift coffins. Except for Mujib's body, which bore as many as seventy bullet holes, all the other corpses were hastily buried in the cemetery in Banani, an upcoming residential zone in the capital. The bodies were placed in one single, long grave and covered over without the rituals of an Islamic burial. Mujib's body, the new regime shrewdly guessed, could not be interred in the capital since there was a chance of the place becoming in time a political shrine for the country. It was flown by helicopter to his village, Tungipara, where the accompanying soldiers made it clear that they wanted a quick burial. They cordoned off the entire village to prevent people from attending the *namaz-e-janaza,* or funeral, as also from a fear of a backlash from a constituency that had been Mujib's own since he decided to make a career of politics in the late 1940s. The soldiers ran into opposition from the cleric who would offer the funeral prayers. The body, said the cleric firmly, could not be buried until it had been washed and placed in a shroud according to Islamic tradition. The soldiers, jittery and nervous, asked him to make it quick. As no soap necessary for bathing the president's body could be found in the village, the cleric made do with a thick ball of rough soap usually used for washing clothes. Late in the afternoon, the body of Sheikh Mujibur Rahman, founder of the independent state of Bangladesh and its president, was laid to rest beside the graves of his parents in the village where he had been born fifty-five years earlier. Before leaving Tungipara, the army officers who had helicoptered to the village with the body made sure that soldiers and policemen would stand guard at the grave and allow no one to approach it.

It rained that evening.

Postscript

The murder of Sheikh Mujibur Rahman has had grave ramifications for Bangladesh. It was, in the immediate sense, an overthrow of constitutional government in the country, and also a reinforcement of the fact that the long struggle Mujib and the Awami League had waged against military rule in Pakistan had in a way come to nought. The *coup d'état* of August 1975 was to be a precursor to other, newer means of removing governments in Bangladesh. The army officers who had organised the large-scale slaughter of the president's family quickly made it clear that they intended to run the show. They ensconced themselves at *Bangabhavan*, the presidential palace, and served as Khondokar Moshtaq's advisors who owed his job to them.

Over the years, much has been made of the fact that it was the Awami League continuing in power after the death of Mujib. Opponents of the party, in their untenable way, have explained why there has been no proper trial and punishment of Mujib's killers, their spurious argument being that Khondokar Moshtaq and everyone else in the government after 15 August were part of the Awami League. The facts were actually rather different. On 15 August, there was technically and legally no Awami League since the party had already been subsumed in the larger BAKSAL that Mujib had formed in January of the year. More importantly, most ministers who worked, or were made to work, with Moshtaq did so as a result of the plain intimidation that was being exercised on them. In the few months the Moshtaq presidency would last, it was not uncommon for the army officers involved in the August mayhem and murder to be present in the room even as cabinet meetings went on.

One of the first moves Khondokar Moshtaq made was to remove General K.M. Safiullah from command of the army, and replace him with his deputy Ziaur Rahman. Another appointment that raised many eyebrows in the country was the return of General M.A.G. Osmany, as defence advisor to the new president. It did not appear to worry him that he was part of a regime that operated on the basis of murder and extra-constitutional rule. He had earlier, in defence of the cause of democracy, resigned from parliament once Mujib formed BAKSAL. In later years, Osmany would try returning to his democratic moorings through a political organisation, the *Jatiyo Janata* Party, which he founded. In 1978, he would seek the support of the Awami League in his bid to defeat General Ziaur Rahman at the presidential elections, an exercise he would lose. After August 1975, Osmany's reputation, built as it had been during the war of liberation and in the early years of Bangladesh, would be on a slide.

Enayetullah Khan, editor of the weekly newspaper *Holiday*, had already made arrangements in the pre-coup period with Sheikh Fazlul Haq Moni to take over as editor of the *Bangladesh Times*. When he took charge of the newspaper, days after Moshtaq seized the presidency, it was given out that he was the new man's appointee, which was misleading. Khan would, in subsequent years, relentlessly carry on anti-Mujib propaganda through his writings. He would serve as a cabinet minister in the Zia regime before serving as General Ershad's ambassador to China and Burma.

The biggest damage done to Bangladesh's democracy and constitutional government was the promulgation of the Indemnity Ordinance by President Moshtaq on 26 September 1975. In his time, General Ziaur Rahman would incorporate the Indemnity Ordinance through the Fifth Amendment into the constitution. The amendment would not only protect the assassins from prosecution but would also pave way for their accommodation in the government.

Except for Farook Rahman and Abdur Rashid, all other officers who had taken part in the coup were appointed to various positions at Bangladesh's diplomatic missions abroad. One of them, Shariful Haq Dalim, would rise to become the country's high commissioner to Kenya. In the course of the nine-year military rule of Bangladesh's second dictator, General Hussein Muhammad Ershad, the leader of the 1975 coup, Colonel Farook Rahman would form the Freedom Party and contest the presidential elections in 1988.

In the three months following the murder of Mujib, the country lurched from one crisis to another. The assassin officers' refusal to return to the barracks impacted the broken chain of command of the army. But by early November, Brigadier Khaled Musharraf and his loyal officers acquired sufficient support from the ranks to force Moshtaq to jettison the junior officers who had installed him in office.

Intriguingly, a Bengali journalist who had co-produced *The Plain Truth*, a Pakistani propaganda tract over Dhaka radio in 1971, let it be known in early November 1975 that he had intercepted letters between Indian intelligence and the imprisoned Tajuddin Ahmed. Alam spread the word that the Indians planned to spring Tajuddin and his colleagues from jail and install them in power. Within hours of Alam's 'revelations', Syed Nazrul Islam, Tajuddin Ahmed, M. Mansoor Ali and A.H.M. Quamruzzaman were brought together in a single cell and bayoneted to death by soldiers. Asked later about the letters, the journalist claimed he had returned them to his source and therefore could not produce them!

Meanwhile on the night of 3 November 1975, Musharraf launched his own coup and was effectively in command of the army, having placed General Zia under house arrest and agreeing to let the coup leaders fly out of the country. Unknown to Musharraf, however, the men who murdered Mujib and his family had made their way to the central jail in Dhaka before their departure for exile abroad and murdered the four leaders of the 1971 Mujibnagar government, imprisoned there since Mujib's assassination. Only after the officers had flown into exile did the ghastly truth become known. The terms under which Moshtaq vacated the presidency had come at a painful price.

On 6 November, having seen Moshtaq appoint him to the rank of Major General and chief of army staff, Khaled Musharraf forced the president to resign on 7 November. He was replaced by the chief justice of the Supreme Court, Abu Sadat Mohammad Sayem. Next morning troops loyal to Zia, drawn to the clandestine propaganda mounted by Colonel Abu Taher, an anti-Mujib independence war hero, about an Indo-Soviet conspiracy to take over the country, mutinied. They were joined by columns of soldiers streaming into Dhaka from Comilla and other cantonments and quickly put Musharraf and his loyalists to flight. General Musharraf, one of the toughest soldiers during the War of Liberation and an avowed believer in secular democracy, took refuge along with Colonel Najmul Huda and Major Haidar in the Savar cantonment on the outskirts of the capital. All three men were soon set upon by those they had sought shelter from and brutally killed.

As the day progressed, Bengalis realised that a new dispensation was at work. Justice Sayem, who had taken over as president only a day earlier, continued in office, though with the additional responsibility of chief martial-law administrator. General Zia, now free and restored to his old job as army chief, was named a deputy chief martial-law administrator, along with Rear Admiral M.H. Khan of the navy and Air Vice Marshal M.G. Tawab of the air force. Power, of course, was in the hands of Zia who, by April 1977, would ease President Sayem out of office and take over as president. In the same month, Zia would organise a referendum seeking his confirmation as Bangladesh's new leader. Predictably his acolytes arranged the results he needed.

The beginning of General Zia's rule was also the period when all references to Mujib and his role in Bangladesh's history would be papered over. As president and martial-law administrator, Zia would tamper with the constitution by replacing its invocations to secularism and Bengali nationalism. In late 1975, he placed Colonel Taher, who had helped free him from house arrest in November, in jail. After a secret trial by a military court, Taher was hanged on 21 July 1976. In September 1978, Zia formed his Bangladesh Nationalist Party (BNP), in which all manner of politicians opposed to the secular Awami League would be accommodated. Men who had opposed Bangladesh's War of Liberation in 1971 and had clearly sided with Pakistan, joined the party, as did a number of adherents of Bhashani and others known for their loyalty to a pro-Chinese brand of socialism. The military ruler removed the ban imposed on communal politics by the Awami League government in December 1971 and thus created the perfect opportunity for all political groups and parties that had actively collaborated with the Pakistan Army in 1971 to enter the Bengali political mainstream.

Zia then carefully undertook to promote a new form of nationalism he chose to define as Bangladeshi nationalism. His critics saw in the move a clear attempt to divide the country and indeed redirect it back to the communalism that Bengalis had spurned in 1971. In his nearly six years of rule, Zia would suppress as many as eighteen coup attempts against him. He succumbed to the nineteenth. On 30 May 1981, he was murdered by troops loyal to Major General M.A. Manzoor, another independence war figure, in Chittagong. Within days, Manzoor's coup would fail and he would go on the run. Pro-government soldiers finally caught up with him in the forests outside Chittagong and killed him. His body was dumped in a ditch in Chittagong cantonment. Twelve army officers, including a brigadier, were court-martialled on charges of involvement in Zia's murder and eventually hanged within months of the assassination.

In November 1981, Justice Abdus Sattar, chief election commissioner in Pakistan in 1970 and Bangladesh's vice president under Zia, defeated Dr Kamal Hossain, foreign minister in the Mujib government, at a new presidential election. Kamal Hossain had been nominated by the Awami League, whose leadership had been taken over a couple of weeks before Zia's assassination by Sheikh Hasina, elder daughter of Sheikh Mujibur Rahman, after her return from exile abroad, as its candidate for the presidency.

On 24 March 1982, President Sattar's government was overthrown in a fresh *coup d'état*, this time led by army chief General Ershad. The new military ruler would exercise power for more than nine years, during which he would form his own political party, the *Jatiyo* Party. Under Ershad, corruption became endemic and Bangladesh lurched increasingly more towards communal politics. He decreed Islam as Bangladesh's state religion and continued the policy of patronising the murderers of Mujib. In time, two political alliances, one led by Sheikh Hasina and the other by Khaleda Zia, the widow of Ziaur Rahman who had in the meanwhile come into active politics by taking over her husband's political party, the BNP, would spearhead a long, sustained movement aimed at driving General Ershad from power.

In December 1990, Ershad's government fell. New elections organised by a caretaker administration in February 1991 placed Khaleda Zia in office as prime minister at the head of a BNP government. Sheikh Hasina, as leader of the Awami League opposition, almost immediately initiated a new movement to dislodge Mrs Zia from power. At the elections in June 1996, the Awami League returned to power for the first time in twenty-one years. The new government quickly repealed the indemnity ordinance incorporated by General Zia in the constitution as a first step toward putting the leaders of the 15 August 1975 coup on trial. The judgement in the August 1975 case was delivered in November 1998. All the army officers involved in the coup were sentenced to death, though a fairly good number of them were, and have remained, fugitive abroad. However, it was not until early 2010, when the Awami League was in office again after five years in Opposition following the elections of October 2001, that five of the assassins, among them Colonel Farook Rahman, Major Bazlul Huda and Major Shahriar, were executed in January 2010.

Moulana Abdul Hamid Khan Bhashani died on 17 November 1976 in his village, Santosh. His National Awami Party disintegrated soon after, with many of his followers making a beeline for General Ziaur Rahman's BNP.

Khondokar Moshtaq Ahmed died of old age in Dhaka three months before the Awami League returned to power under Sheikh Hasina in June 1996. Towards the end of his life, he went on making assertions of his innocence in the murder of Mujib and his four wartime colleagues in 1975. He was quickly and quietly buried in his village.

Taheruddin Thakur, having spent a number of years in prison on charges of conspiracy to kill Mujib and four other national leaders, is out on bail in Dhaka. Curiously, the courts have not been able to prove his involvement in the 1975 tragedy.

Mahbubul Alam Chashi, one of the conspirators against Mujib in 1975, died in a road accident in Saudi Arabia years later.

Major General K.M. Safiullah, chief of army staff in the Mujib government, would go on serving as Bangladesh's ambassador in various countries under General Zia and General Ershad. He won a seat in parliament as an Awami League nominee in 1996 but lost it in 2001.

Dr Kamal Hossain, who played an instrumental role in bringing Mujib's daughter Sheikh Hasina home from exile in 1981, later fell out with her and left the Awami League. He subsequently formed his own political party, the *Gono* (people's) Forum. He remains a leading lawyer in Bangladesh.

Tofail Ahmed, the fiery student leader who first conferred on Mujib the honorific 'Bangabandhu' in February 1969 and later was political secretary to him between 1972 and 1975, is a senior figure in the Awami League and served as a minister in Sheikh Hasina's administration between 1996 and 2001.

A.S.M. Abdur Rab and Shahjahan Siraj, two of the four influential student leaders in the build-up to the independence movement in 1971 who would form the JSD in 1972, subsequently went their separate ways. Rab would serve as leader of the Opposition in Parliament in the Ershad years and then would become a minister in Sheikh Hasina's government. Siraj would abandon the JSD and join the BNP, serving as a minister in Khaleda Zia's cabinet. Of the two other student leaders from the 1971 period, Nur-e-Alam Siddiqui would remove himself from politics and spend time in business. Abdul Kuddus Makhan, the most selfless among the four, died quietly decades after liberation.

Ataur Rahman Khan, Awami League politician and chief minister of East Pakistan in the late 1950s, would serve as prime minister in General Ershad's regime before falling out with the dictator. In a similar fashion, Mizanur Rahman Chowdhury, a leading figure behind the Six Points movement in 1966 and later minister in Mujib's government, would team up with Ershad and become prime minister in his government. Towards the end of his life, he would return to the Awami League and serve on its board of advisors. He died in 2006.

Justice Abu Sayeed Chowdhury, as foreign minister in the Moshtaq regime, would leave the country before the Khaled Musharraf coup of 3 November 1975 and repudiate the government. He presided over a rally in London on 9 November 1975 to condemn the killings of Mujib and his four colleagues that year.

Mohammadullah, speaker of Parliament, president of the republic and cabinet minister in the Mujib years, subsequently joined Zia's BNP. He was appointed vice president by President Sattar but went out of office a day later when General Ershad mounted his coup in March 1982.

In 2010, the Bangladesh government established the International Crimes Tribunal (ICT), under a 1973 act of parliament. It has indicted nine suspects who are prominent Jamaat-e-Islami leaders, and two who are BNP leaders. The government was responding to popular support to have the trials and settle longstanding accusations dating to the War of Liberation in 1971.

In the first judgement, the ICT sentenced a well-known Muslim cleric Abul Kalam Azad to death for crimes against humanity during the independence war. The trial was held in absentia because Azad went into hiding hours before the tribunal issued an arrest warrant against him on 3 April 2012. He is believed to have fled to India or Pakistan. Azad was indicted on eight counts for murder, rape and genocide. Investigators said they had identified fourteen people murdered by Azad; three were women he had raped and nine were abducted civilians. Testimony was offered by twenty-two prosecution witnesses, including friends and families of the victims. The prosecution said that Azad had burnt down at least five houses, looted fifteen, and forced at least nine Hindu persons to convert to Islam. On January 2013, he was convicted of war crimes, on six of eight counts, including murder of unarmed civilians and rape committed during the war. On 21 January 2013 Azad was sentenced to the death. The verdict led to violent protests by major Islamist organisations and political parties in Bangladesh.

Acronyms

Bangladesh Academy of Rural Development (BARD)

Bangladesh Krishak Sramik Awami League (BAKSAL)

Central Students Action Council (CSAC)

Central Treaty Organisation (CENTO)

Combined Opposition Parties (COP)

Communist Party of Bangladesh (CPB)

Democratic Action Committee (DAC)

East Pakistan Communist Party (EPCP)

East Pakistan Students League (EPSL)

East Pakistan Students Union (EPSU)

Elective Bodies' Disqualification Ordinance (EBDO)

Jatiyo Rakkhi Bahini (JRB)

Jatiyo Samajtantrik Dal (JSD)

Jatiyo Smriti Shoudho (JSS)

Legal Framework Order (LFO)

Members of the National Assembly (MNAs)

Members of the Provincial Assembly (MPAs)

National Awami Party (NAP)

National Democratic Front (NDF)

North West Frontier Province (NWFP)

Organisation of Islamic Countries (OIC)

Pakistan International Airlines (PIA)

Pakistan People's Party (PPP)

Round Table Conference (RTC)

South East Asia Treaty Organisation (SEATO)

Unilateral declaration of independence (UDI)

Index